The
Sacred Sites
Bible

The

Sacred Sites
Bible

Anthony Taylor

The definitive guide to spiritual places

STERLING

New York / London
www.sterlingpublishing.com

STERLING and the distinctive Sterling logo are
registered trademarks of Sterling Publishing Co., Inc.

10 9 8 7 6 5 4 3 2 1

Published by Sterling Publishing Co., Inc.
387 Park Avenue South, New York, NY 10016

First published in Great Britain in 2010 by
Godsfield, a division of Octopus Publishing Group Ltd.

Distributed in Canada by Sterling Publishing
c/o Canadian Manda Group, 165 Dufferin Street,
Toronto, Ontario, Canada M6K 3H6

Printed and bound in China

Sterling ISBN: 978-1-4027-7748-6

For information about custom editions, special sales,
premium and corporate purchases, please contact
Sterling Special Sales Department at 800-805-5489
or specialsales@sterlingpublishing.com.

CONTENTS

INTRODUCTION

We know very little about the lives of pre-agricultural people, who left no writings for us to decode, but one thing seems clear: they had a profound sense of the divine. Historians believe that by 10,000 BCE human beings had colonized virtually all the primary ice-free land masses of the Earth, including Africa, Asia, Europe, the Americas, and Oceania; from what we can gather, they told fantastic stories about the creation of the Earth that involved anthropomorphic gods, whom they perceived in the heavens above and the land below. For our early Neolithic ancestors, it would appear that the entire planet was sacred: the world was the creation of the gods, who were always and everywhere present.

The Anangu people had been long settled in central Australia by 10,000 BCE. In an oral tradition that has survived to this day, they speak of the creation of the Earth, which they say was formless until the first ancestral beings appeared. In the Dreamtime mythology, as their tradition is known, the bewildering landscapes of the world bear testimony to the activities of these early beings, who roamed the formless Earth, hunting, playing, fighting, and love-making, thus creating all the significant features of the land that we see today. The Anangu tell stories about rivers, caves, and the great rocks of Katajuta and Uluru, which they have always held to

Devils Tower in Wyoming has long been sacred to Native Americans, who call it "Bear's Lodge."

be deeply sacred. By touching the rocks and performing sacred ceremonies in their caves, the Anangu were able to make direct contact with the gods and thus bring favor upon themselves and their tribe.

THE SACRED EARTH AND SACRED MONUMENTS

The belief that the land itself is sacred—or at least its significant features are—has been evident since the dawn of civilization in all corners of the globe. The indigenous Americans tell creation stories about sacred landforms, such as Devils Tower in Wyoming and Crater Lake in Oregon; and in India, the first Hindus told stories about the great holy Rivers Ganges and Yamuna, which they viewed as living gods. In Europe, the ancient Greeks created a pantheon of gods, who were said to live on Mount Olympus, then the tallest known peak in the world; they also told creation stories about the Earth, such as the birth of Zeus in a great cave, which gave rise to an early shrine on Mount Ida in Crete. Meanwhile in ancient

Some of the oldest passage-tombs found at Carrowkeel are more than 5,000 years old.

Japan, followers of the indigenous Shinto tradition believed that forests were especially sacred, and they cut down cypress trees to mark sacred spots where the gods had touched the Earth, establishing the first shrines at the base of Mount Fuji and in the forests near Ise, where the creation gods are still worshipped today.

A little more than 5,000 years ago the Neolithic peoples of northern Europe began to construct a vast array of mysterious earth and stone monuments that not only identified sacred spots, but also appear to have served as sites for important religious ceremonies. In Ireland, elaborate stone monuments were erected above and below man-made earth mounds, giving rise to the sacred sites of Knowth, Newgrange, and Carrowkeel; and in England, huge stones were dragged great distances to create the wondrous stone circle of Stonehenge, while other vast monoliths were arranged in roughly 1 mile (1.6 km)-long lines at Carnac in France.

The great Inca city of Machu Picchu rises high above a lush green valley, overlooked by snow-capped peaks.

At first it was assumed that these vast monuments were simply burial sites, but recent advances in archeoastronomy have shown them to be perfectly aligned with the sun, moon, and stars. We know almost nothing of the religious rites that took place at these sacred monuments; however, many of the stones were engraved with hieroglyphs, which indicate that the people who created them had detailed knowledge of the movements of the sun, planets, and stars, which had attained a supreme importance in their lives. By an impossible coincidence, at roughly the same time vast stone pyramids were being built thousands of miles away in Egypt, which likewise were initially assumed to be tombs for the dead, although many modern scholars now believe that these awe-inspiring monuments served another purpose: they were initiation sites that enabled a person to die symbolically and thus resurrect as a living god. At these sacred monuments, it is widely believed that the true mysteries of life and death were revealed.

Approximately 3,000 years later the indigenous peoples of Central and South America began building great cities in stone. Not only did they build pyramids at Chichen Itza, Tenochtitlan and later at Machu Picchu, but they also carved their sacred stones with hieroglyphs, which were likewise aligned with the movements of the stars. Further north, in North America Native Americans in Wyoming constructed a medicine wheel using simple stones, which bears a striking resemblance in design to the stone circles in northern Europe; and in Ohio, the Adena people built a mound in the shape of a serpent, which is not unlike the great snake represented by the massive standing stones passing through the stone circle at Avebury in southern England, or the giant snake Vasuki carved by Hindus at Angkor Wat in Cambodia.

Hewn from rocky cliffs, the Dazu Rock Carvings are ornate Buddhists sculptures.

WORSHIPPING THE DIVINE

It is as if the ancient peoples of the world had a common wisdom and symbolism, which in the course of modern history was somehow lost. One explanation is the emergence in the Middle East of monotheism—the belief in a single creator god—which gave rise to the Abrahamic faiths of Judaism, Islam, and Christianity, which have shaped the sensibilities of the modern Western world. At roughly the same time, the pantheon of lesser gods that dominated life in the East was being replaced by the increasingly organized and doctrine-based religions of Taoism, Buddhism, and Hinduism, which did not so much believe in a single creator god as in the possibility of transcendent enlightenment,

Left The stunning Takstang Monastery is perched precariously on a steep Himalayan mountain.

Right Hindu pilgrims pray in the River Ganges at Varanasi.

leading to a personal experience of the divine. For the first time in history there was a supreme divinity, and through a plethora of prophets, saints, gurus, and holy men, his words could be heard and written down in sacred books that were no longer open to dispute. Henceforward, places were no longer sacred in themselves, but because of their association with the lives and deeds of holy men and women, such as Moses, Lao Tzu, Jesus, the Virgin Mary, the Buddha, and Muhammad, who to their followers were immortal gods in human disguise.

Jews revered Mount Sinai in Jerusalem, Taoists the sacred mountains of China, Christians the Church of the Nativity in Bethlehem, Buddhists the holy towns of Lumbini, Bodhgaya, Sarnath, and Kushinara in India, and Muslims the cities of Mecca and Medina in Saudi Arabia. At these supremely sacred sites, beautiful temples, stunning cathedrals, and lavish mosques were built, which became increasingly important places for holy pilgrimage. During the Middle Ages and beyond, vast numbers of Christian pilgrims flocked to Santiago de Compostela in Spain to worship the holy relics of St. James the Apostle, while Hindu pilgrims assembled in massive numbers on the banks of the River Ganges in Varanasi (Benares) to worship Shiva, and Shia Muslims congregated in great numbers in Karbala to honor the martyred Imam Hussain.

THE SEARCH FOR SPIRITUALITY

As the great religions grew, so did the temples where God and his prophets were venerated. In Europe great cathedrals were built in France, Italy, Spain, and Germany, often to house the relics of Jesus and his apostles, while in Arabia huge mosques were erected where Muhammad had lived and died.

11

In Tibet the stupendous Potala Palace was built as a home for the Dalai Lama, and at Bagan in Burma a vast complex of temples was constructed to honor the four incarnations of the Buddha. As the main orthodox religions grew, so did the priestly class, who were now needed to nurture and convey spiritual truth to the laity, who lacked direct access to God. Throughout the world, monasteries and nunneries began to flourish, where devoted men and women gave their lives in service. Sacred sites were chosen not only because of momentous events that had occurred, such as miracles and divine apparitions, but also because they were conducive to meditation and prayer. The early Christians in Britain chose the holy islands of Lindisfarne, Iona, and Devenish to retreat from life, because these places were beautiful, peaceful, and remote. In the Far East monasteries flourished on inaccessible mountains, such as Samye in Tibet and Takstang in Bhutan, where monks were cordoned off from the hustle and bustle of the world and could sit in an empty wilderness in quiet contemplation of eternal truth.

Today, as the great Western faiths find themselves increasingly embroiled in scandal, politics, and nationalism, many young people are turning away from religion, but the spiritual longing they feel has not died, nor has the need to visit places conducive to spiritual experience. This had led to a renewed appreciation of sacred sites, such as the magnificent landforms in

Buddhist pilgrims gather before the Mahabodhi Temple in Bodhgaya.

Asia, America, and Australia, the great pyramids in Egypt, pre-Christian sites such as Glastonbury Tor in England, and the Hill of Tara in Ireland, and the sacred stone cities of Central America. Many people now travel the world to marvel at the sacred sites of foreign cultures, such as the Hindu temples in India, the beautiful Buddhist monasteries in South East Asia, and the lavish Shia mosques in Iran and Iraq.

The stunning churches at Lalibela are carved directly from the rocky ground.

No book can do justice to all the great sacred sites around the world, but in this one I have done my best to give a taste of the most inspiring, visually impressive, and best-loved sites, in the hope that readers will want to travel the world to visit them for themselves.

13

LANDFORMS

JEJU ISLAND

LOCATION	South Korea
SPIRITUAL TRADITION	Jeju
ASSOCIATED DEITY	SeulMunDae HalMang
DATE	1000 BCE
WHEN TO VISIT	Any time of year

Jeju Island is a wondrous volcanic island located in the Korea Strait, south of mainland Korea and west of Japan. Adorned with thousands of basalt statues known as "stone grandfathers," this exceptionally beautiful island is dominated by Halla San, a sacred mountain highly revered by the indigenous Jeju people.

According to Jeju mythology, the creation goddess SeulMunDae HalMang made Halla San with seven giant spadefuls of earth. It is said that one day she made a huge cauldron of soup for her 500 children, but accidentally fell into it and drowned. Her sons ate the soup, and when the youngest explained what had happened, the boys couldn't stop crying until they turned into stones.

Mount Halla San rises to almost 6,560 ft (2,000 m) in the middle of the island, making it the tallest peak in South Korea. A lake has formed in its central crater, where hundreds of spirits are said to live. Lower down the

mountain is a Buddhist cave shrine, which is reputed to have special healing powers. But perhaps the most extraordinary feature of Halla San is that a sacred mushroom used to grow abundantly all over its forested slopes. Many people believe that the sacred fungus was fly agaric, a poisonous mushroom that produces psychotropic effects. The visions induced by ingesting the mushroom may explain why Halla San has for so long been attributed with special spiritual powers. The ancient Chinese referred to it as "the island of the blessed," and their myths claim that the mountain is so powerful that it pulls the Milky Way towards the Earth.

As well as the ubiquitous stone grandfathers, Jeju Island is adorned by many small round towers made from loose stones. Known as Bangsatap, the local people have erected them to ward off evil spirits and to protect against misfortune. The precise location is considered especially important, and sites are chosen where geomancers believe the flow of spiritual energy is blocked.

Jeju Island is also home to the world's finest lava tubes, with which the volcanic rock is riddled. At Samseonghyeol, three caves enable visitors to enter the underground network, which islanders claim leads to the secret home of the gods.

Jeju Island is covered with dol hareubang *(stone grandfathers): ancient rocks carved from basalt in the shape of old men.*

ULURU/AYERS ROCK

LOCATION	Northern Territory, Australia
SPIRITUAL TRADITION	Aboriginal Dreamtime
ASSOCIATED DEITY	Tjukuritja/Waparitja
DATE	Prehistoric
WHEN TO VISIT	Any time of year, but best in the cooler weather in April/May; it is occasionally closed for spiritual ceremonies

Uluru—named Ayers Rock by European settlers in the region—is a colossal sandstone mound rising from flat land in the Northern Territory of central Australia. It has a circumference of more than 5½ miles (9 km), and rises over 1,115 ft (340 m) from the ground, even though the bulk of the rock lies beneath the surface.

For tens of thousands of years Uluru has been sacred to the local Pitjantjatjara and Yankunytjatjara peoples, who to this day still decorate the surface with beautiful and evocative paintings. They follow the indigenous spiritual tradition of the Anangu—the indigenous Australians—known to outsiders as Dreamtime.

According to Anangu mythology, the world was completely formless until ancestral beings appeared and journeyed across the Earth, leaving their mark wherever they went. It is said that their travels began in central Australia, meaning that Uluru is one of the most important of their sacred sites, because its various cliffs, caves, ravines, and gullies are all evidence of their early activities. There is a Dreamtime story associated with every significant feature of the rock, and these are taught to adolescent Anangu during initiation ceremonies, but are usually kept secret from outsiders. The local Anangu tribes believe that they can make a direct connection with Dreamtime—the spiritual reality underlying physical reality—by performing sacred rites on the rock. They believe the land is still inhabited by the spirits of the ancestral creator beings, whom they refer to as Tjukuritja or Waparitja, and that it is their responsibility to pass this wisdom on to the young.

For modern-day visitors one of Uluru's most impressive features is that it appears to change color according to the time of day and season of the year; at sunset the rock seems to shimmer a deep reddish-orange, and after rain it can appear to be a metallic gray-blue color streaked with black.

Many tourists make the dangerous climb up Uluru against the wishes of the local Anangu people, who want to preserve the spiritual significance of Dreamtime paths that traverse the rock. When a tourist dies or is hurt climbing Uluru, the Anangu regard it as a tragic personal loss.

The beautiful rock is sacred to indigenous Australians, who have decorated it with spiritual etchings and paintings.

THE GRAND CANYON

LOCATION	Arizona, USA
SPIRITUAL TRADITION	Hopi Native American
DATE	Prehistoric
WHEN TO VISIT	Any time of year

The Grand Canyon in northern Arizona is one of the most inspiring wonders of the natural world. A spectacular gorge more than 280 miles (450 km) long and in places almost 1¼ miles (2 km) deep, this immense rock canyon was carved by the great Colorado River during a period of more than five million years. The site is sacred to Native Americans, who believe that the spirits of their ancestors reside there.

There is evidence of human habitation in the canyon and its caves dating back to 2000 BCE. It is known that the ancestors of the modern-day Hopi tribe lived in the canyon for thousands of years, but for unknown reasons—possibly a drought—they left around the 12th or 13th century, although they continued to make pilgrimages to the site. In 1540 Spanish conquistadors led by Hopi guides explored the canyon for the first time. They never made it to the bottom, probably because their guides chose not to reveal any routes to the river, believing that the pathways were too sacred for the Spanish to walk. More than 200 years passed before Europeans visited the canyon again, when two Spanish priests supported by soldiers traveled the north rim while seeking, and finding, a route from New Mexico to California.

In the late 19th century there was a surge of interest in the Grand Canyon as a possible site of valuable natural resources, which led to the Grand Canyon Railway opening in 1901. However, once Americans actually saw the spectacular vista and immersed themselves in its natural wonder, mining quickly gave way to tourism. In 1903, President Roosevelt visited and declared that he wished the Grand Canyon to be left untouched for future generations to enjoy, which led to the creation of the Grand Canyon National Park in 1916. Today, millions visit the Grand Canyon every year, and for many it is an unforgettable and life-changing spiritual experience.

The Grand Canyon has been sacred to Native Americans for thousands of years. Today, it attracts nearly five million visitors annually from all over the world.

DEVILS TOWER

LOCATION	Wyoming, USA
SPIRITUAL TRADITION	Native American
ASSOCIATED ANIMAL	Bear
DATE	Triassic period
WHEN TO VISIT	Any time of year; although a voluntary ban on rock-climbing is imposed during the month of June

Devils Tower is a huge stone monolith near the Belle Fourche River in the Black Hills of north-eastern Wyoming. An edifice of gypsum-covered volcanic rock, the tower rises more than 1,245 ft (380 m) from its surroundings. In 1906 President Roosevelt made Devils Tower the first United States National Monument, acknowledging what an awe-inspiring sight it is.

Devils Tower has long been sacred to many Native American tribes, who worshipped here well before European settlers arrived. The Cheyenne and the Crow call it "Bear's Lodge," the Lakota call it "Grizzly Bear's Lodge," and the Arapaho "Bear's Tipi," emphasizing its strong spiritual association with bears. Recently, Native Americans have attempted to have the monument renamed, but without success.

The local tribes have many legends concerning the origins of "Bear's Lodge." An old Sioux story tells how two young girls were picking flowers by the river when they were chased by hungry bears. The Great Spirit felt sorry for the terrified girls and raised the ground beneath them, leaving the bears scratching the rock below. Their scratch-marks are the deep grooves that can be seen in the rock today.

Every year Native Americans come here to perform sacred ceremonies, including sweat lodges, vision quests, prayer offerings, and the Sun Dance. Traditionally, the most important rituals take place during summer, which has resulted in a voluntary ban on rock-climbing in June, so that these rites can be performed without interruption. Some climbers and mountain-gear manufacturers have opposed this "self-imposed" ban, but in a unique judgement, it was upheld by a federal judge, who asserted that the Government had a duty to protect religious practices and could do so without violating the First Amendment.

"Bear's Lodge" is highly sacred to Native Americans, who still perform rites there.

GLASTONBURY TOR

LOCATION	Glastonbury, England
SPIRITUAL TRADITION	Celtic pagan
DATE	Prehistoric
WHEN TO VISIT	Any time of year

Glastonbury Tor is a sacred hill that rises mysteriously from verdant green plains in Somerset, in south-west England. It is crowned by a roofless stone tower—all that remains of St. Michael's Church, which was built in the early 14th century to replace an earlier church destroyed by an earthquake in 1275.

Modern-day archeologists have found Neolithic tools on the Tor, suggesting that people have visited this sacred site throughout human history. Until roughly 2,000 years ago the surrounding land would have been submerged by water, so that the Tor would have appeared like an island to all who visited. Perhaps this explains why so many people believe the Tor is the ancient Isle of Avalon, the final resting place of King Arthur and Queen Guinevere. According to Celtic mythology, Avalon is home to Gwyn ap Nudd, Lord of the Underworld and King of the Fairies. As a consequence, many modern-day Celtic pagans view Glastonbury Tor as an entrance to the fairy-world and come to the Tor to perform sacred rites and to interact with fairies.

Although the Tor is a natural formation, a number of terraces are clearly visible. According to Geoffrey Russell, they form a massive spiral labyrinth that may be walked in a sacred journey to the summit. In total, seven terraces encircle the Tor, creating a distinct pattern found at many Neolithic sites.

Archeologists have also found evidence of a 5th-century CE fort on the Tor, with two burials aligned north–south, indicating that the site was pagan before St. Michael's Church was built. In 1539 the Tor was the site of a grizzly execution, when the last Abbot of Glastonbury, Richard Whiting, was hanged, drawn, and quartered here. Thereafter the church fell into disuse.

Today, the Tor is visited by followers of different spiritual traditions (and none), who enjoy the wonderful views, stretching for miles in all directions. At the foot of the Tor are the magical Chalice Well gardens, where a holy spring gushes red water, believed by many to be the blood of Christ. This is a very special sanctuary, where visitors can come to rest and refresh themselves with delicious cool water after a hike up the Tor. And, if they pay special attention, they might even see a fairy.

The Tor is regarded by many in the New Age movement as one the most magical sacred sites in England.

25

KASHA-KATUWE

LOCATION	New Mexico, USA
SPIRITUAL TRADITION	Cochiti Pueblo Native American
DATE	Prehistoric
WHEN TO VISIT	Daytime only; occasionally closed for the performance of sacred rites

Kasha Katuwe—also know as the "Tent Rocks National Monument"—is located roughly 37 miles (60 km) south of Santa Fe, a thriving New Age hub in New Mexico in the American south-west. A truly awe-inspiring natural landform, this desert monument has long been sacred to the Cochiti Pueblo people, on whose land it sits.

The sacred site comprises a collection of spectacular canyons and magnificent cone-shaped tent rocks that have formed over millions of years, due to the erosion of softer layers from hard volcanic rock. The smallest tent rocks are only 3⅓ ft (1 m) high, while the tallest rise to 98 ft (30 m). Most of the tent rocks are adorned with conical boulder-caps, which protect the supporting structures (referred to as *hoodoos*) below. The hoodoos are covered by a layer of pumice and hard tuff (light porous rock) that give them a pink-and-beige appearance, apart from occasional bands of gray. Shards of volcanic glass are embedded in their surface, which creates a stunning effect close up.

Archeological evidence indicates that Native Americans have lived near the site for at least 4,000 years. During the 14th century large pueblos, or villages, were established by the ancestors of the modern-day Pueblo de Cochiti. Less than 1,000 Cochiti tribespeople live on the lands surrounding Kasha-Katuwe today. Despite enormous outside influences, they still observe the Native American form of governance, wear traditional clothes, practice sacred rites, and perform ancient religious ceremonies. The Cochiti people welcome visitors to Kasha-Katuwe, although they ask that guests observe a number of rules: for example, the rocks should be approached on foot, which means a roughly 1¼ mile (2 km) trek from the entrance to the site. Dogs and mobile phones are forbidden, and visitors are asked to adopt a respectful attitude, especially if they come upon tribespeople engaged in sacred rites. The Cochiti perform a number of dances near the site to re-enact their sacred myths, and ask that these are not interrupted, although they may be watched. Applause is inappropriate.

The Tent Rocks of Kasha-Katuwe, sacred to the local Cochiti people, are one of the most spectacular natural landforms in the American south-west.

MOUNT ATHOS

LOCATION	Macedonia, Greece
SPIRITUAL TRADITIONS	Ancient Greek mystery, Eastern Orthodox Christian
DATE	3rd century CE (Eastern Orthodox element)
WHEN TO VISIT	Any time of year, but male visitors require a permit and women are not allowed

Mount Athos is a rocky tree-lined mountain just over 6,560 ft (2,000 m) high at the eastern edge of a mountainous peninsula protruding into the Aegean Sea. It is prominent in ancient Greek mythology, and today is home to 20 Eastern Orthodox Christian monasteries.

In classical Greek mythology, Athos hurled a rock at Zeus or Poseidon, who sent it crashing to the Earth near Macedonia, where it became Mount Athos. In another myth, the sun god Apollo fell in love with Daphne, who fled to Mount Athos to escape his unwanted advances, giving her name to the main port.

In the Christian tradition, storms are said to have forced the Virgin Mary and John the Evangelist—one of Christ's 12 disciples—to stop at the port of Klement enroute to meet Lazarus in Cyprus. Mary was so enamoured of Mount Athos that God presented it to her as a gift, and ever since the mountain has been known as the Garden of the Virgin Mary, and all other women have been forbidden to visit it. In the 11th century Eastern Orthodox Christian monks built the Monastery of Iviron near the port in her honor.

Possibly as early as the 3rd century CE Christian monks settled on Mount Athos, its remote setting perfect for communion with God. Archeological evidence indicates that both Christians and pagans lived together on Mount Athos during the early part of the 4th century CE. But in the second half of that century, the Christian churches were destroyed. Later, during the reign of Theodosios I (383–395 CE), almost all of the pagan temples were demolished and the churches restored. During the 9th century CE a decree was issued by Basil I asserting that only monks could live on Mount Athos, and this is still observed today.

Mount Athos is sacred to the Virgin Mary; all other women are forbidden entrance.

CRATER LAKE

LOCATION	Oregon, USA
SPIRITUAL TRADITION	Klamath Native American
DATE	*c.* 4600 BCE
WHEN TO VISIT	Any time of year, but be prepared for heavy snow in winter

Crater Lake is the main attraction of the Crater Lake National Park in Oregon, which is part of the Cascade Mountains in the north-west United States. This exceptionally clear, stunningly blue lake is formed by volcanic rock and sinks as deep as 1,970 ft (600 m). Surrounded by rugged tree-lined mountains, the lake's striking color and naked natural beauty make it a wonder to behold.

Crater Lake has always been sacred to the Klamath tribe of Native Americans, who may have lived in the area 7,000 years ago when the lake was formed by the sudden eruption and collapse of a large volcano, Mount Mazama. A Klamath sacred myth recounts how the lake was created during a fierce battle between the god of the sky, Skell, and the god of the underworld, Llao, which destroyed the volcano in spectacular fashion.

Crater Lake was first seen by non-Native Americans in 1853, when a party of gold prospectors stumbled upon it by chance. Within ten years American settlers in their droves began traveling in freight-wagons for hundreds of miles to see the enchanting lake for themselves. According to recorded accounts, many people would fall to the ground and weep upon seeing the lake, awed by the breathtaking stillness and sanctity of the site.

Visitors to Crater Lake often see a tree bobbing vertically in the water. This tree is known as the "Old Man of the Lake," and has been patiently treading water for more than a hundred years, peacefully preserved by the icy current.

For a long time it was held that Native Americans were frightened of Crater Lake and would not travel anywhere near it, but this is not true. On the contrary, the lake has been an important site for vision quests for many thousands of years and it is still used for this sacred purpose today. On occasion, Native American men will swim in the cold waters, with the express intention of acquiring shamanic powers.

Crater Lake is sacred to the Klamath Native Americans, who perform vision quests and other sacred rites at the site.

31

MOUNT OLYMPUS

LOCATION	Border of Macedonia/Thessaly, Greece
SPIRITUAL TRADITION	Ancient Greek pagan mystery
ASSOCIATED DEITIES	The 12 Olympian gods
DATE	700 BCE
WHEN TO VISIT	Any time of year

Mount Olympus rises almost 9,840 ft (3,000 m) above sea level and the surrounding land, making it the highest mountain in Greece, and one of the tallest mountains from base to summit in the whole of Europe. It is the renowned home of the 12 Olympian gods of the ancient Hellenistic world, referred to by the poet Homer in both the *Iliad* and the *Odyssey*, composed around 700 BCE.

It is likely that Mount Olympus only became identified as the actual mountain referred to in mythology many centuries after Homer, for the little evidence we have suggests that the hermits who first lived in its caves and under the trees on its rocky slopes believed it held special powers only by association, not because the Olympian gods were actually living there.

King of the mighty Olympians was Zeus, who sat on his throne on Mount

The sacred peak of Mount Olympus was once home to the 12 Olympian gods.

Olympus with his wife, Hera, and their many children: Apollo, the sun god; Artemis, the chaste huntress; Ares, the god of war; Athena, the warrior goddess; Hermes, the winged messenger-god; Aphrodite, the goddess of love and sexual passion; and Hephaestus, the blacksmith god associated with the arts. Zeus's sisters Demeter, goddess of the earth, and Hestia, goddess of the hearth, also lived on Olympus, as well as Zeus's brother, Poseidon, ruler of the oceans. Zeus's other brother, Hades, lived in the underworld, where he was King.

With the advent of Christianity, Mount Olympus lost its special status as a supreme sacred site. The hermits left, and followers of the ancient mystery cults no longer flocked to its forested slopes to perform their secret rites. Today, however, Mount Olympus is attracting visitors once more. Tourists and spiritual seekers alike make the journey from the town of Litochoro to the sacred mountain.

MOUNT AGUNG

LOCATION	Bali, Indonesia
SPIRITUAL TRADITION	Balinese Hindu
ASSOCIATED DEITY	Shiva
DATE	1000 CE
WHEN TO VISIT	Any time of year

Mount Agung is an active volcano and the tallest peak on the island of Bali, Indonesia. Shaped like a perfect cone, this awe-inspiring mountain is universally regarded as the most sacred site in Bali. It is home to many holy temples and shrines, including the all-important Pura Besakih—the Mother Temple of Besakih—which is built on its gentle slopes.

According to Balinese Hindu tradition, the God Pashupati (Shiva) struck Mount Meru—the mythological home of Brahma and the semi-devas—causing a fragment to tear off. The fragment fell to Earth and formed Mount Agung. Followers of Tibetan Buddhism, Jainism, and the Bon faith share a belief in the supreme sacredness of Mount Agung.

More than a thousand years ago the Besakih Temple was built 3,280 ft (1,000 m) above sea level on the slopes of Mount Agung. Three-tiered shrines modeled on Mount Meru rise high in the central courtyard overlooking the sea. The three shrines symbolize Brahma, Vishnu, and Shiva, although devotees of Shiva see all three as different emanations of him. Today, pilgrims of many faiths come to worship at the Besakih Temple. Unlike other Hindu temples, the Mother Temple welcomes Hindus of all castes.

Further up the slopes of Mount Agung are two additional temples related to the Mother Temple of Besakih. The Kiduling Kreteg is dedicated to Brahma, and the Batu Mddeg to Vishnu.

In 1963 Mount Agung erupted. Huge plumes of smoke rose from its deep crater, followed by waves of molten lava pouring down the northern slope. Great explosions followed, sending rocks high into the air, which soon came crashing down the mountains slopes, causing mayhem. As the lava flows gathered pace, whole villages were destroyed, leaving more than 1,500 people dead. Almost miraculously, the Mother

Temple avoided destruction by a few feet, leading many to suspect that Shiva had intervened to protect the shrine built by the Balinese people.

Mount Agung is an active volcano, greatly revered by Buddhists, Hindus, Jains, and followers of the Bon faith.

THE KATAJUTA/THE OLGAS

LOCATION	Northern Territory, Australia
SPIRITUAL TRADITION	Aboriginal Dreamtime
DATE	Prehistoric
WHEN TO VISIT	Any time of year, but best in the cooler weather in April/May

Katajuta is an Australian Aboriginal term meaning "many heads," and refers to the 36 dome-shaped red rocks that rise mysteriously from flat plains in the Northern Territory of central Australia. The tallest rock in the group is Mount Olga, standing 1,508 ft (460 m) above the plain, which gives rise to the European name, The Olgas.

The Katajuta cover an area of 11 sq miles (28 sq km). The enormous rocks are the visible outcrop of a much larger piece of rock beneath the ground. Covered by a thick coat of granite, they have the remarkable ability to appear to change color dramatically, according to the weather and time of day. Mostly red, they can turn blueish-black in an instant, as clouds gather and rain falls.

Along with Uluru (see pages 18–19) and nearby Mount Conner, the Katajuta are probably the most sacred of all sites to the Anangu, the indigenous Australians, who may have lived in the area for more than 20,000

years. According to their sacred Dreamtime mythology, at the beginning of creation the ancestors roamed the formless earth, in the process creating the myriad features of our present-day landscape. They believe that the hills, rivers, lakes, and valleys we see today all tell of these ancient activities. To reconnect to the Dreamtime, the Anangu walk the paths the ancestors took, performing sacred rites along the way. These "walkabouts" invariably require them to journey from one sacred site to another, and the Katajuta have a special importance in this nomadic tradition. Upon arrival, pilgrims would invoke the spirits by singing songs and performing sacred dances in an effort to obtain blessings for themselves and their tribe.

The Katajuta are sacred to the indigenous Anangu people, who perform sacred rituals there.

MOUNT KAILASH

LOCATION	Tibet, China
SPIRITUAL TRADITIONS	Hindu, Buddhist, Jain, Ayyavazhi, Bon
ASSOCIATED DEITIES	Lord Shiva, Khorlo Demchog, Rishabhadeva, Sipaimen
DATE	4500–2500 BCE
WHEN TO VISIT	Mount Kailash is considered too sacred to climb

Mount Kailash is a stunning peak in the Himalayas in western Tibet. Rising to more than 21,650 ft (6,600 m), it lies near the source of several of the most sacred rivers in the East, including the Indus, the Sutlej, the Brahmaputra, and the Ghaghara, which runs through Nepal before flowing into the Ganges in India. The peak is sacred to Hindus, Buddhists, Jains, Ayyavazhis (a 19th-century Hindu sect from southern India), and followers of the Bon faith.

According to some branches of Hinduism, Mount Kailash is the home of Shiva and his consort Parvati. Some believe that the mountain is Shiva's lingam, or male sex organ, and that the nearby Lake Manasarowar is Parvati's yoni, or female sex organ. They say that Mount Kailash is the spiritual center of the universe.

Tibetan Buddhists believe that Mount Kailash is the abode of the great three-eyed god Khorlo Demchog, who embodies both wisdom and compassion. In their tradition, Khorlo Demchog battled with Lord Shiva long, long ago and displaced him from the peak.

In the Jain tradition, Mount Kailash is where Rishabhadeva, the first Tirthankara and founder of Jainism, attained enlightenment. To Ayyavazhis, Mount Kailash is sacred as the home of Shiva, whom its followers revere. In the Bon faith, Mount Kailash is the abode of the great sky goddess Sipaimen, and the spiritual center of the world. Even Sikhs regard Mount Kailash as sacred, for it is said that Guru Nanak, the first of the Ten Gurus and founder of Sikhism, climbed the peak during his quest for enlightenment.

Mount Kailash is one of very few peaks deemed too sacred to climb. There is no conclusive evidence that anyone has ever climbed to the top. However, the mountain's centrality in the mythologies of the Eastern spiritual traditions has ensured its place as a major site for holy pilgrimage. Pilgrims trek around the mountain's base.

Mount Kailash is widely held to be the spiritual center of the universe.

MOUNT FUJI

LOCATION	Honshu, Japan
SPIRITUAL TRADITION	Shinto
ASSOCIATED DEITY	Sengen-Sama
DATE	At least since the 1st century CE
WHEN TO VISIT	During the warmer summer months of July and August; climbing at night makes for a spectacular sunrise at the summit

At 12,385 ft (3,776 m), Mount Fuji is the tallest mountain in Japan. On clear days it can be viewed from the city of Tokyo, rising majestically in cone-like fashion towards a single ice-capped peak from the lake-filled flatlands that surround its base. Although Mount Fuji takes its name from the Buddhist fire goddess, Fuchi, it is especially sacred to followers of the indigenous Shinto religion, which has the worship of nature at its heart. Mount Fuji is universally regarded as the holiest of Japan's sacred mountains and is climbed every summer by tourists and spiritual seekers alike.

In ancient times samurai warriors trained in forest camps at the base of Mount Fuji, although the first human ascent is not thought to have taken place until 663 CE, when it was climbed by a Shinto monk. The summit itself is regarded as especially sacred, and the first shrine to the goddess who presides over this sacred mountain, Sengen-Sama, is believed to have been built as early as the 2nd century CE. Today, the beautiful Sengen Temple at the foot serves as the starting point for pilgrims making the climb to the summit. Three ancient trees protect the sacred grove next to the shrine; they have girths in excess of 75 ft (23 m) and are more than a thousand years old.

The forest at the foot of Mount Fuji is called Aokigahara or Sea of Trees. Long ago, poor people would abandon unwanted babies and elderly relatives in the forest to die. As a consequence, Aokigahara is widely believed to be haunted by ghosts and other demons. In recent years, a large number of people have taken their own lives in the forest.

Mount Fuji is an active volcano, with the capacity to wreak such terrible devastation on the city of Tokyo that it has become the most closely watched volcano in the world. The last major eruption took place in 1707, and scientists anticipate that it will erupt again in the not-too-distant future. That danger is clearly not in the minds of Mount Fuji's many visitors, for more than 200,000 people climb the peak every year to enjoy the spectacular views from its slopes.

Mount Fuji is an active volcano, sacred both to followers of the indigenous Shinto tradition and to Buddhists.

THE SACRED MOUNTAINS OF CHINA

LOCATION	Shandgong, Shanxi, Hunan, and Henan provinces, China
SPIRITUAL TRADITION	Taoist
DATE	3000 BCE–600 CE
WHEN TO VISIT	Any time of year, but best to avoid Heng Shan Bei in the winter, when it is very cold

In ancient China, holy men and women often retreated to the mountains to nurture their relationship with the divine. Not only do mountains rise up to the heavens where the gods are thought to reside, but they are typically places of outstanding natural beauty, where one can truly appreciate the supreme wonder of creation. In Taoism, five peaks are considered to be especially sacred: Tai Shan in Shandong province, Heng Shan Bei and Hua Shan in Shanxi province, Heng Shan Nan in Hunan province, and Song Shan in Henan province.

Mount Tai Shan has long been a pilgrimage destination for kings, poets, and commoners, who perceived it as a living god. Thousands of Chinese still climb the mountain every day, paying their respects at the two temples built

Mount Hua Shan is situated in the Shanxi province in China.

on its summit. To this day, the Temple of the Princess may be the most important pilgrimage site for women in China.

Mount Heng Shan Bei is the most inaccessible of the five sacred mountains and therefore the least visited. For many, this is its single greatest attraction. An ancient temple shrine was built on its slopes roughly 2,000 years ago, and has been in constant use ever since.

Mount Heng Shan Nan is most famous for the huge temple at its foot, dedicated to the mountain spirit; most unusually, this accommodates both Taoist and Buddhist worshippers.

Mount Hua Shan is formed by five peaks. From a distance they look like the petals of a flower, thus giving rise to its Chinese name, which means Flower Mountain.

Mount Song Shan is home to the world-famous Shaolin Temple, where Zen Buddhism was founded.

SHRINES AND GROVES

THE AJANTA CAVES

LOCATION	Maharashtra state, India
SPIRITUAL TRADITIONS	Theravada and Mahayana Buddhist
DATE OF CONSTRUCTION	2nd century BCE
WHEN TO VISIT	Open Tuesday through Saturday

The Ajanta Caves are a wonderful collection of 29 Buddhist temples carved into a cliff near the village of Ajanta in the Indian state of Maharashtra. The ancient caves were once used as sacred shrines and monasteries for Buddhist monks and house some of the finest Buddhist art in India.

It is generally thought that construction of the first Ajanta Caves began in the 2nd century BCE and continued into the 4th or 5th centuries CE, when work came to an abrupt halt with the decline of the Vakataka dynasty. It seems likely that the entrances to the caves were obscured by quickly growing trees, so that all knowledge of their existence was lost until they were rediscovered by Europeans in 1819.

The earliest caves belong to the Theravada tradition in Buddhism, known as the Lesser Vehicle, while the later caves are part of the Mahayana tradition, or Greater Vehicle, which

developed in the 1st century CE. The Theravada caves house beautiful stupas—sacred monuments whose precise geometry and intricate detail symbolize key aspects of the Buddha's life and teachings. The Mahayana caves, by contrast, typically contain a shrine with a large sculpture of the Buddha, where devout monks would meditate and worship.

For the convenience of modern-day visitors and scholars, the Ajanta Caves have been numbered 1 to 29, although this is not the order in which they were constructed. Every cave is truly remarkable, but some stand out for their exceptional murals and sculpture. Cave 1, for example, a Mahayana temple is adorned with beautiful paintings that depict important scenes from the Buddha's life, while its inner shrine houses an enormous sculpture of the Buddha preaching. Cave 9, on the other hand, is a Theravada prayer hall, with beautifully sculpted windows to allow sunlight into the cave. It contains a large monolithic stupa carved from the rock of the cliff, and its remarkable wall paintings are some of the oldest to survive in India.

Cave 26 is another prayer hall in the Mahayana tradition. It contains a huge carved statue of the Buddha in the reclining position, symbolizing the moment of his death, a seminal event for Buddhists.

The Ajanta Caves lay hidden by trees for more than a thousand years until they were discovered accidentally. They contain truly exceptional Buddhist art.

THE DAZU ROCK CARVINGS

LOCATION	Szechuan province, China
SPIRITUAL TRADITIONS	Buddhist, Confucian, Taoist
DATE OF CONSTRUCTION	7th century CE
WHEN TO VISIT	Any time of year

The Dazu Rock Carvings are one of the most extraordinary collections of rock carvings and sculptures to be found anywhere in the world. Located in Szechuan province near the city of Chongqing in China, these exquisitely crafted stone structures were hewn from a large number of steep rocky cliffs as long ago as 650 CE. They are remarkably well preserved, in large part due to their remote location, which helped to save them from the ravages of China's Cultural Revolution.

The most impressive carvings and statues are located at the sites of Bei Shan and Baoding Shan. The carvings at Bei Shan are older, dating from the late 9th century CE. The earliest were commissioned by Wei Junjing, a military commander stationed in the province to quell a local insurgency. Among this group is a life-sized sculpture of Wei Junjing himself, which was sculpted in full military regalia by a defeated adversary.

The newer sculptures at Bei Shan date from the 12th century and have been carved into an overhanging cliff-face that extends for more than 1,640 ft (500 m). Most of the statues depict Kuan Yin, the Buddhist goddess of compassion and mercy, who is usually surrounded by devoted nuns and monks. In most instances she is shown as a loving, peaceful presence, sometimes gazing at the moon's reflection. However, in niche 130 this many-armed goddess is uncharacteristically portrayed holding weapons, along with the severed head of an enemy. In niche 245, the story of the Amitabha Sutra is beautifully depicted and shows the Amitabha Buddha in the Land of Bliss, surrounded by bodhisattvas on clouds.

The Baoding Shan carvings are wholly distinct from those at Bei Shan. Designed by the monk Zhao Zheifeng, they were carved in the 12th and 13th centuries and are painted in bright colors. The many delightful sculptures here depict scenes from Mahayana Buddhist scripture, including images that are both amusing and terrifying from the Eighteen Layers of Hell, plus a 65 ft (20 m)-long reclining Buddha.

The Baoding Shan carvings at Dazu include a 65 ft (20 m) reclining Buddha, symbolizing the moment of his death.

A Hindu worshipper prays before the great Shiva lingam made of ice.

THE AMARNATH CAVES

INDIA

LOCATION	Amarnath, Jammu and Kashmir, India
SPIRITUAL TRADITION	Hindu
ASSOCIATED DEITY	Shiva
DATE OF CONSTRUCTION	3000 BCE
WHEN TO VISIT	Pilgrimage is undertaken in July/August to coincide with the festival of Shravani Mela; at other times the entrance to the caves may be blocked by snow

The Amarnath Caves form a spectacular high-altitude Hindu shrine in the state of Jammu and Kashmir. Dedicated to the great god Shiva, they have played a prominent role in Hindu mythology for up to 5,000 years.

The main Amarnath cave is home to a huge ice stalagmite, which grows every summer before shrinking again in the winter months. The enormous white monolith is strangely shaped like a male phallus, and for Shiva worshippers it represents the divine lingam of Shiva himself. Two smaller stalagmites also wax and wane in the caves every year, and are said to represent Parvati, Shiva's consort, and the elephant-headed god Ganesha, who is his son.

According to Hindu mythology, it was in the caves at Amarnath that Shiva shared the secret of creation with Parvati. It is said that two white doves overheard them talking and learned the secret themselves, thereby gaining the power to be reborn again and again. Many pilgrims have reported seeing a pair of doves flying together as they make the long pilgrimage to the caves.

The Amarnath Caves attract nearly half a million pilgrims every year, the vast majority walking 26 miles (42 km) of difficult mountain terrain from the town of Pahalgam during the warmer months of July and August. Older pilgrims frequently make the arduous journey on a horse, and in the last few years wealthy visitors have avoided the arduous four- to five-day trek altogether by taking a helicopter.

Since 2007, possibly because of global warming or because of the vast number of pilgrims inside the cave at the same time, the ice lingam has completely melted before the end of summer, much to the despair of visiting Hindu pilgrims. The Indian government is urgently exploring ways of remedying this situation.

THE ERAWAN SHRINE

LOCATION	Bangkok, Thailand
SPIRITUAL TRADITION	Hindu
ASSOCIATED DEITY	Lord Brahma
DATE OF CONSTRUCTION	1956 CE
WHEN TO VISIT	Any time of year

The Erawan Shrine is located within the Grand Hyatt Erawan Hotel in downtown Bangkok. It houses the famous Phra Phrom statue, which is greatly revered by Hindus in Thailand. Ritual dancers are regularly commissioned to perform sacred dances at the shrine, in the hope that prayers made to Phra Phrom—a representation of the supreme Hindu god, Lord Brahma—will be answered.

It is said that during the construction of the Erawan Hotel in 1956 an evil force was at work, causing innumerable delays and the deaths of many workmen. An astrologer advised that a shrine should be built to counter this trend, and by all accounts it succeeded, for upon the shrine's completion no further deaths or delays were reported, and soon afterward the hotel opened and began to thrive. Word spread concerning the magical powers of the Phra Phrom, and it became a major site for Thai Hindu pilgrimage. In 1987 the Erawan Hotel was demolished to make way for the Grand Hyatt Erawan Hotel, but the sacred shrine was preserved.

The Phra Phrom depicts a golden Lord Brahma seated on a raised platform. He has four arms, symbolizing the four Vedas (the primary sacred texts of Hinduism), and four faces, which point in each of the cardinal directions so that he can fully behold his creation. Lord Brahma is said to love jasmine, which is given freely to him by worshippers. He is also said to love Thai classical music, which is played more or less constantly in the shrine. Pilgrims sometimes place wooden elephants beneath the altar to honor him.

In 2006 the Erawan Shrine attained notoriety when a deranged man attacked the Phra Phrom and broke it to pieces. Onlookers were so incensed that they beat him to death.

The Phra Phrom statue depicts the four aspects of Lord Brahma in gold.

THE ISE GRAND SHRINE

LOCATION	Ise, Japan
SPIRITUAL TRADITION	Shinto
ASSOCIATED DEITIES	Amaterasu, Toyouke
DATE OF CONSTRUCTION	4th century BCE
WHEN TO VISIT	Any time of year

A Shinto priest worships in the Inner Shrine at Ise carved from sacred cypress trees.

The Ise Grand Shrine—commonly known simply as "The Shrine"—is a stunning complex of sacred Shinto shrines in and around the city of Ise in eastern Japan. It comprises two main shrines—the Inner and Outer Shrines —along with another 123 lesser shrines dotted around the city and its suburbs.

In the Japanese religion of Shinto, cypress trees are especially sacred, and they grow in abundance in the forests around Ise. According to tradition, in the 4th century BCE two sacred trees were cut down and made into posts to mark the precise spot of the Inner and Outer shrines, which stand roughly 3¾ miles (6 km) apart. These sacred posts still play a key role in the shrines today. According to Shinto custom, the main shrine buildings at Ise must be ritually destroyed and rebuilt on the adjacent site every 20 years, in an act of symbolic renewal. The ceremony is known as Shikinen Sengu; it was first performed in the 7th century CE and last performed in 1993. After the ceremonial destruction of the shrines, the sacred posts are placed in the ground to mark the old site, and white pebbles are cast around it. The ground is thus protected until the shrine is returned to its previous spot in 20 years' time.

The Inner Shrine is called Naiku and is one of the most sacred sites in Japan. Located just south of the city of Ise in Uji-tachi, it is dedicated to the sun goddess, Amaterasu-omikami, from whom the imperial Japanese family is said to be descended. Shrouded in secrecy, this shrine is watched over by the Supreme Priestess, who is always a member of the Japanese imperial family, according to strict Shinto tradition. She acts as an intermediary between Amaterasu and the people, and prays for the well-being of the Emperor and of Japan. The Inner Shrine is home to the Sacred Mirror, which plays a key role in ceremonial rites performed by the Emperor, and is jealously guarded by temple priests. According to Shinto mythology, Amaterasu once hid from her brother Susanoo in a cave, causing all the light in the world to disappear. The goddess of dawn, Ame-no-Uzume, then placed jewels and a mirror outside the cave, thereby tempting Amaterasu to step outside. As she gazed at her reflection, the other gods grabbed her, thus ensuring that the world would remain light. The mirror was eventually given to the Emperor of Japan and then kept at Naiku in the inner sanctuary, known as the *honden*. Members of the public are never allowed to see this prized relic, which as far as anyone knows has never been drawn or photographed. Visitors and pilgrims may pass through the Torii gate, where they can see the roofs of the most holy buildings rising

from behind trees, but only priests and members of the imperial family may actually enter the *honden*.

The Outer Shrine of Ise is called Geku and is also one of Japan's most sacred sites. Located a short bus journey from Naiku, this shrine is dedicated to the goddess of food and housing, Toyouke, who supervises offerings to Amaterasu. Twice a day, food is dedicated to the goddess in an ancient ritual that involves drawing water from a sacred well and kindling fire by turning wood on wood. Shinto pilgrims traditionally walk the 4 miles (6.4 km) from Geku to Naiku along a specially constructed pathway through the Sacred Forest of Ise Jingu, which is thick with cypress trees. Upon arriving at the shrine, the pilgrim is expected to bow twice, to clap the hands twice, and then to press the hands together in worship, before bowing twice more. During major festivals, such as Kanname-sai, when the first fruits are offered to Amaterasu, Shinto pilgrims may enter the main hall of the shrine for special ceremonies.

The Outer Shrine is dedicated to the Shinto goddess Toyouke, who supervises offerings to the great goddess Amaterasu.

MONTE GARGANO

LOCATION	Apulia, Italy
SPIRITUAL TRADITION	Christian
ASSOCIATED SAINT	Archangel Michael
DATE OF CONSTRUCTION	492 CE
WHEN TO VISIT	Festivals take place on May 8 and September 28–30

The Sanctuary of Monte Sant'Angelo sul Gargano—often referred to simply as Monte Gargano—is an historic cave shrine on the slopes of Mount Gargano in the Italian region of Apulia. Dating back to the late 5th century CE, the shrine is dedicated to the Archangel Michael, who is said to have appeared at the site on four separate occasions.

According to local tradition, the Archangel Michael first appeared at Gargano in 492 CE. One day, so the story goes, a bull was grazing on the mountain when it suddenly disappeared. It was eventually found hiding in a cave. An arrow was shot into the cave to chase the bull out, but the arrow flew back and struck the man who had shot it. Alarmed, the local people consulted the Bishop of Sipontum to ask what the strange occurrence meant. He ordained three days of fasting at the site of the cave, after which the Archangel Michael appeared, saying that the cave was under his protection. News of this extraordinary event reached Pope Gelasius I, who ordered that a church dedicated to the archangel be built at the site. The bishop entered the cave to perform the consecration, but found a temple already laid out, with a purple cloth on the altar and the archangel's footprint in the rock. The miracle was deemed proof that the cave had already been consecrated by St. Michael.

The final apparition of Michael occurred in 1656 when a terrible plague was raging in the area. Archbishop Alfonso Puccinelli prayed for help, and St. Michael appeared again and declared that stones from his grotto should be marked with his initials. Anyone who prayed to the stones would be granted immunity from the plague. The local people performed the penance and were saved. In gratitude, they erected a monument to Michael in the town square. The monument and the grotto shrine have attracted millions of Christian pilgrims over the centuries and may still be enjoyed today.

It is said that Francis of Assisi once visited Monte Gargano, but upon arriving chose not to enter the grotto itself, believing himself unworthy. Instead, he carved the sign of the cross on a stone outside and kissed it.

The shrine at Monte Gargano is dedicated to the Archangel Michael, who is said to have appeared there on four separate occasions.

THE TORII OF ITSUKUSHIMA

LOCATION	Off Itsukushima Island, Japan
SPIRITUAL TRADITIONS	Shinto, Buddhist
ASSOCIATED DEITIES	Princesses Ichikishima, Tagori, and Tagitsu
DATE OF CONSTRUCTION	16th century CE
WHEN TO VISIT	Any time of year; the Island of Itsukushima is approached by a 10-minute boat trip

The Torii of Itsukushima is a much-loved and iconic representation of Japan's indigenous Shinto tradition. Located just off the shore of the holy island of Itsukushima—also known as Miyajima—near Hiroshima, the Torii is an elegant monumental gateway painted deep red, which appears to float on the water at high tide. According to Shinto belief, the spirits of the dead pass through the shrine as they are swept in from the sea.

The Torii is built at the water's edge in front of the wooden Itsukushima shrine, which was constructed in the 16th century and modeled on its 12th-century predecessor. No one knows when the first shrine was erected, but historians believe that it was probably during the 6th century CE or earlier. The Itsukushima shrine is dedicated to the Shinto goddesses Ichikishima, Tagori, and Tagitsu, three powerful princesses who are viewed as divine protectors of sailors. Itsukushima has always been sacred in the Shinto tradition and, in Japan's ancient past, common folk were forbidden to walk on the island. Instead they had to approach by boat and sail through the Torii to participate in spiritual activities. Today, births and cremations are still forbidden on the island, which is viewed by many as a living god. Japanese visitors often walk around the shrine at low tide, placing coins in the cracks of the gate's wooden legs while making a wish.

The main shrine is part of a complex of shrines dotted around the perimeter of the island and a nearby theatre stage, which is used for performances of sacred Noh plays. Just along from the Itsukushima shrine is the Gojunotu shrine, which combines a surprising fusion of Shinto and Buddhist traditions.

The Torii of Itsukushima is an iconic landmark sacred to followers of Shinto.

PATMOS

LOCATION	Dodecanese Islands, Greece
SPIRITUAL TRADITIONS	Ancient Greek pagan, Christian
ASSOCIATED DEITIES/ SAINT	Apollo and Artemis, St. John the Theologian
DATE OF CONSTRUCTION	4th century BCE, 1st century CE
WHEN TO VISIT	Most tourist boats arrive from April to October

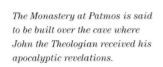

The tiny Greek island of Patmos is located near the coast of Turkey in the Aegean Sea. Much loved for its outstanding natural beauty, Patmos is most famous as the place where John the Theologian received divine revelations and wrote the fourth Gospel of the Christian New Testament.

According to Greek mythology, Patmos was once a sunken island lying at the bottom of the sea. The moon goddess Selene persuaded Artemis to ask her brother, Apollo, to bring it to the surface. Apollo asked Zeus for help, and Zeus raised the island out of the water. Ever since, Patmos has been sacred to Artemis (worshipped by the Romans as Diana) and Apollo.

People have lived on Patmos for 4,000 years, although the first Greek temples dedicated to Artemis and Apollo were not constructed until the 4th century BCE. The Romans took over the island in the 2nd century BCE, and gradually the population of Patmos declined, until it was used solely as a place of banishment for criminals and religious troublemakers. According to Christian tradition, in 95 CE John the Theologian, one of Christ's original disciples, was exiled to Patmos with his helper, Prochorus. John made a home for himself in a cave below the mountain temple of Artemis, and there he received a series of apocalyptic divine revelations that were transcribed by Prochorus. These writings later became the Book of Revelation in the New Testament, which foretells the second coming of Christ. It is said that John also wrote the fourth Gospel here, although some historians doubt this was the same John.

In the 4th century CE Greek Christian monks built a church above the Temple of Artemis. During the next few hundred years the church was destroyed many times by Arab invaders, until the monk Christodolous built a monastery above the sacred cave in the 11th century. The monastery has been in operation ever since, and is a major site for Christian pilgrimage. Built like a fortress to protect the monks from invaders, it contains some of the world's earliest transcriptions of the works of ancient Greek philosophers.

The Monastery at Patmos is said to be built over the cave where John the Theologian received his apocalyptic revelations.

THE MOGAO CAVES

LOCATION	Gansu province, China
SPIRITUAL TRADITION	Buddhist
ASSOCIATED DEITY	The Buddha
DATE OF CONSTRUCTION	366 CE
WHEN TO VISIT	Any time of year, but the caves may only be visited on an official tour

The fabulous Mogao Caves—known variously as the Mogao Grottoes, the Dunhuang Caves, and the Caves of the Thousand Buddhas—are located near Dunhuang in the Gansu province of northern China. They contain a wealth of Buddhist treasures, including exquisite murals and once-lost renditions of sacred texts.

According to Buddhist tradition, in 366 CE a monk by the name of Le Zun was walking near Dunhuang in search of enlightenment when he had a vision of a thousand Buddhas. Shortly afterwards Le Zun began excavating the first cave shrine, which over the next thousand years grew in number, until they housed a thousand Buddhas.

In the early days the caves were used to store Buddhist scripture and art. They proved highly popular with Buddhist pilgrims keen to find sanctuary from the world in their quest for enlightenment. Many of them painted murals on the inner cave walls,

which they used to aid their meditation, but also to teach local people about Buddhism.

By 700 CE Buddhism was flourishing in China, and Dunhuang was a growing city on the all-important Silk Road. Money poured into the local Buddhist monasteries, and before long more than a thousand cave shrines had opened for worship. For unknown reasons, many of the caves were sealed at some time after the 11th century, possibly as late as the 14th century. By then the Silk Road had given way to maritime trading routes, and Dunhuang had lost its importance. The caves were apparently forgotten.

In the early 20th century a Taoist by the name of Wang Yuanlu was investigating one of the caves when he found a false wall. Carefully removing it, he discovered a chamber full of ancient Buddhist, Taoist, and Confucian manuscripts in many different languages, ranging from 1,300–900 years old. He also found many statues of the Buddha, paintings, and numerous other sacred artefacts. Soon afterward major excavation work began on the caves. Today 30 of the caves are open to the public.

The lost Buddhist treasures buried in the Mogao Caves were discovered accidentally. Many walls feature exquisite murals.

THE SHRINE OF SAYIDDA ZEINAB

LOCATION	Damascus, Syria
SPIRITUAL TRADITION	Shia Muslim
ASSOCIATED SAINT	Sayidda Zeinab
DATE OF CONSTRUCTION	7th century CE
WHEN TO VISIT	Any time of year; non-Muslims are allowed into the courtyard outside, but they may find the intense grieving of the Shia pilgrims overwhelming

The Shrine of Sayidda Zeinab is located within a beautiful onion-shaped mosque in the suburbs of Damascus in Syria. For Shia Muslims, the shrine is one of the most sacred sites in the world; it ranks just after the cities of Najaf (see pages 256–257) and Karbala (see pages 72–73) as a destination for holy pilgrimage.

According to Islamic tradition, when the Prophet Muhammad died in 632 CE, a disagreement broke out over who should be the new ruler of Islam. One group, who became known as the Sunnis, wanted to elect a leader, while another group, who became known as the Shia, wanted to choose someone from Muhammad's family. Before long, fighting broke out between the rival factions. In 680 CE Sayidda Zeinab,

The shrine is decorated with beautiful blue tiles and topped with a golden dome.

granddaughter of the Prophet Muhammad and daughter of the great Shia leader Imam Ali, was present at the decisive Battle of Karbala, when her brother Hussain and both her sons were martyred. It is said that she gathered up their bodies before being captured and taken to Damascus, where she suffered great deprivations before eventually being freed.

For Shia Muslims, the Battle of Karbala was a defining moment in their history, for their leader Hussain and his followers had given their lives to safeguard the true word of the Prophet. As a consequence, when Shia pilgrims visit the Shrine of Sayidda Zeinab, they do not mourn in silence, but wail and scream and beat their chests, overcome by intense emotions stirred by memories of the great sacrifices made by their ancestors, especially Hussain and Sayidda Zeinab.

THE SHRINE OF OUR LADY OF EINSIEDELN

LOCATION	Near Zurich, Switzerland
SPIRITUAL TRADITION	Christian
ASSOCIATED SAINT	The Virgin Mary
DATE OF CONSTRUCTION	861 CE
WHEN TO VISIT	Any time of year, but the main pilgrimages take place from Easter until the beginning of October

The Shrine of Our Lady of Einsiedeln is located roughly 19 miles (30 km) from Zurich in the hills of central eastern Switzerland. Housing a sacred Black Madonna statue reputed to have magical powers, this beautiful marble shrine has attracted pilgrims for more than a thousand years.

According to Christian tradition, in 835 CE a nobleman named Meinrad left Zurich for the woods south of the city, in possession of a wooden Black Madonna statue. There he lived for 26 years as a hermit, making friends with two ravens. One day two villains stumbled upon Meinrad and killed him. The ravens followed the killers back to Zurich, shrieking loudly, causing the villains' capture. Almost a hundred years later a group of Benedictine monks found the Black Madonna at the site of Meinrad's hermitage, where they built a small monastery. In 948 CE they built the Chapel of Grace to house the Black Madonna. During the consecration of the shrine, it is said that Christ appeared in the form of a bright white light. News of the miracle spread quickly, and in 964 CE the Pope issued a papal bull confirming the miracle. This led to a huge number of pilgrims visiting Einsiedeln, and over time a magnificent abbey church was built to accommodate them, along with an ever-growing monastery, both of which can enjoyed today.

Although the abbey church at Einsiedeln is an impressive building in its own right, the main attraction has always been the Chapel of Grace, otherwise known as the Shrine of Our Lady. Made from marble, it stands alone at the west end of the church. Inside, the Black Madonna dressed in fine robes stands above the altar. It is said that the present statue is a replica, the original having been destroyed by a fire in the 15th century.

The Shrine houses a highly revered Black Madonna. It is said that Christ himself appeared when the shrine was first consecrated.

Outside the church is an enormous painting known as the Panorama, which depicts Christ's crucifixion; and beside it is the Diorama Bethlehem, a massive holy crib, consisting of more than 500 carved wooden figures.

THE VIRGIN OF CHARITY

SHRINES AND GROVES

LOCATION	El Cobre, Cuba
SPIRITUAL TRADITION	Christian
ASSOCIATED SAINT	The Virgin Mary
DATE OF CONSTRUCTION	1608 CE
WHEN TO VISIT	Any time of year

The Shrine of the Virgin of Charity—La Virgen de la Caridad—is located in the town of El Cobre, near Santiago in south-western Cuba. It has long been regarded as Cuba's most sacred site, as it houses a statue of the Virgin Mary that is said to cause miracles.

According to legend, in around 1610 two Indians accompanied by an African slave were sailing in a boat off the coast of El Cobre when they came upon a statue of the Blessed Virgin floating in the water. She was carrying a tiny baby Jesus and a gold cross, and attached to her was the inscription "I am the Virgin of Charity" in Spanish. At the time, St. James was the most revered saint on the island, so the Virgin was quietly stored in a hut. But in the morning she was gone, only to be found on top of the hill overlooking El Cobre. She was returned to the hut, but mysteriously reappeared on the hill again. On the occasion of her third appearance there, it was decided to house her in a shrine.

In 1630 all the slaves in El Cobre were freed, and the Virgin was taken from her shrine and placed above the altar in the town's church, replacing St. James in a startling symbolic gesture. Ever since she has been reputed to cause miracles, and is as sacred to followers of Santeria—the island's African religious tradition—as she is to Catholics, as well as to people who say they are non-believers.

In 1916 the Pope visited Cuba and travelled to El Cobre to behold the Virgin, whereupon he declared her the patron saint of Cuba. As a result, a new triple-domed church was built to house her, which opened in 1927. Among her more famous devotees have been the novelist Ernest Hemingway, who gave her his Nobel Prize, and the mother of Fidel Castro, who prayed to Mary for her son's success during the Cuban revolution.

The Church of Our Lady of Charity in El Cobre houses The Virgin of Charity.

KARBALA

LOCATION	Karbala, Iraq
SPIRITUAL TRADITION	Shia Muslim
ASSOCIATED SAINT	Imam Hussain
DATE OF CONSTRUCTION	684 CE
WHEN TO VISIT	This site is currently extremely difficult to visit because of the fighting in Iraq following the occupation by the American-led coalition

Karbala is a holy Islamic city located approximately 62 miles (100 km) south-west of Baghdad. For Shia Muslims—who are the largest religious grouping in Iraq—Karbala is the fourth most sacred city in the world, after Mecca (see pages 232–235), Medina (see pages 236–237), and Najaf (see pages 256–257). It is the site of the all-important pilgrimage to the Shrine of Imam Hussain, the grandson of the Prophet Muhammad and a hugely popular Shia martyr.

According to tradition, when the Prophet Muhammad died in 632 CE, a disagreement broke out over who should be the new ruler of Islam. One group, who became known as the Sunnis, wanted to elect a leader, while another group, known as the Shia, wanted to chose someone from Muhammad's family. Before long fighting broke out, and Imam Hussain, Muhammad's grandson and potential heir, was martyred along with many other Shia men in 680 CE, during the Battle of Karbala. Four years later a mosque was built over Hussain's tomb, which soon became the focal point of the city and a major site for Shia holy pilgrimage. Over the centuries many mosques were built to replace the original one, and in the 10th century a wooden sepulchre was made for Hussain's tomb. The present-day mosque dates from the 11th century, although the walls and dome were greatly improved in the 14th century, with large amounts of gold being added to the minarets and roof.

A second important destination for Shia pilgrimage is the Shrine of Hadrat Abbas, dedicated to Hussain's half-brother, who was also martyred in the Battle of Karbala. A third is al-Makhayam, believed to be where Hussain made camp before the decisive battle.

Pilgrimage to Karbala takes place on the day of Ashura, a Muslim holiday that usually occurs in January. During Saddam Hussein's rule of Iraq, Shia pilgrimages were heavily suppressed, but in recent years they have become increasingly popular. Male pilgrims often re-enact Imam Hussain's death by cutting themselves with knives so that they draw blood as they throng together in procession. Older pilgrims sometimes walk to the shrine and wait for death, believing that Hussain's tomb is a portal to paradise.

Every year thousands of Shia pilgrims flock to the Mosque of Imam Hussain to commemorate the Battle of Karbala.

THE CAVE CHURCH

LOCATION	Budapest, Hungary
SPIRITUAL TRADITION	Christian
ASSOCIATED SAINT	St. Istvan
DATE OF CONSTRUCTION	1926 CE
WHEN TO VISIT	Any time of year, except during services

The Cave Church is a beautiful and tranquil grotto sanctuary in Gellert Hill in Budapest. Dedicated to St. Istvan, a monk who reputedly lived in the cave a thousand years ago, the church was built in the 1920s and extended in the 1930s. The chapel houses a revered painting of the Black Madonna, which attracts pilgrims from all over Hungary.

St. Istvan was the first Christian King of Hungary, canonized by the Pope in 1083. Whether or not he was the same Istvan who is said to have lived in the grotto at Gellert Hill, no one can know for sure. According to tradition, the hermit Istvan was a healer, famous for curing the sick with hot water that gushed from a spring outside his cave. In 1926 a church dedicated to St. Istvan was founded in the grotto by an order of Pauline monks. The Archbishop of Kalocsa extended the church ten years later by

The Cave Church in Budapest houses a beautiful grotto carved deep into the hill.

digging further into the cave, which enabled the congregation to grow. In 1951 the communist government of Hungary shut down the church and arrested all the monks, executing the superior. A thick concrete wall was erected to conceal the church from view. In 1989, following the widespread revolutions in the Eastern Bloc, the wall was dismantled and the church once again opened its doors.

Pauline monks have long been associated with Marian worship, and the many hollows in the grotto walls are adorned with statues of the Virgin Mary and other Christian icons. On one wall is a replica of the famous painting of the Black Madonna at Czestochowa in Poland, which is said to possess miraculous powers.

The church walls are shaped by the rocky interior of the cave, which creates an amazing acoustic for singing and music during church services, and a profound stillness at other times, which is highly conducive to prayer.

THE SHWEDAGON PAGODA

LOCATION	Yangon (Rangoon), Burma
SPIRITUAL TRADITIONS	Buddhist, Burmese astrological
ASSOCIATED DEITIES	The past four Buddhas
DATE OF CONSTRUCTION	Allegedly *c.* 460 BCE
WHEN TO VISIT	Any time of year; however, trips to Burma require careful planning and the necessary permits must be obtained

The Shwedagon Pagoda—also known as the Golden Pagoda—is the most sacred Buddhist temple in Burma. Rising majestically to nearly 33 ft (100 m) from Singuttara Hill, it radiates golden light over Lake Kandawgyi in Yangon (Rangoon) in southern Burma.

According to Buddhist tradition, the Pagoda is 2,500 years old, having been constructed before the Buddha's death in 486 BCE. However, modern-day archeologists dispute this, claiming that the stupa was probably built closer to 1,000–1,500 years ago. It is possible that both are correct, and that the present stupa was built on the site of an earlier temple.

Local Buddhists tell of two merchant brothers who met the last Buddha, Gautama, and were given eight of his precious hairs to enshrine. They traveled to Singuttara Hill, where relics of the three preceding Buddhas had been enshrined by King Okkalapa. The King opened the casket containing the Buddha's hairs

and a great miracle occurred: lightning flashed, the earth shook, and rain poured from the skies along with masses of precious stones. All at once the blind could see, the deaf could hear, and the mute could speak. Trees blossomed and bore fruit. In response, the King ordered a shrine to be built, and a series of pagodas was constructed on top of each other to house the holy hairs. Over time it became the most sacred pilgrimage site in Burma.

The present gold-plated temple rises to a beautiful spire set with precious stones. There are four entrances; at the top of one is an image of the second Buddha, Konagamana, seated on a gold-plated plinth. Above him are terraces for monks, and at the very top is the crown. Burmese astrology dictates exactly where in the temple each devotee must worship.

The pagoda is believed to be built over a casket containing the Buddha's hairs.

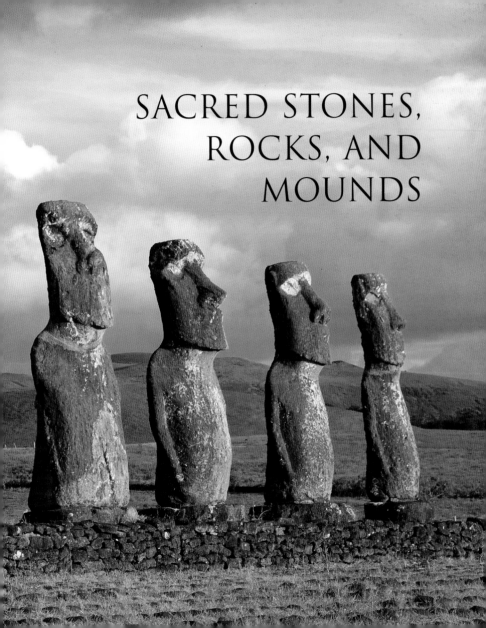

SACRED STONES,
ROCKS, AND
MOUNDS

THE ALTA ROCK CARVINGS

LOCATION	Finnmark county, Norway
SPIRITUAL TRADITION	Not known
DATE OF CONSTRUCTION	4200–500 BCE
WHEN TO VISIT	Summer

The Alta Rock Carvings are a magnificent collection of more than 5,000 paintings and petroglyphs—pictures carved into rocks—along an ancient fjord near the Arctic Circle in the far north of Norway. The earliest were probably made from 4200 BCE, while the latest are dated around 500 BCE. These extraordinary carvings provide conclusive evidence of extensive human activity in the far north of Europe in prehistoric times.

The carvings were first discovered in 1967 and have since been extensively studied by scientists who are keen to understand more about the people who created them. In the main, the paintings and petroglyphs depict everyday human activities, such as hunting, fishing, and sailing, but also religious rituals, some of which appear to be sexual in nature. In addition, there are a large number of geometric shapes and symbols, the meanings of which still remain a mystery. In the later carvings, animals

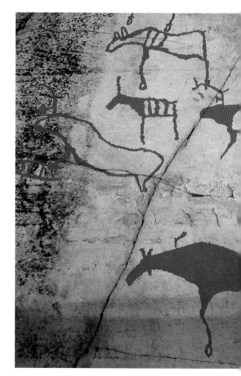

like reindeer are pictured behind fences, suggesting that the people who carved these extraordinary images had become more settled than nomadic.

Most historians believe the creators of this astonishing artwork are the direct predecessors of the indigenous Sami people, who still hunt and fish in northern Norway and beyond. The designs on their clothes and tools bear a strong resemblance to patterns found on the rocks. However, this belief is only conjecture, as there is no DNA or other physical evidence to prove it definitively.

One of the most interesting aspects of the petroglyphs is the unique depiction of polar bears. While almost all the other animals—moose, reindeer, and elk—are shown with horizontal tracks behind them, some bears have vertical tracks, often crossing those of other animals, as if they have magical powers. Curiously, after 1700 BCE bears are no longer depicted in this way; from then on they are shown in exactly the same way as other animals. This has led to the theory that bears were worshipped as an important totemic animal with access to the afterlife until for some reason there was an abrupt change in religious belief.

The Alta Rock Carvings date from around 4200 BCE. They depict intricate geometric shapes, humans, and animals, including elk, reindeer, and bears.

AVEBURY

LOCATION	Wiltshire, England
SPIRITUAL TRADITIONS	Ancient pagan, Druidic
DATE OF CONSTRUCTION	2600 BCE
WHEN TO VISIT	Any time of year, although the summer and winter solstices are deemed to be especially magical

Located in the county of Wiltshire in the west of England, Avebury boasts the largest ancient stone circle in the world. Although it is older even than the neighboring site of Stonehenge (see pages 118–121), the precise purpose of this magnificent monument remains as mysterious as the people who constructed it some 4,000–5,000 years ago.

Avebury consists of a circular chalk-stone bank 20 ft (6 m) high and more than 1,312 ft (400 m) wide. The ditch has four distinct entrance points —north, east, south, and west—and just inside the ditch is a circle of huge sarsen stones, some of which are 23 ft (7 m) tall and weigh up to 40 tons each. Unfortunately, only 27 of the original 98 remain, largely because of vandalism, as opposed to natural erosion caused by long exposure to the elements.

Inside the large stone circle are two smaller stone circles, and archeologists believe these were probably constructed just before the large circle. The northerly inner circle was made of 27 stones, of which only four have survived, while the southerly one was originally made of 29 stones, of which only five are still standing today.

Before many of the stones were destroyed in the late 18th century, a local historian, Dr. William Stukeley, made drawings of Avebury, which clearly show that it was designed to represent a giant snake passing through a circle—an extremely potent spiritual symbol. The head and tail were represented by standing stones that stretched for more than 1 mile (1.6 km) into the surrounding countryside, and these stones were arranged in patterns connecting them to yet more stones further away.

In recent times modern-day historians and archeologists have presented evidence to show that the stone circle at Avebury forms part of an interconnected latticework of stone monuments all over southern England, including Glastonbury Tor (see pages 24–25), Stonehenge, and St. Michael's Mount in Cornwall. It is possible that these mysterious monuments are themselves connected to other stone monuments throughout Europe, with Avebury as the spiritual core.

The standing stones at Avebury form the largest ancient stone circle in the world.

MACHU PICCHU

LOCATION	Urubamba Valley, Peru
SPIRITUAL TRADITION	Inca
DATE OF CONSTRUCTION	1430–1530 CE
WHEN TO VISIT	June through September

Machu Picchu is an ancient Inca site north of the city of Cuzco in southern Peru. Perched on a high mountain ridge more than 7,870 ft (2,400 m) above sea level, this stunning stone city overlooks the sacred Urubamba Valley, which runs from east of Pisac to Ollantaytambo, beautifully enclosed by snow-capped mountain peaks.

Archeologists believe that construction began around 1430, and was still ongoing when the Spanish conquered Peru in 1532, although the site was sacred to the Incas since their earliest history. Fortunately the Spanish never found Machu Picchu, so this extraordinary site was left unharmed, unlike so many other Inca monuments. It was not until the 20th century that knowledge of Machu Picchu became widely known, when an indigenous tribe living there made contact with an American historian.

There are many beautiful stone structures to enjoy at Machu Picchu, including temples, houses, water fountains, and more than a hundred flights of stone steps, often carved from a single piece of granite. The beautiful stone structures display an astonishing degree of architectural sophistication and building mastery; the huge slabs fit so perfectly together that the joins are practically invisible. Archeologists have ascertained that a large area within the city was set aside for religious activities, and in this district three principal buildings have been identified. They are known as the Temple of the Sun, the Room of the Three Windows, and the Intihuatana, a breathtaking sundial made from polished stone, constructed so that it points directly to the sun during the winter solstice. Each of these three monuments was dedicated to the Inca sun god, Inti, who played a central role in the Inca religion.

Theories abound about the role of Machu Picchu in Inca society, but no one can be absolutely sure. What seems clear, however, is that the site was chosen at least in part for its position in relation to other mountains and their alignment with the sun, moon, and stars, which was highly important to the Incas. Today, many tens of thousands of spiritual seekers take the three-day hike along the Urubamba Valley to the remote city every year, making Machu Picchu the most-visited sacred site in Peru.

Machu Picchu is an awe-inspiring Inca stone city, overlooking a lush valley and surrounded by snow-capped peaks.

An artist's impression of the Great Pyramid at Giza, which is one of the most sublime sacred sites to be found anywhere in the world.

THE GREAT PYRAMID OF GIZA

LOCATION	Cairo, Egypt
SPIRITUAL TRADITION	Ancient Egyptian
ASSSOCIATED DIGNITARY	King Khufu
DATE OF CONSTRUCTION	2560 BCE, or possibly much earlier
WHEN TO VISIT	Any time of year

The Great Pyramid of Giza is located on the outskirts of modern Cairo in Egypt. An extraordinary monument of the ancient world, this magnificent stone structure is shrouded in myth and mystery. Indeed, theories abound concerning its method of creation and its sacred purpose, with each new discovery adding to, rather than diminishing, the controversy.

Egyptologists typically date the Great Pyramid to 2560 BCE, and claim it was built as a tomb for the Egyptian King Khufu. However, independent researchers dispute this, arguing that in 2560 BCE the Egyptians lacked the technology to build such a structure—as evidenced by the two smaller, more primitive pyramids built next to it at around that time. Furthermore, no human remains were ever laid to rest inside the Great Pyramid. The most common alternative view is that the Great Pyramid was built as long ago as 10,000 BCE, when it would have been perfectly aligned with certain stars in the constellation of Orion, who was a sacred god for the ancient Egyptians. Many of these researchers believe that the main chamber was used for sacred initiation rites, and that the precise shape and construction of the pyramid served to enhance the intensity of the religious experience.

If the 2560 BCE date is correct, the Great Pyramid was the tallest building in the world for more than 3,800 years. It was made from two-and-half million limestone blocks, which weighed on average more than 2½ tons each. The structure that can be seen today was once encased by smooth white granite slabs, which fitted perfectly together over its whole surface area, so that the pyramid would have gleamed in the hot desert sun. At that time it was capped by a huge pyramid-shaped onyx carving.

THE VALLEY OF THE KINGS

LOCATION	Luxor, Egypt
SPIRITUAL TRADITION	Ancient Egyptian
ASSOCIATED DEITIES	Isis, Selkis, Nepththys, Neith, and other Egyptian gods
DATE OF CONSTRUCTION	1539–1075 BCE
WHEN TO VISIT	Any time of year

The Valley of the Kings is a vast burial site on the west bank of the Nile River, adjacent to the city of Luxor in Egypt. Here, great tombs were built more than 3,000 years ago to store the remains and artefacts of pharaohs and other important people. Sadly, most of the treasures housed in the tombs have since been plundered, but the awe-inspiring stone burial chambers adorned with extraordinary hieroglyphs may still be enjoyed today.

The Valley of the Kings was begun in 1539 BCE, when the tomb of Thutmose I was built. Construction continued for roughly 500 years, during which time more than 60 tombs were dug out, ranging from simple pits to veritable palaces, with the last great tomb being that for Rameses X or Rameses XI.

Most of the tombs are found in the East Valley, with only the tomb of Ay in the West Valley currently being open to the public. His red-quartzite sarcophagus is decorated with beautiful carved images of Egyptian gods, including Isis, Selkis, Nepththys, and Neith, who would have protected him in the afterlife.

In the East Valley the largest tomb was built for Rameses II, which contains 67 separate burial rooms. Rameses II ruled for 66 years, making him the longest-serving monarch in dynastic Egypt. The stone walls of his burial chamber are engraved with scenes from the Book of Gates and the Amduat, two ancient texts that describe the fate of the soul when it reaches the afterlife.

The most famous tomb in the East Valley is that of Tutankhamun, discovered in 1922. It is neither the grandest nor the biggest tomb to be discovered, but it is certainly the best preserved and thus reveals more about ancient Egyptian funerary rites than any other. In total, a staggering 3,500 treasures were found in this tomb, suggesting that even more treasure would have been buried with greater kings. The walls of his burial chamber are adorned with scenes depicting his arrival in the underworld, where he would have been greeted by the gods Hathor, Anubis, and Isis.

The Tomb of Tutankhamun was discovered in 1922. Very well-preserved, it has revealed much information about ancient Egyptian spiritual beliefs.

CHICHEN ITZA

LOCATION	Yucatan state, Mexico
SPIRITUAL TRADITION	Mayan
ASSOCIATED DEITY	Kukulcan/Quetzalcoatl
DATE OF CONSTRUCTION	7th–12th centuries CE
WHEN TO VISIT	Any time of year

Chichen Itza is a remarkably well-preserved Mayan stone city in the Yucatan peninsula in southern Mexico. Its early construction began in the 7th century CE, with significant additions being made for the next 500 years, until it was captured by neighboring city Mayapan. Although no further building work was subsequently carried out, Chichen Itza appears to have continued as a site for Mayan pilgrimage until the 16th century, when the city was conquered by the Spanish and abandoned. Major excavation work began in the 1920s, and today the site is one of the most visited sacred destinations in Mexico.

From the 7th to the 9th centuries CE many stone temples and palaces in the highly decorative Puuc style were erected in honour of the rain god, Chaac. In the 10th century, however, a new style of grand architecture

90

The Pyramid of Kukulcan is one of the most impressive structures at the site.

suddenly appeared, generally attributed to the city coming under the influence of the Toltecs. From then on, Chichen Itza became a focal point for worship of Kukulcan, the feathered serpent god known to the Aztecs as Quetzalcoatl. Great temples in his honor and stone sculptures depicting his form sprang up all over the city. During this time Chichen Itza became the center of power in the Yucatan.

There are a great many important sacred stone structures at Chichen Itza, but arguably the most impressive is the Pyramid of Kukulcan, which is modeled on the Mayan calendar. This huge monument has four great stairways each of 91 steps, which—when added to the central platform—make 365 steps, a complete solar year.

BAIAME CAVE

LOCATION	New South Wales, Australia
SPIRITUAL TRADITION	Aboriginal Dreamtime
ASSOCIATED DEITY	Baiame
DATE OF CONSTRUCTION	1000 BCE
WHEN TO VISIT	The cooler summer months of July and August are best

Baiame Cave is one of many rock shelters sacred to Aboriginal tribes near the town of Singleton in New South Wales. It takes its name from a large rock painting of Baiame, the Sky Father and creator god in the local Dreamtime mythology, although there are many other Aboriginal paintings at this site, which have been carbon-dated to around 1000 BCE.

Close to the entrance of the cave, Baiame's narrow body is painted a deep red ochre, which has faded over time. He is depicted facing the viewer head-on, a feature of all Aboriginal paintings of him. In this instance he is shown with disproportionately long arms stretching outward in a gesture of protection. He has no mouth, as the Sky Father speaks only from the heart. His low hanging member leaves no doubt that he is male—important because Baiame played a key role in

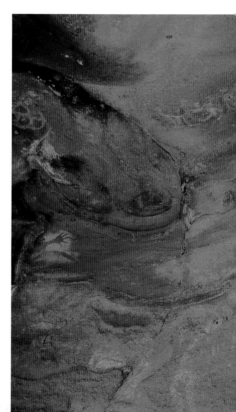

The Sky Father Baiame is shown with arms outstretched in a protective gesture.

male initiation ceremonies; the cave would have been forbidden to women.

According to the local Wanaruah people, Baiame arose during the time of the Dreaming to create everything beautiful in the world—the rivers, mountains, and lakes, as well all the striking animals of the valley, including the wallaby, emu, and kangaroo. At the same time another god, Marmoo, created all things ugly and harmful to humans, such as illness and pestilence. In response, Baiame created a sacred bird, Eaglehawk, to protect the people of the valley. He also invented songs, laws, and culture, as well as the first *bora*, an initiation site for boys. Once his creation was complete, he flew up to the sky where he has remained ever since as the Sky Father.

THE BIG HORN MEDICINE WHEEL

LOCATION	Wyoming, USA
SPIRITUAL TRADITION	Crow Native American
DATE OF CONSTRUCTION	1300 CE
WHEN TO VISIT	The northerly location and high elevation make the site inaccessible due to snow, in all but the summer months

The Big Horn Medicine Wheel is located on a flat ridge on Medicine Mountain in the Bighorn National Forest in Wyoming at an elevation of more than 9,840 ft (3,000 m). It appears to have been made entirely from rocks gathered from the surface of the mountain some 700 years ago.

The wheel consists of a central cairn some 10 ft (3 m) across surrounded by a large, uneven circle of rocks approximately 230 ft (70 m) in circumference. There are six smaller cairns dotted along this outlying rim, which is joined to the central cairn by 28 spokes made of small rocks. Just like the stone circles in Europe, the Big Horn Medicine Wheel is aligned with the sun, moon, and stars. The outer cairns are big enough to hold a seated person, and they are aligned

The Big Horn Medicine Wheel has been used for vision quests for centuries.

with the rising and setting sun during the summer solstice, as well as with the stars Aldebaran, Rigel, and Sirius, which are visible from Medicine Mountain at dawn. The 28 spokes of the wheel appear to represent the days in a lunar cycle.

No one knows who built the medicine wheel, although members of the local Crow tribe say that it was made by a boy called Burnt Face, who got his name from being badly scarred by a fire as a baby. According to the Crow myth, when Burnt Face reached adolescence, he went on a vision quest in the Big Horn Mountains and built the medicine wheel. As the quest progressed, he helped to save some baby eaglets that were being stalked by an animal. His good deed was seen by an eagle flying overhead, which carried him off and removed the blemishes from his face in a gesture of gratitude.

THE CARNAC STONES

LOCATION	Brittany, France
SPIRITUAL TRADITION	Pre-Celtic
DATE OF CONSTRUCTION	4500–2000 BCE
WHEN TO VISIT	Any time of year

The Carnac Stones are an ancient burial site near the village of Carnac in north-western France. More than 3,000 standing stones were erected here, making it one of the most multitudinous megalithic monuments in the world. Archeologists believe the first stones were hewn as early as 4500 BCE, although the majority date to around 3300 BCE. Other stones may have been added as late as 2000 BCE.

The Carnac Stones are arranged over a wide area in what appear to be remarkably straight lines. Archeologists have classified them into three distinct groups, known as the Menec, Kermario, and Kerlescan alignments. The Menec alignment consists of solitary stones (menhirs) arranged in rows that extend for more than 3,280 ft (1,000 m) long by 328 ft (100 m) wide. The tallest of these stones is 13 ft (4 m) high and the shortest just 1½ ft (0.5 m). Further east, the Kermario alignment consists of 1,029 stones arranged in ten fan-like

rows roughly 4,264 ft (1,300 m) in length. The remains of a stone circle can be seen from the air at the far eastern end of this alignment. Further east again is the Kerlescan alignment, which consists of 555 stones arranged in 13 distinct rows roughly 2,624 ft (800 m) long. At the far west of this alignment is a stone circle, and archeologists believe there was probably another stone circle built further north. They have discovered a much smaller collection of stones, called the Petit-Menec alignment, even further east, but these are largely hidden by trees and ivy.

Carnac also has a number of dolmens (collections of stones resting upon each other) as well as tumuli (stones set within burial mounds), including the tumulus of Saint-Michel, a huge burial chamber upon which a Christian chapel was built in 1663. As with other Neolithic monuments, there is an undoubted spiritual significance to the precise arrangement of these stones, but exactly what this is remains as mysterious as the sun, moon, and stars whose precise movements they seem designed to record.

A local Celtic myth claims that the Carnac stones were created by the magician, Merlin, who petrified a visiting Roman legion, thus explaining why they are arranged in such wonderfully straight lines.

The Carnac Stones are arranged in remarkably straight lines for purposes that seem to elude modern historians.

CARNARVON GORGE

LOCATION	Queensland, Australia
SPIRITUAL TRADITION	Aboriginal Dreamtime
DATE OF CONSTRUCTION	2500 BCE
WHEN TO VISIT	Any time of year, but not accessible during times of heavy rain

Carnarvon Gorge is a spectacular site sacred to the Anangu—the indigenous Australians—located near the towns of Roma and Emerald in Queensland, Australia. This beautiful gorge is adorned by impressive sandstone edifices, which rise like the pointing fingers of a great creator god. The caves and cliff-side ravines of the gorge are covered with sacred paintings and etchings, making Carnarvon Gorge an awe-inspiring place to visit.

Archeologists have determined that the uplands were inhabited more than 19,000 years ago, although the area does not appear to have been properly settled until the arrival of the Bidjara tribe around 2500 BCE. They are thought to be responsible for the amazing art found at the site, which appears to serve a great number of purposes: to mark out land, to narrate Dreamtime myths, to share knowledge, and to honor important people.

The main site for art at Carnarvon is a huge rock chamber known as Cathedral Cave. The most prolific artform is stencil art, which appears to have been made simply by blowing primitive paint over an object pressed on the wall. Many hands are pictured, along with boomerangs and other weapons. Some of the hands are thought to point to burial chambers, because the first Europeans to enter the cave found the remains of a child in a hole surrounded by pointing hands.

In addition to the stencil art, there is also some free drawing and rock engraving. A common motif is the female vulva, which presumably played a major role in fertility or sexual rites. These sacred images are also found in abundance along a sandstone cliff known as the Art Gallery, as well as at Baloon Cave. The most common color of the artwork at Carnarvon is red; amazingly, the pigments have not faded with age.

Stunning Carnarvon Gorge is decorated with ancient paintings and etchings.

CARROWKEEL

LOCATION	County Sligo, Ireland
SPIRITUAL TRADITION	Ancient Celtic pagan
DATE OF CONSTRUCTION	3400–3100 BCE
WHEN TO VISIT	Any time of year

Carrowkeel is an outstanding passage-tomb cemetery located on ridges of the Bricklieve Mountains in County Sligo in the north-west of Ireland. Known locally as the Pinnacles, Carrowkeel consists of 14 extremely well-preserved cairns, under which 14 tombs have been discovered.

The burial chambers were first opened and excavated in 1911. Archeologists used to believe that the most recent tombs were dug as late as 2000 BCE, but modern dating methods suggest that all the tombs were first constructed more than 5,000 years ago. The burial chambers appear to have been in use by prehistoric people as late at 1500 BCE; they were used again in the Christian era for the burial of children who had not been baptized.

Each chamber has a doorway that may be entered by crawling along a small passageway. The largest of the chambers is 98 ft (30 m) wide, the smallest around 26 ft (8 m). The roof of each chamber was made of large limestone slabs, onto which many smaller stones were piled to form the distinctive cairns. Inside these chambers, pottery and primitive tools

made from deer antlers were found alongside the bones of the deceased.

The spiritual purpose of the tombs at Carrowkeel remains a mystery. However, it has been shown that one of the cairns—known as Cairn G—was built with a light box above the doorway, so that the chamber would be lit by the setting sun for one month before and after the summer solstice, and by the moon for one month either side of the winter solstice. Another chamber—Cairn K—contains a rock known as the Croach Patrick Stone, since it closely resembles Croach

Patrick Mountain 75 miles (120 km) away. From Cairn K, the sun can be seen setting directly behind Croach Patrick Mountain on Samhain (November 1), the first day of the Celtic new year, and again on Imbolc (February 2), which falls halfway between the winter solstice and the spring equinox, suggesting a profound celestial significance to the design.

The oldest passage-tombs that were dug at Carrowkeel are more than 5,000 years old.

CERNE ABBAS

LOCATION	Dorset, England
SPIRITUAL TRADITION	Pagan
ASSOCIATED DEITY	Cernunnos/Heracles
DATE OF CONSTRUCTION	Not known
WHEN TO VISIT	Any time of year

The village of Cerne Abbas sits on the banks of the sleepy River Cerne, a few miles north of Dorchester in the west of England. In 987 CE a large Benedictine abbey was founded in Cerne Abbas, but unfortunately it was almost completely destroyed by Henry VIII. Ever since, religious life in the village has centred around St. Mary's Church, built in the late 13th century and still retaining many original features. But what makes Cerne Abbas most famous as a sacred site is neither the abbey nor the church, but the Rude Man adorning one its steep hills.

The Rude Man—or Rude Giant, as he is also known—is an enormous carved figure of a naked man brandishing a large club. Standing 180 ft (55 m) tall and 167 ft (51 m) wide, he is clearly visible from miles around, and may be best viewed by standing in the valley opposite. This extraordinary carving was made by digging a small trench into the chalky ground, creating a white-line effect that is characteristic of many hill drawings that are in England. The most striking feature of this pagan piece is the vivid portrayal of the man's member, which rises proudly in vertical fashion and reaches all the way to his ribs. What the local monks must have thought of this rude sight is hard to imagine!

No one knows who made the Giant, although records show that a spot above the Giant's head was used for maypole dancing—an important pagan fertility ritual—up until 1635, when it was suppressed by the Christian Church. To this day, barren couples will sometimes make love on the giant under the stars in the hope of conceiving a child.

Some believe the Giant is the Celtic fertility god, Cernunnos, and others that he is Heracles, who is often depicted brandishing a club.

The Rude Man of Cerne Abbas is an ancient fertility symbol.

EASTER ISLAND

LOCATION	South-eastern Pacific Ocean
SPIRITUAL TRADITION	Rapanui
DATE OF CONSTRUCTION	After 300 CE
WHEN TO VISIT	Any time of year

Easter Island is a tiny volcanic island in the south-eastern Pacific Ocean some 2,200 miles (3,540 km) from the coast of Chile, making it the most remote inhabited island in the world. It was first discovered by Europeans in 1722, when it was home to an estimated 2,000–3,000 Rapanui people. Today the island is world-famous for the many hundreds of huge stone torsos that the first visitors found adorning its many hills and coves.

It is not known precisely when the island was first settled or when the torsos were erected, with estimates varying from between 300 and 1200 CE. Sadly, almost all the islands' inhabitants were killed or died of natural causes in the 1860s, either at the hands of ruthless Peruvian slavers or as a result of the diseases they brought with them. Those who survived fought against each other over their rights to the land of the deceased, leading to the demise of almost everyone. Although the population of the island has since recovered, virtually all knowledge of its history was lost.

Archeologists have since determined that almost all the large stone statues, known as *moai*, were probably carved at around the same time from volcanic ash from within the Rano Raraku volcano. Primitive stone hand-chisels have been found at this site, and these appear to be the main tools for these extraordinary creations. Each statue is thought to represent a chief or other important person, and the largest one, known as Paro, weighs more than 80 tons, as do several others. The biggest ones would have required upwards of 200 men to drag and raise them off the ground, indicating that the stone statues were of supreme importance to the Rapanui, who positioned them roughly ½ mile (0.8 km) apart looking out to sea, to form a more or less unbroken line around the island.

As well as the stone statues, Easter Island possesses one of the world's finest collections of petroglyphs—that is, images carved into rock. These variously depict important people or events, as well as religious symbols and totemic figures.

The iconic stone torsos—known as Moai—gaze out towards the ocean in an almost unbroken line around the island.

KNOWTH

LOCATION	County Meath, Ireland
SPIRITUAL TRADITION	Prehistoric pagan
DATE OF CONSTRUCTION	3000 BCE
WHEN TO VISIT	Any time of year

Knowth is an extraordinary set of early Bronze Age passage-tombs located near the prehistoric site of Newgrange in County Meath, Ireland. Rising from moist green land, a massive burial mound stretching almost 328 ft (100 m) across is surrounded by 19 smaller burial mounds, constructed from beautifully decorated stones.

The main mound was built more than 5,000 years ago with a border made of more than 100 decorated stones. It is formed of two separate chambers with access from the east and the west, although they stop short of meeting in the middle. The passageways and tombs are decorated with ornamental stones, known as orthostats, which depict a variety of geometric shapes, including spirals, concentric rectangles, and circles. Interestingly, the chambers were not used for burying human remains, but rather housed the ashes of the dead, who were cremated during sacred ritual ceremonies that took place outside.

During the period that preceded the construction of the mounds (3800–3400 BCE) the local people built rectangular wooden houses and a huge wooden enclosure approximately 328 ft (100 m) across. However, at the

time of the building of the tombs (3300–2900 BCE), they switched to living in circular wooden houses for reasons that are not clear. For the next several hundred years the passage-tombs fell into disuse, and the local people built a timber circle known as "Woodhenge." By 2500 BCE a new tribe had taken over Knowth.

Later peoples used the great mound as a fort and dug deep ditches around it to protect it from attack. By 800 CE it was the home of the King of North Brega, and in the 12th century the Normans fortified the site still further, erecting protective walls.

However, by 1400 Knowth was completely abandoned.

No one can say what purpose the sacred mounds served, although the decorated stones reveal deep insights into their creators; for example, an orthostat found in the eastern chamber is carved with a map of the moon, clearing showing the Mare Crisium. All we can do is marvel at the awe-inspiring mystery.

The massive burial mound at Meath was built more than 5,000 years ago. Many of its stones are intricately carved.

LOUGHCREW

LOCATION	County Meath, Ireland
SPIRITUAL TRADITION	Neolithic
DATE OF CONSTRUCTION	4000–3200 BCE
WHEN TO VISIT	Any time of year, but the spring and autumn equinoxes are considered to be especially sacred

Loughcrew near Oldcastle in the county of Meath is one of the most important sacred-stone sites in Ireland. In all, more than 30 large cairns have been found there, making it one of the most intensely used Neolithic sacred sites in the world. One of the cairns has been shown to be aligned with the rising sun during the autumn equinox.

Loughcrew is spread out over three distinct areas: two hilltop sites known as Carnbane West and Carnbane East, and the slopes of nearby Patrickstown Hill, although the stone monuments there have been largely destroyed. The cairns that can be seen today are thought to date from about 3200 BCE; however, the recently perfected art of archeo-astronomy dates them much earlier, possibly to 4000 BCE, when certain of the inner passages would have been correctly aligned with solar events at significant times of the year. This may explain why human remains have only been found in a few of the "burial" chambers, for their primary purpose may not have been funerary, but astronomical.

Beneath the mounds that have been opened are cross-shaped chambers supported by stones decorated with petroglyphs, which include geometric shapes and leaves. One of the most popular cairns with spiritual seekers is known as Cairn T on Carnbane East, which has a beautiful back-stone decorated with solar symbols including sun-wheels. During the spring and autumn equinoxes this stone is lit up at sunrise by light shining through the entrance of the passageway, an event now witnessed by many modern sun-worshippers. A similar event is believed to occur in Cairn L on Carnbane West, where a free-standing monolith in the chamber is said to be lit up at sunrise on the cross-quarter days in November and February; however, access to this cairn is currently not possible, making this claim difficult to prove.

The intricately carved back-stone in Cairn T is lit up at sunrise on the spring and autumn equinoxes by sunlight shining through the entrance of the passageway.

THE NAZCA LINES

LOCATION	Nazca Desert, Peru
SPIRITUAL TRADITION	Nazca
DATE OF CONSTRUCTION	200 BCE–700 CE
WHEN TO VISIT	Any time of year

The Nazca Lines are a truly extraordinary collection of ancient images carved into the Nazca desert off the southern coast of Peru. These fascinating geoglyphs, which stretch across an area more than 50 miles (80 km) wide, depict mysterious geometric shapes, alongside animals, fish, insects, and birds. One of the most striking features of the Nazca Lines is their size, making them impossible to apprehend except from the air.

The lines are thought to have been created up to 2,700 years ago by the Nazca people, who lived in the area till around 700 CE. It is believed that they used primitive tools to dislodge a surface layer of red stones from the desert, leaving the lighter-colored lines to show through. To create the astonishing visual accuracy of the images, historians think the Nazca people used string attached to wooden posts to map out their grand designs. Most of the huge shapes are extremely well preserved, in large part due to the

incredibly dry and windless condition of the desert.

Most historians agree that the primary function of the lines is religious, but as to their precise meaning, no one is completely sure. Some say they have an astronomical function, lining up with the sun, moon, and stars. Others say that the Nazca people used the lines to point to water sources that otherwise would have been lost. Some historians believe the animals may have been totems invoked to aid in this important task. Others say that the lines prove the Nazca had mastered flight, and they conjecture that the Nazca built hot-air balloons to view them, although there seems to be no evidence to prove or disprove this. One of the most extraordinary claims is made by the famous Swiss author, Erich von Däniken, who asserts that the lines were used as ancient landing strips, possibly for alien spacecraft. He refers to one of the round-headed figures as "the astronaut." The Nazca people left behind them no written language, so we may never know what the Lines' true purpose was. But thousands of years after their creation they still delight us.

The ancient line carvings at Nazca are so large that they can be properly apprehended only from the air.

NEWGRANGE

LOCATION	County Louth, Ireland
SPIRITUAL TRADITIONS	Neolithic pagan, Celtic pagan
DATE OF CONSTRUCTION	3000 BCE
WHEN TO VISIT	Any time of year, but visitors can only witness the extraordinary lighting up of the tomb on the winter solstice if they win an annual lottery to participate in this event

Newgrange is located in the green hills of County Louth about 43 miles (70 km) north of Dublin and about 9 miles (15 km) from the Irish Sea. An enormous burial mound that is more than 5,000 years old, Newgrange is widely considered to be one of the most significant prehistoric sacred sites anywhere in the world. Recent studies have shown that it served an astronomical as well as a funerary purpose.

Newgrange is more than 246 ft (75 m) wide and 39 ft (12 m) high. The stone perimeter is indented at one point, where a small entrance leads into a stone passageway almost 66 ft (20 m) long, which in turn leads into a cross-shaped burial chamber. In the corners of the chamber the cremated remains of human beings were found. The walls of the chamber are decorated with astonishing megalithic art, including an amazing triple-spiral motif. Most of the kerbstones supporting the mound are also decorated, featuring circles, zigzags, lozenges, and other geometric shapes. Some 1,000 years later a large stone circle was erected around the mound, but only 12 of these standing stones remain today.

Newgrange features heavily in Celtic mythology, where it is described as an ancient fairy mound that was home to the Tuatha De Danann, once god-like people who worshipped the goddess Danu. The ancient myths tell of how the great fairy mound was built by Dagda, the King of the Gods; however, the mound predates these Iron Age myths by at least 2,000 years.

On December 21, 1967 Professor M. J. O'Kelly was standing in the burial chamber when he observed that the floor was suddenly lit by the rising sun sending light down the long passageway through a roof-box sited above the entrance. Astronomical calculations have shown that this event would have occurred exactly at sunrise on the winter solstice 5,000 years ago, and not four minutes later as it does today. This remarkable event is re-enacted for modern-visitors. At the end of each tour, the guide assembles the guests inside the mound and turns off the lights. Then a single light is switched on, simulating the effect of the sun. But to witness the real thing, visitors must win a lottery.

The huge stone mound at Newgrange serves an astronomical as well as funerary purpose.

THE PETERBOROUGH PETROGLYPHS

LOCATION	Ontario, Canada
SPIRITUAL TRADITION	Algonkian shamanic
DATE OF CONSTRUCTION	900–1400 CE or earlier
WHEN TO VISIT	The park opens in May and closes in November every year

The Peterborough Petroglyphs are an outstanding collection of sacred rock carvings located about 31 miles (50 km) north of Peterborough in Ontario, Canada. In total, more than 900 distinct images carved into limestone rock are currently visible, variously depicting turtles, snakes, the sun, shaman, geometric patterns, and ceremonial boats. All knowledge of this sacred site was lost until a chance discovery in the 1950s.

The dominant academic view is that the images were carved roughly a thousand years ago by the Algonkian people, now classified as a First Nations tribe. However, a number of researchers dispute this, pointing out that the boats depicted do not look like those used by Native Americans, instead closely resembling shamanic boats depicted in ancient Russian and Scandinavian petroglyphs thousands of miles away. These researchers believe that some of the petroglyphs are much older, possibly more than 5,000 years old.

Modern-day Native Americans such as the local Ojibwa tribe describe the carvings as *Kinomagewapkong*, which translates as "the rocks that teach," and use them to instruct their young during pilgrimages to the site. They claim that it is not the carvings that are sacred, but the large 164 x 98 ft (50 x 30 m) rock into which they are carved. They say that it is possible to enter the spirit world through cracks in the rock, and that the sounds of underground water are the voices of spirits speaking. Although they claim the images were carved by their ancestors, they do not appear able to shed much light on what the European-looking images mean, or why the site was forgotten for so long.

Modern-day archeologists have evidence that humans lived in the area long before the First Nations tribes are thought to have arrived, and it is these people that the maverick researchers credit with carving the images. Some see in the carvings an elaborate solar map made by Viking explorers, which they use to give the site a precise dating of 3117 BCE.

The origin and spiritual purpose of the extraordinary rock carvings at Peterborough are shrouded in mystery.

THE SERPENT MOUND

LOCATION	Ohio, USA
SPIRITUAL TRADITION	Native American
DATE OF CONSTRUCTION	1000–1500 CE
WHEN TO VISIT	Any time of year

The Serpent Mound is an awe-inspiring, man-made monument that stretches more than 1,130 ft (400 m) along a flat ridge of the Serpent Mount Crater in Adams County, Ohio. Rising more than 3⅓ ft (1 m) high and shaped like an uncoiled, undulating snake about to swallow an egg, this stunning earthwork was probably created around a thousand years ago.

Archeologists have determined that the area around Serpent Mound was first settled by the Adena people more than 2,500 years ago. Tools they left behind indicate that they erected two conical burial mounds near where the serpent stands today, as well as building many other burial mounds in the vicinity, typically consisting of log- or clay-lined chambers, often brightly painted and housing sacred treasures.

From around roughly 1000–1500 CE the site was settled by the Fort Ancient people, who erected an elliptical-shaped burial mound near the serpent's tail. For a long time no

one could tell whether the serpent was created by the Adena or the Fort Ancient people, for not a single artefact was found. The customary view was that it belonged to the Adena people, until recent radiocarbon dating indicated that at least parts of the mound's construction took place in the 11th century, proving that it was the work of the Fort Ancient. However, they were at least inspired by the mounds of the Adena, so perhaps it is fair to say that the serpent is a creation of both peoples and both cultures.

Intriguingly, the head of the serpent lines up with the setting sun at the summer solstice, and a coil of the serpent may be aligned to the rising sun at the winter solstice, although this is less certain. As to what purpose the great serpent served, no one really knows. It was not used for burials, like the other mounds, and can only be seen clearly from the air, suggesting that it may have been created simply to please the gods, so that they might look more kindly on the mortals below. The snake is also a potent symbol of re-birth in many ancient spiritual traditions.

An extraordinary effigy, Serpent Mound was probably constructed around 1,000 years ago. It depicts an undulating snake about to eat an egg.

STONEHENGE

LOCATION	Wiltshire, England
SPIRITUAL TRADITION	Originally unknown, but recently considered Druidic pagan
DATE OF CONSTRUCTION	3100–2200 BCE
WHEN TO VISIT	Any time of year

ENGLAND

Stonehenge is an ancient stone circle located on open fields near the town of Amesbury in south-western England. There is some debate about precisely when the stones were first erected, although archeologists are certain that the circular earth bank that surrounds them was initially constructed more than 5,000 years ago, and that the site served primarily as a burial chamber. The other possible purposes of Stonehenge are the subject of much mystery and debate.

According to an ancient legend, first recorded by Geoffrey of Monmouth in the 12th century, Stonehenge was brought to England from Ireland by Merlin, the magician who served King Arthur and the Knights of the Round Table. The stones were said to have originated in Africa and to have been erected by

Stonehenge is a mysterious stone circle in south-western England, aligned with the movement of the sun, moon, and stars.

giants on Mount Killaraus, a mythical Irish mountain, because of their special healing properties. Initially knights attempted to drag the stones to England, but they proved too heavy, so Merlin was called upon to employ magic. Geoffrey further related that the remains of Uther Pendragon (King Arthur's father) as well as those of Constantine III (a legendary king and a relative of Arthur) were buried inside the stone circle.

The archeological evidence suggests that around 2600 BCE 80 standing stones, known as blue stones, were brought from Wales and arranged in two concentric circles within the raised earth bank. Remnants of 43 of these stones are visible today. At the same time, a great

stone known as the Heelstone was erected just outside the north-eastern entrance to the circle, and two or three large stones were erected just inside. Only one of these great monoliths—the Slaughter Stone—has survived. Significantly, the north-eastern entrance is perfectly aligned with where the sun would have appeared during the midsummer and midwinter solstices, suggesting a profound celestial purpose to the stone circle. At around this time, 56 pits known as Aubrey Holes were also dug inside the circle, but what their purpose was is widely contested.

During the next 200 or so years, 30 enormous sarsen stones were brought to Stonehenge and arranged in a large circle around the blue stones. Massive lintel stones were places atop them, bringing the height of the circle to nearly 16½ ft (5 m). Inside this circle, five huge trilithons—sets of two stones with a lintel on top—were erected, each stone weighing up to 50 tons. How these massive stones were brought to the site remains a profound mystery, just like the spiritual significance of the circle.

It is believed by most people that Stonehenge served as an astronomical observatory where religious rituals

An artist's impression shows the earth mound, main stone circle, inner trilithons, and standing stones c. 2500 BCE.

were performed, which probably included the cremation and burial of the dead. In the late 20th century an American astronomer named Gerald Hawkins published extensive research into the alignment of Stonehenge, which claimed that the standing stones and trilithons could be used to predict moonrises and moonsets at the winter and summer solstices, as well as sunrises and sunsets. He further demonstrated how it was possible to predict lunar eclipses occurring every 19 years using the Aubrey Holes. Since then, other astronomers have built on his work, using the stones to predict solar and lunar events with an extraordinary degree of accuracy. Much of the objection to their theories has arisen from those who claim that such a detailed knowledge of mathematics and astronomy would have been impossible for primitive people who almost certainly had no written language.

Today, Stonehenge is visited by large numbers of tourists all year round, many of whom can be seen standing in awe on the surrounding grass, contemplating the unfathomable mystery of the stones. Modern-day Druids view Stonehenge as a place of pilgrimage, and have been given permission to carry out sacred rites during the midsummer and midwinter solstices, as well as at the spring and autumn equinoxes.

THE STANDING STONES OF STENNESS

LOCATION	Orkney Islands, Scotland
SPIRITUAL TRADITION	Neolithic and Norse pagan
DATE OF CONSTRUCTION	*c.* 3100 BCE
WHEN TO VISIT	Any time of year

The Standing Stones of Stenness are a beautiful Neolithic monument on the Orkney Islands off north-eastern Scotland. Located on the south-eastern shore of the Loch of Stenness, only a few of the original standing stones remain, but they are singularly impressive. Other stone monuments, such as the Ring of Brodgar and the Cairn of Maeshowe, are found only about ½ mile (1 km) away, suggesting that the site was deemed especially sacred to its ancient Neolithic builders.

Most of the standing stones were originally laid out in an ellipse consisting of 12 stones, although archeologists suspect that the monument may have been abandoned before the last two stones were in place. Only four of these monoliths remain, and they rise to a height of almost 16½ ft (5 m), but are only 12 in (30 cm) thick, making them extraordinarily thin and elegant.

A deep ditch was cut around the circle into rock, and around this an earth bank was constructed. Beyond the circle is the Watch Stone, which rises to nearly 20 ft (6 m) tall. Inside the circle many smaller stones were laid, and on the central stone cremated bones have been found. Some 5,000 years have passed since the stones were first erected, so it is very difficult to ascertain their precise spiritual purpose. However, there is evidence that the stones were being used in the 17th century for Norse marriage rites and other ceremonies, when they were known as the "Temple of the Moon."

In 1988 archeologists found the socket of the famous Odin Stone, which had been destroyed in 1814 by Captain W. Mackay, much to the anger of the local people. According to local lore, a News Year's feast lasting five days was held at Stenness every year. During the festivities, young couples visited the stone circle to perform sacred marriage rites. The woman would kneel and pray to the god Odin, before the couple traveled to the Ring of Brodgar to repeat her prayer. Then they would travel to the Odin Stone to finalize the marriage. This great stone had a hole bored through its middle, so that the young couples could join hands through it to announce their marriage vows.

The Standing Stones of Stenness are unusually thin and elegant. They were erected more than 5,000 years ago.

TENOCHTITLAN

LOCATION	Mexico City, Mexico
SPIRITUAL TRADITION	Aztec
ASSOCIATED DEITY	Quetzalcoatl
DATE OF CONSTRUCTION	1325–1521 CE
WHEN TO VISIT	Any time of year

The ancient city of Tenochtitlan was once the capital of the Aztec empire in Central America. Built on an island in Lake Texcoco in the early 14th century, the city was thriving until it was conquered in the early 16th century by the Spanish, who settled there and used the site as an administrative base for their operations throughout Mexico. Today, the ruins of old Tenochtitlan can be found in the center of Mexico City.

According to an ancient Aztec prophecy, the site of a great future city would be revealed by the vision of an eagle sitting on a cactus eating a snake. In 1325 precisely this apparition is thought to have been witnessed by Aztecs on marshy land in Lake Texcoco. Immediately they began planning and building a grand symmetrical city, which necessitated expanding the island by drying the land. As the city grew, so did the prosperity of the Aztecs, who came to dominate all nearby tribes. During the reign of Ahuitzotl a great flood occurred but, undeterred, the Aztecs built an even greater city to replace it.

When the Spanish laid siege to the city in 1519, Tenochtitlan was one of the largest cities in the world—much larger than almost all European cities—with an estimated population of more than 200,000, and possibly as many as 350,000. There were many public buildings, schools, a great pyramid, and lavish temples dedicated to Aztec gods, including the great feathered serpent, Quetzalcoatl. There was a great palace for Montezuma, the ruler of Tenochtitlan, which had more than a hundred rooms, all equipped with their own baths. There were zoos for mammals, reptiles, and birds of prey, along with an aquarium for exotic fish. Regrettably, the Spanish conquistadors destroyed almost everything in the city. Recently, excavations have been carried out, revealing many of the old buildings, including a huge stone calendar.

At the time the Spanish laid siege to the island city of Tenochtitlan in 1519, it was one of the greatest cities in the world.

THE STONE RING OF CALLANISH

LOCATION	Isle of Lewis, Scotland
SPIRITUAL TRADITION	Ancient pagan
DATE OF CONSTRUCTION	3400–2600 BCE
WHEN TO VISIT	Any time of year

The Callanish Stones—otherwise known as the Stone Ring of Callanish—are located on the west coast of the Isle of Lewis, which is part of the Outer Hebrides in Scotland. In total, 13 silver-white, elegantly shaped stones rise from a grassy plain to form a circle just over 131 ft (40 m) in circumference. In addition, four avenues of stones lead to the circle from the four points of the compass, the longest and most defined approach coming from the north. The tallest stone is just over 16½ ft (5 m) high and the shortest barely 3⅓ ft (1 m) in height, with the majority of the slender stones being taller rather than shorter.

Archeologists believe the stone circle was built from 3400 to 2600 BCE, although there is evidence that the site has been in use even longer. A burial cairn has been discovered beneath the tallest stone containing human remains, although this appears to have been a later addition and not the principal purpose of the site. According to a local legend, St. Kieran of Ireland traveled to Callanish where he found a clan of giants, who refused to embrace the Holy Spirit. Their punishment was to be turned into stones.

Speculation abounds as to why this spectacular monument was erected, with most theories concentrating on the movement of the sun, moon, and stars. Significantly the skies above Callanish would have been crystal-clear prior to 1500 BCE, when the weather in northern Europe cooled, leading to cloudy skies. Some scholars claim that the north avenue is aligned with the setting midsummer full moon as it sinks behind the distant mountain of Clinash, but conclusive proof of this is lacking. Others have noted that the precise position of stones would have created alignments with the Pleiades, Capella, and Altair prior to the clouding of the skies, but again this may be more by accident than design. We may never know why the ancients built the stone circle at Callanish, although it seems certain they had a spiritual purpose in mind, for just to stand in their midst usually evokes feelings of mystery and awe.

The Stone Ring of Callanish consists of 13 silver-white stones that rise gracefully from a grassy plain on the Isle of Lewis.

TIWANAKU

LOCATION	Lake Titicaca, Bolivia
SPIRITUAL TRADITIONS	Tiahuanaco, Inca
ASSOCIATED DEITY	Viracocha
DATE OF CONSTRUCTION	*c.* 300–900 CE
WHEN TO VISIT	Any time of year; an annual Winter Solstice Festival takes place on June 21

The ancient city of Tiwanaku is located on the shores of Lake Titicaca in western Bolivia. Built by an early pre-Inca Andean civilization known as the Tiahuanaco, the city is home to temples, monumental gates, a pyramid, and standing stones, many of which have been carved with mysterious faces that look uncannily like aliens. Today, followers of New Age spirituality travel to Tiwanaku to participate in ritual ceremonies at the winter solstice.

The land around Tiwanaku has been settled by farmers for at least 2,500 years, but the large monumental buildings that can be seen today were not built until the 5th century CE, when the Tiahuanaco people began to flourish. For the next 500 years they fashioned an extensive empire in the region, with Tiwanaku as their capital city. It appears that a massive drought occurred around 1000 CE, which resulted in the near-total demise of their civilization. During the 15th century the Incas took over the city, believing it had been built by their great god, Viracocha, who lived in neighbouring Lake Titicaca. The Incas succumbed to the Spanish conquest of Bolivia in the mid-16th century, when most of the city's treasures were either dispersed or destroyed. Fortunately they left some of the largest stone statues in place and sold a small number of artefacts, which have since found their way into local museums.

One of the most unusual monuments at Tiwanaku is the Akapana pyramid. Little remains of it today because of extensive looting over the centuries, but archeologists have determined that in around 700 CE all other building work ceased in the city, to focus on the pyramid's construction. Even so, the great pyramid was

never finished. Archeologists speculate that it may have been intended to be a reservoir for water, as if the inhabitants had foreknowledge of the impending climatic disaster. One of the most interesting temples in the city is the subterranean temple made of red sandstone. Its walls are carved with more than 100 faces, all of which bear a striking resemblance to aliens.

An artist's impression of the breathtaking pre-Inca city of Tiwanaku, soon after it was built in the 5th century CE.

COPAN

LOCATION	Copan Ruinas, Honduras
SPIRITUAL TRADITION	Mayan
DATE OF CONSTRUCTION	5th–9th century CE
WHEN TO VISIT	Any time of year

Copan is a Mayan city in western Honduras, next to the modern village of Copan Ruinas. Close to the Guatemalan border, the ruined city sits peacefully in a lush green valley surrounded by forested mountains, teeming with jungle animals. Copan is today admired for possessing some of the finest pre-Columbian art anywhere in the Americas, being especially noted for the exquisite stone sculptures adorning its surviving buildings.

The ancient Mayan kingdom of Xukpi was founded at Copan in the 2nd century CE. By the 5th century Copan had become the center of power in the region, and over the next several hundred years, many great palaces, step-pyramids, temples, and processional ways were constructed all over the city. These buildings were uniformly decorated with intricate combinations of elaborately carved stone slabs—known as portrait stelae —creating a stunning effect, which may be enjoyed by visitors today.

The last great monuments were erected at Copan in 822 CE, and by 900 CE the city was in serious decline, although historians have not been able to ascertain why. Whether due to invasion, revolution, environmental disaster, climatic deterioration, or simply the fact that its inhabitants had lost favor with the gods, the fall of Copan remains a mystery. When the Spanish arrived in the 16th century the city had long been abandoned.

Among the many ruins that may be explored today, the Acropolis, the Ball Court, the Hieroglyphic Stairway, and the Great Plaza are among the most exceptional. The Great Plaza is truly enormous. It is adorned with many altars and lavishly decorated by elaborate portrait stelae. The Hieroglyphic Stairway consists of 63 steps, many of which have fallen out of place. These were inscribed with thousands of glyphs, creating the longest Mayan text that has ever been found, although its precise meaning has yet to be discerned. The Acropolis contains several noteworthy temples, one of which served as a portal to the world of the gods, and the Ball Court is the second-largest ever found in Central America. It is believed that the players had to move a small rubber ball through raised hoops without using their hands. Victory may have been rewarded by being chosen for ritual sacrifice.

An artist's impression of the Mayan city of Copan, noted for its stunning stone sculpture.

THE OCMULGEE NATIONAL MONUMENT

LOCATION	Georgia, USA
SPIRITUAL TRADITION	Mississippian Native American
DATE OF CONSTRUCTION	900–1350 CE
WHEN TO VISIT	Any time of year

The Ocmulgee National Monument in Macon, Georgia, consists of a number of ancient burial and temple mounds and an earth lodge near the Ocmulgee River. Although the area around the site has been inhabited for more than 11,000 years, the temple mounds were constructed just over a thousand years ago by the highly successful Mississippian people, who flourished from around 900 to 1350 CE from Wisconsin to Georgia to Florida.

The Great Temple Mound rises some 59 ft (18 m) above the Macon Plateau, which is itself 49 ft (15 m) above the river bank below, meaning that the mound provides an unparalleled view of the surrounding area. Evidence suggests that a fire was burning at all times in this temple, and that it may also have served as the home of a priest or chief. A large wooden effigy used to sit on top of the mound, with steps leading up to it

from the ground. But who or what was worshipped here, no one knows for sure. Many other temple mounds have

been found in the area, but none as large or grand as this one.

The Great Earth Lodge is shaped like a large flattened cone, with an entrance on one side built from wooden pillars. This grassy mound is largely reconstructed, although the floor inside is wholly original. Artefacts found at the site suggest it was some kind of meeting place. Exactly 50 people would have gathered in the great chamber in a wide circle, presumably to discuss and make decisions about the issues of the day.

By 1350 the Mississippian culture was in decline, and a new set of mounds known as the Lamar Mounds were built. These include the only example of a spiral mound in North America, although two strikingly similar ones have been found in Mexico. This has led archeologists to suggest that the Mississippian people originally traveled west in canoes all the way down the Ocmulgee, which translated from Muscogean means "where they sat down."

The great earth lodge is shaped like a flattened cone and has wooden pillars marking the entrance.

MONTE ALBAN

LOCATION	Oaxaca, Mexico
SPIRITUAL TRADITIONS	Zapotec, Mixtec
DATE OF CONSTRUCTION	500 BCE–700 CE
WHEN TO VISIT	Any time of year

Monte Alban is an ancient pre-Mayan site, roughly 6 miles (10 km) west of Oaxaca City in southern Mexico. Perched on low mountainous hills, the spectacular stone ruins at Monte Alban overlook a green plain that stretches towards majestic mountains visible in the far distance. At present only about one-tenth of this mysterious site has been excavated.

Monte Alban was founded in around 500 BCE by the Zapotec people. Over the next 500 or so years it grew to become the political and religious capital of an empire that dominated much of Oaxaca. By 500 CE the city was diminishing in importance, and three hundred years later it had been abandoned. Before the Spanish arrived in the 16th century the site was reused by the Mixtec people, who performed ritual ceremonies in the sacred structures they inherited.

The most significant ruins at Monte Alban are built on and around a man-made ridge roughly 1,312 ft (400 m) from the plain below. This vast ridge was home to the Main Plaza, which was —and still can be—reached by climbing monumental stone staircases from the north or south. To the east and west are mounds where great temples and a great ball-court once stood. Throughout the Main Plaza carved stone monuments have been found, many of them depicting extraordinary and unsettling images, such as tortured prisoners, some of whom have been genitally mutilated. Other stones are marked with place names, presumed to be cities that the Zapotec conquered. More than a hundred stone tombs have been uncovered, which were later reused by the Mixtecs.

The pre-Mayan city of Monte Alban was founded by the Zapotecs around 500 BCE.

THE HILL OF TARA

LOCATION	County Meath, Ireland
SPIRITUAL TRADITION	Ancient Celtic pagan
ASSOCIATED DIGNITARIES	The High Kings of Ireland
DATE	3500 BCE–1200 CE
WHEN TO VISIT	Any time of year

The Hill of Tara consists of a series of earthwork and stone monuments near the River Boyne in County Meath, Ireland. Today an inconspicuous stretch of raised grassy mounds on deserted green hills, the site once played a central role in the ceremonial rites of the ancient Kings of Ireland.

The most important monuments on the Hill of Tara are found on its summit, within an area enclosed by a ditch and raised earthbanks known as Raith na Riogh, or the Fort of the Kings. Two linked circular mounds form the centrepiece of this extraordinary site. One is the Teach Chormaic, or Cormac's House; the other is the Forradh, or Royal Seat. At the middle of the Forradh is the Lia Fail, or Stone of Destiny, a simple standing stone about 3¼ ft (1 m) tall. According to Celtic tradition, any would-be King had to symbolically marry the goddess Maeve during sacred ceremonies that took place at the stone. It is said that the stone

would scream out in pleasure if touched by a man who was a rightful King—a noise so loud that it could be heard all over Ireland.

Just north of the Teach Chormaic and the Forradh is Dumha na nGiall, otherwise known as the Mound of Hostages. This is the oldest monument so far found on Tara, possibly dating to as early as 3500 BCE. An extremely well-constructed and astronomically aligned ancient passage-tomb, this mound once stored the ashes of venerated individuals who had been cremated nearby. It takes its name from the supposed custom of the ancient kings of seizing hostages from neighboring tribes to ensure their peaceful cooperation.

The Hill of Tara once played a central role in the ceremonial rites of the ancient Kings of Ireland.

PLACES OF RETREAT

PLACES OF RETREAT

MOUNT SHASTA

LOCATION	California, USA
SPIRITUAL TRADITIONS	Native American, New Age
ASSOCIATED DEITY	The Great Spirit
DATE OF CONSTRUCTION	*c.* 2500 BCE
WHEN TO VISIT	Any time of year, but visitors are asked to stay away from Native American rituals

Mount Shasta is a breathtaking, snow-capped mountain peak sacred to Native Americans, rising to a height of more than 13,120 ft (4,000 m) in the far north of California. In recent years an increasing number of New Age seekers have been drawn to the mountain and its outlying areas, which are reputed to induce both healing and mystical experiences.

The north slope of Mount Shasta may have been inhabited for 4,500 years, while its immediate environs have been home to Native Americans for up to 9,000 years. All the various local tribespeople believe that Mount Shasta is sacred, and it features predominantly in Native American creation mythology. According to the Shasta tribe, when the Great Spirit decided to create the world, he took a stone and carved a hole in the sky, then thrust down ice and snow to make Mount Shasta. He then climbed down through the clouds onto the mountain, before pressing his fingers into the surrounding land, causing trees to rise up from the earth. He told the sun to shine, which caused the snow on the mountain to melt, providing much-needed water for the trees, and rivers to flow and springs to rise. He breathed on the leaves of the trees to make birds, and took a branch, which he broke into many pieces and threw into a river, creating fish. He then created all-powerful grizzly bears before retiring to Mount Shasta to live with his family. According the local Modoc tribe, humans are the offspring of these early mountain bears and the Great Spirit's daughter.

Today, Mount Shasta has become a focal point for New Age spirituality. A Buddhist monastery has been built on its slopes, and many spiritual retreat centers have grown up in the vicinity. In 1987 Mount Shasta was chosen as a site of harmonic convergence by the New Age movement, which attracted thousands of believers to the mountain where they performed ceremonies intended to usher in a new era of world peace. Unfortunately, the ever-increasing popularity of Mount Shasta has recently created tensions with the local Native Americans, who believe that their sacred sites are sometimes disturbed by modern-day visitors and their rituals. They ask that all visitors treat the sacred land with respect and care.

The snow-capped peaks of Mount Shasta draw New Age spiritual seekers from around the world.

141

SEDONA

LOCATION	Arizona, USA
SPIRITUAL TRADITION	New Age
DATE OF CONSTRUCTION	Prehistoric
WHEN TO VISIT	Any time of year

The Red Rocks of Sedona are a spectacular and rather awe-inspiring collection of immense sandstone deposits in the Upper Sonoran Desert of northern Arizona. Visitors are treated to an empty desert landscape framed by stunning mesas (flat-topped hills with steep sides) and deep canyons that glow red and orange at sunrise and sunset. In recent years Sedona has become a highly popular place for spiritual retreat, especially for New Age seekers, who are drawn by the large number of apparent energetic vortices, which are thought to induce mystical experiences.

The rocky formations at Sedona were created over hundreds of millions of years by the steadily eroding Colorado plateau. The first humans appear to have come here roughly 6,000 years ago, and by 300 BCE the Hohokham people had begun to farm the dry soil. They later developed an intricate irrigation system, but for unknown reasons they abandoned the area in around the 10th century CE. Their departure led to the area being settled by the Sinagua people, who built impressive stone pueblos decorated with intricate petroglyphs. In the 15th century they too abruptly abandoned Sedona, which led to Yavapai and Apache tribes moving in. In 1583 the Spanish conquistadors arrived looking for gold, but they too moved on. In 1902 the small town of Sedona was established, but remained largely undeveloped until Hollywood filmmakers arrived in the 1940s, having found the perfect backdrop for Western movies. In the 1960s the first tourists came, and in the 1980s New Age seekers began arriving in droves, many choosing to settle in the area. They have given the red rocky formations new names, for example, Coffeepot, Cathedral, and Thunder. Today, Sedona offers a wide array of spiritual workshops and retreats and is the most-visited New Age site in the United States. Of particular interest are the spiritual vortexes, which are said to be found across the landscape. They cannot be demonstrated by scientific means, but are "felt" by experienced practitioners. It is widely believed that as well as inducing experiences of the divine, they can facilitate emotional and physical healing. In addition, a number of churches have been built into the landscape, specially designed to take advantage of the spectacular views.

The inspiring Red Rocks of Sedona are the most-visited New Age sacred site in the United States today.

IONA ISLAND

LOCATION	Inner Hebrides, Scotland
SPIRITUAL TRADITIONS	Christian, Celtic Christian
DATE OF CONSTRUCTION	563 CE
WHEN TO VISIT	Any time of year, but the best weather is in spring and summer

Iona is a small island of outstanding natural beauty near the Isle of Mull, forming part of the Inner Hebrides off the west coast of Scotland. In 563 CE St. Columba of Ireland founded a monastery on peaceful Iona, and the island soon became a focal point for Christian activities in Scotland, in spite of its remote location.

In the centuries that followed, Christian pilgrims from all over northern Europe traveled to Iona, and the island served as an important burial site for kings and other dignitaries. Historians believe that much of the world-famous Book of Kells was written and illustrated on Iona. Sadly, the island's remote location made it specially vulnerable to attack, and in 849 CE the monastery was abandoned following repeated raids by Viking invaders, who stole many of its sacred treasures.

In 1203 a Benedictine abbey (which still survives as an ecumenical church) was built on Iona, followed by a Benedictine nunnery in 1208, the restored ruins of which may be seen today. In the 16th century the Reformation reached Iona, and almost all the buildings along with hundreds of beautiful hand-carved stone crosses were destroyed. Fortunately St. Martin's Cross, which stands in front of the charming abbey, survived, for it is an outstanding example of 9th-century Celtic Christian art. The abbey graveyard houses the graves of many Scottish, Irish, French, and Norwegian kings, including Mac Bethad mac Findlaich, popularized by Shakespeare as Macbeth.

Just before the onset of the Second World War an ecumenical community was founded on Iona by George MacLeod. The Iona Community, as it is known, offers a wide selection of residential retreats for spiritual seekers from all over the world and has undoubtedly helped to create the resurgence of interest in Celtic Christianity seen in Britain today.

A view of St. Martin's Cross—a fine example of 9th century CE *Celtic Christian Art—in front of the peaceful Benedictine Abbey.*

LINDISFARNE/HOLY ISLAND

LOCATION	Northumberland, England
SPIRITUAL TRADITIONS	Christian, Celtic Christian
DATE OF CONSTRUCTION	635 CE
WHEN TO VISIT	Any time of year, but visits can only be made at low tide

Lindisfarne is a tiny, tidal island off the coast of north-eastern England. Known locally as Holy Island, it has an adult population of fewer than 200. At low tide, Lindisfarne is attached to the mainland by a causeway; at high tide, it becomes an island again. Although small, Lindisfarne boasts an ancient castle, a ruined monastery and the exquisite Lindisfarne Gospels.

Lindisfarne has been a sacred site for Christians since 635 CE when King Oswald—the most powerful king in England at the time—instructed St. Aidan of Ireland to travel from the holy island of Iona (off the west coast of Scotland, see pages 144–145) to Northumbria to spread the Christian message in England. St. Aidan traveled to Lindisfarne with a group of fellow monks from Iona, who helped him to found a monastery. Lindisfarne quickly became the focal point for all Christian activities in the North-East.

In 793 CE Lindisfarne was attacked by Viking invaders and the monastery was destroyed. However, the community reassembled and in the early 8th century CE an artist believed to be Eadfrith—subsequently Bishop of Lindisfarne—made a highly illustrated copy of the Gospels of the New Testament in Latin, now well-known as the Lindisfarne Gospels.

Three hundred years later a monk known as Aldred wrote an Anglo-Saxon version of the Gospels, which was added to the original version. This text is now the oldest surviving version of the Gospels in Old English, and is greatly appreciated by visitors today.

Lindisfarne has always attracted a large number of pilgrims and other visitors. In the 19th century the island and its amazing seascape were painted by the celebrated British artist J. M. W. Turner. More recently Lindisfarne has become an important center for Celtic Christianity in England, with many modern-day spiritual seekers staying on the island for revitalizing retreats.

The tidal island of Lindisfarne has been a sacred Christian site since 635 CE.

DEVENISH ISLAND

LOCATION	County Fermanagh, Northern Ireland
SPIRITUAL TRADITION	Christian
ASSOCIATED SAINT	St. Molaise
DATE OF CONSTRUCTION	6th century CE
WHEN TO VISIT	Any time of year; take the Devenish Ferry from Enniskillen

Devenish Island is a beautiful, tranquil stretch of green land in Lough Erne in County Fermanagh in Northern Ireland. The site of a Christian monastery since the 6th century CE, the island is a perfect spot for meditation and retreat. It has attracted Christian pilgrims for centuries.

According to Christian tradition, St. Molaise was on a pilgrimage to Croach Patrick when he visited Devenish Island and founded the first monastery. The story goes that he stopped building one day to listen to a bird singing, which he sensed was a communication from the Holy Spirit. Wholly enraptured, St. Molaise closed his eyes and listened for a hundred years. Upon looking up, he found that the monastery had been completed.

Christian monks were living on Devenish Island by the late 6th century CE, attracted by its peace and

The slim stone tower on Devenish Island rises between the monastery and church.

remoteness. The monastery flourished, becoming a major center for Christian scholarship. In 837 CE the island was attacked and the monastery sacked by Viking invaders. The monks rebuilt, only to experience a devastating fire in 1157, which led them to build a new monastery, chapel and unique stone tower that can still be enjoyed today. During the 13th century another church was added nearby, and in the 15th century St. Mary's Augustinian Priory was built to replace the monastery, with wonderful views of Lough Erne and the surrounding land.

The stone tower on Devenish Island is 98 ft (30 m) tall. Slender and smooth, it rises between the monastery and church to the skies, as if reaching for God. The tower doorway faces the west doorway to the church, but it is not clear what purpose the tower served. Many theories abound, but the most popular is that it was a belfry, housing the church bell long ago.

MONT SAINT-MICHEL

FRANCE

LOCATION	Normandy, France
SPIRITUAL TRADITION	Christian
ASSOCIATED SAINT	Archangel Michael
DATE OF CONSTRUCTION	708 CE
WHEN TO VISIT	Any time of year

Mont Saint-Michel is a tiny tidal island located just off the coast of northern France in the region of Normandy. A cluster of huge rocks bedecked with a beautiful medieval Benedictine abbey and Christian church rise from the shallow waters in glorious fashion.

According to Christian tradition, Bishop Aubert of Avranches had an apparition of the Archangel Michael in 708 CE. The archangel asked him to build a church on the island, but the bishop refused, so the archangel pressed one of his fingers against Aubert's skull, causing a hole to appear. The bishop immediately saw the error of his ways and dedicated a church to the Archangel Michael the very same year.

In the 11th century many underground chapels were built to support the building of a large abbey on the very top of Mont Saint-Michel. During the 12th century a new facade was added to the church, and in the 13th century a refectory and cloister were added. The Benedictine abbey flourished and became a major site of Catholic pilgrimage for many hundreds of years. This glorious building still crowns the Mount today.

With the spread of the Reformation in France during the 16th century, the abbey went into serious decline. By the time of the French Revolution it had all but been abandoned, and the revolutionaries used the abbey as a prison for their enemies. It seemed destined to remain a prison, until a restoration campaign spearheaded by the French poet Victor Hugo, who was extremely fond of the island, finally led to the prison's closure in 1863.

In 1879 a causeway from the mainland to the island was built. Some visitors make the mistake of trying to walk to the island at low tide, but the tides come in so quickly that many pilgrims have died.

The tiny island of Mont St.-Michel has long been a sacred site for Christian pilgrimage.

SAMYE MONASTERY

CHINA

INDIA

LOCATION	Tibet, China
SPIRITUAL TRADITION	Tibetan (Vajrayana) Buddhist
DATE OF CONSTRUCTION	8th century CE
WHEN TO VISIT	April through October is best, on account of the extreme climate

Samye Monastery is located a few miles from Dranang in southern Tibet. Beautifully arranged on a low-lying mountain above a rocky plain, it is overlooked by steep mountains of exceptional beauty, their presence creating a perfect environment for meditation and retreat.

The monastery was commissioned in 775 CE by King Trisong Detsen in an attempt to revive Buddhism, which was at that time beginning to decline in Tibet. It is said that he employed an Indian monk, Shantarakshita, who chose the auspicious site near Dranang to commence work. Unfortunately, the building kept collapsing once it reached a certain height, until another monk, Padmasambhava, a master skilled in the art of sacred ritual music, arrived. He performed the sacred Vajrakilaya dance, after which construction proceeded without obstacle until the monastery was completed in 779 CE. As a consequence of Padmasambhava's success, a new form of Buddhism, known as Vajrayana, began to gain prominence in Tibet.

Over time, the monastery has grown to the size it is today. Surrounded by a large wall, it is arranged in the form of a giant mandala—a complex circular design that represents the layout of the universe. The principal building symbolizes Mount Meru, the mythological center of all things, where Brahma resides. Rising to an impressive six stories high, the prayer hall is on the first floor. Its entrance is adorned with statues of Shantarakshita and Padmasambhava, and its chapel houses an image of the Buddha.

The Samye Monastery on a low rocky plain in Tibet is the perfect place for meditation and retreat.

TAKSTANG MONASTERY

LOCATION	Near Paro, Bhutan
SPIRITUAL TRADITION	Tibetan Buddhist
ASSOCIATED SAGE	Guru Rinpoche
DATE OF CONSTRUCTION	1692
WHEN TO VISIT	September through November is best; the monastery can only be reached on foot or the back of a mule, and all trips must be pre-booked well in advance

Takstang Monastery is perched precariously on the slopes of a steep Himalayan mountain 12 miles (20 km) north of Paro in western Bhutan. Behind this beautiful monastery sits a sacred cave, where the monk Padmasambhava—otherwise known as Guru Rinpoche, the founder of Buddhism in Bhutan—is believed to have meditated for four months in the 8th century CE.

According to Buddhist tradition, Padmasambhava came to Bhutan by flying over the Himalayas on the back of a flying tigress in 748 CE. At that time, the people were possessed by demons, and Rinpoche performed many sacred rites to heal them. While living in Bhutan, he meditated in numerous different caves, including the famous one at Taktsang, which literally means "tiger's nest."

The present-day monastery was completed in 1692. It is a work of breathtaking beauty and bravery, for the exquisite complex of buildings seems almost to hang in the air, 2,295 ft (700 m) above the valley below. It consists of seven separate temples, one of which—the Kundung Chorten—is said to have been built above the remains of Guru Rinpoche, which were left deep in the rocks by his disciples as treasures to be found by later generations. The other temples are associated with other important Tibetan Buddhist masters, who visited Taktsang over the centuries and likewise meditated in the various caves. Each temple is adorned with fine statues and decorated with exquisite murals depicting various Buddhist gods and revered Buddhist teachers. Every year the cave in which Guru Rinpoche meditated is opened, and the monks of the order perform a sacred ceremony that lasts for 21 days.

The Takstang Monastery is perched precariously on a steep mountain cliff.

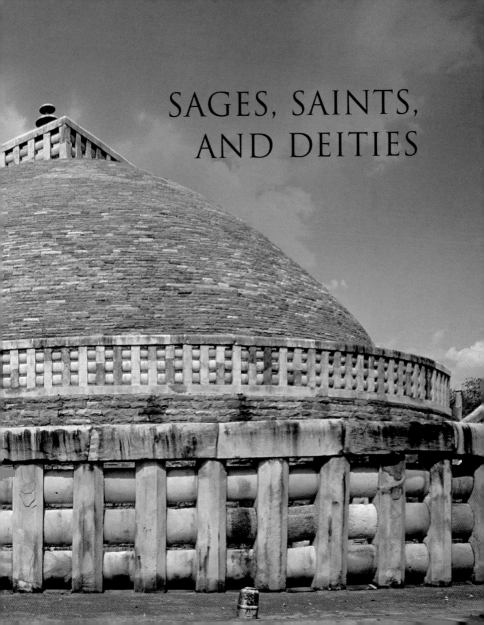

SAGES, SAINTS,
AND DEITIES

THE ELEPHANTA CAVES

INDIA

LOCATION	Elephanta Island, India
SPIRITUAL TRADITION	Hindu
ASSOCIATED DEITY	Shiva
DATE OF CONSTRUCTION	7th century CE
WHEN TO VISIT	Any time of year, by means of a short boat trip from Mumbai harbor

The Elephanta Caves—also known as the "Caves of Gharapuri"—are found on the peaceful island of Elephanta in the Arabian Sea, roughly 6 miles (10 km) off the coast of Mumbai. Part of an extensive complex of magical shrines and grottoes, these unique caves contain beautiful carvings of deities that are sacred to worshippers of the Hindu god Shiva. The cave temples are carved from solid rock, making the site a truly extraordinary creation.

No one knows the precise origins of the cave temples on Elephanta, but the earliest are thought to date to the 7th century CE, when Mumbai was a thriving and opulent city. They were greatly added to by the Silhara kings, who ruled from the 9th until the 13th centuries.

The whole complex covers an area of 6,698 sq yards (5,600 sq m), and comprises a magnificent main chamber with two side chambers, and numerous other shrines of lesser importance, which nonetheless contain priceless treasures. The main chamber is supported by large pillars and houses the massive Mahesamurti statue—also known as the Trimurti Sadashiva—which shows Shiva in the three manifestations of Creator (Brahma) facing right, Protector (Vishnu) facing forward, and Destroyer (Shiva) facing left. As Creator, he is shown with youthful, sensuous lips, evoking a sense of creativity and pleasure; as Protector, he is shown with a peaceful face, evoking both contemplation and compassion; and as Destroyer, he is shown as an angry young man, ready to set the world on fire.

To the side of the Mahesamurti is the Ardhnarishvara statue, which shows Shiva with his consort, Parvati, as a single deity. Shiva's left side is female and his right side is male, indicating that Shiva embodies within him the unity of all opposites. Another sculpture in the main temple depicts him as Yogisvara, the Lord of all Yogis, seated on a lotus; yet another shows him as Shiva Nataraja, the many-armed dancer, readying the world for Lord Brahma's creation. In February of every year, a large dance festival is held on Elephanta Island in honor of Lord Shiva.

The Shiva Lingam shrine with its carved door-keepers in the rock-hewn Elephanta Caves.

THE POTALA PALACE

LOCATION	Tibet, China
SPIRITUAL TRADITION	Tibetan Buddhist
ASSOCIATED DEITY	Bodhisattva Chenresi/Chenrezig
DATE OF CONSTRUCTION	637 CE
WHEN TO VISIT	Any time of year, but spring and autumn are best; tickets must be obtained from the Chinese Government at least one day in advance

The Potala Palace is a truly spectacular sacred monument built on Marpo Ri hill in the Lhasa Valley in Tibet. The official residence of a succession of Dalai Lamas, it was the seat of the Tibetan Government prior to the Chinese invasion in 1959, when the present Dalai Lama fled to India after a failed uprising against the People's Republic of China. In the 1970s the Potala Palace miraculously managed to escape the routine destruction of Tibetan sacred sites that took place during China's Cultural Revolution, and it may still be visited today.

According to legend, a cave on Marpo Ri hill is the abode of the Bodhisattva Chenresi, the greatest Buddhist protector of Tibet. This mythological Tibetan god has 11 heads and 1,000 hands, each with an eye in its palm to give him penetrating vision, which he uses compassionately to seek out human distress so that he can give succor. Tibetan Buddhists believe the present Dalai Lama is an incarnation of the Bodhisattva Chenresi.

In 637 CE the Emperor Songtsen Gampo is said to have built a palace on Marpo Ri hill for the purposes of meditation and retreat. This stood for more than a thousand years, when work on the current palace commenced under the direction of the 5th Dalai Lama. The Potrang Karpo, or White Palace, was completed in 1648; and the Potrang Marpo, or Red Palace, in 1694; it is thought that more than 7,000 workmen and 1,500 artisans were employed to create the Red Palace. In 1922 the 13th Dalai Lama built a further two stories on top of the Red Palace and carried out extensive renovations, creating the imposing facade that greets visitors today.

The Red Palace is used almost exclusively for religious ceremonies and study. It houses a wealth of Tibetan art and scripture, as well as the tombs of eight former Dalai Lamas. The mummified body of the greatly revered 5th Dalai Lama lies deep within the palace, inside an enormous stupa set with precious gems within literally tons of gold. Scenes from his life are beautifully depicted in murals on the walls of the lavish palace rooms. At the far west of the palace is the Hall of the Holy Stupa, which was completed in 1935 to honor the 13th Dalai Lama, who died in 1933 after making Tibet an independent country. Inside this great hall, which contains his golden tomb, is an extraordinary mandala made from 200,000 pearls. It makes an

The Potala Palace is the official home of the Dalai Lama, widely held to be Tibet's spiritual leader.

161

astonishing altar for worship.

The White Palace was built primarily as the living quarters for the Dalai Lama, and as a place to conduct important matters of state. It is separated from the Red Palace by a courtyard that is painted yellow. On the fourth story is the huge Eastern Hall, which is supported by 38 colossal pillars. This is where a specially chosen boy is ritually enthroned as the reincarnated Dalai Lama and subsequently appointed to begin his official reign at the age of 18. The White Palace is also home to two sacred chapels that date back to the 7th century CE. One of these, the Phakpa Lhakhang, houses one of the most holy images in Tibet, the Arya Lokeshvara. This sacred statue attracts thousands of pilgrims each day, who travel clockwise throughout the vast Potala Palace from chapel to chapel, chanting

"Om mani padme hum." This mantra is very difficult to translate exactly, but it expresses the deep compassion that the Bodhisattva Chenresi feels for the world. Today the Potala Palace is officially a museum, but the huge number of pilgrims ensures its status as a most sacred site. During China's Cultural Revolution, starting in 1966, it escaped serious damage thanks largely to the personal

An artist's impression of the original Potala Palace, showing both the Red and the White Palaces.

intervention of Premier Zhou, who opposed the wanton damage carried out elsewhere by the Red Guards; this drew admiration not only from Tibetans, but also from many Chinese people.

163

THE HAJI ALI DARGAH

INDIA

LOCATION	Mumbai, India
SPIRITUAL TRADITION	Muslim
ASSOCIATED SAINT	Sayed Peer Haji Ali Shah Bukhari
DATE OF CONSTRUCTION	1431 CE
WHEN TO VISIT	Any time of year, but most pilgrims visit on Thursdays and Fridays; the mosque can only be reached on foot at low tide

The Haji Ali Dargah is a sacred Islamic mosque located on a tiny tidal islet in Worli Bay in southern Mumbai. A beautiful Indian landmark, it houses the remains of Sayed Peer Haji Ali Shah Bukhari, a revered holy man who came from Persia.

According to tradition, in the early 15th century CE the wealthy merchant Sayed Peer Haji Ali Shah Bukhari gave up his riches and made a holy pilgrimage to Mecca. He returned to live in Mumbai, where he soon amassed many followers, who recognized him as a saint. Today, many stories are told about the great Haji Ali. In one story, he died while making a holy pilgrimage to Mecca, and his casket was washed back to Mumbai. In another, Haji Ali met a poor woman sobbing in the road, who told him she had dropped the oil she was carrying and would be beaten by her husband. Taking pity on her, Haji Ali stuck his finger in the ground and oil spouted out, which the woman collected and took home. Later Haji Ali had a recurring dream that he had violated

the earth by acting in this way and he became seriously ill. Filled with remorse, he knew that he would die. He asked his disciples to bury him in the Arabian Sea, and they chose the islet in Worli Bay.

The Haji Ali Dargah can be reached only on foot at low tide. On Thursdays and Fridays thousands of pilgrims of many different religious traditions make the trip across the narrow causeway to the vast temple, which is spectacularly adorned by an exquisite stone minaret rising nearly 98 ft (30 m) high. Pilgrims walk across a marble courtyard to enter the main prayer hall, which is supported by pillars decorated with colored glass to spell out the 99 names of Allah. In the inner shrine, Haji Ali's tomb is covered by a red and green sheet supported by an ornate silver frame and beautiful marble pillars.

The Haji Ali Dargah is a sacred Islamic mosque that can be reached only by pilgrims on foot at low tide.

SAGES, SAINTS, AND DEITIES

MOUNT IDA

LOCATION	Crete, Greece
SPIRITUAL TRADITION	Ancient Greek pagan
ASSOCIATED DEITIES	Rhea, Zeus
DATE OF CONSTRUCTION	2000 BCE
WHEN TO VISIT	Any time of year, but the climb to the summit is particularly hard in midsummer because of the intense heat

Mount Ida is the highest mountain on the Greek island of Crete, rising to almost 8,200 ft (2,500 m) above sea level. In ancient times it was sacred to the goddess Rhea, and a cave on its slopes is said to be the birthplace of Zeus. Today, a simple stone church sits on the summit, overlooking the arid rocky slopes, which at high altitude are completely bereft of plants and trees.

According to an ancient Greek legend, the earth goddess Rhea gave birth to Zeus in a cave on Mount Ida, her sacred mountain. After Zeus's birth, his jealous father, Cronus, demanded that she hand the baby over, so that he could swallow him. Rhea wrapped up a stone in a blanket and gave it to Cronus instead, pretending it was Zeus. The deception worked, and Zeus grew up to overthrow his father and become the ruler of the Olympian gods.

The huge cave where Zeus was supposedly born is known as Idaion

166

Antron and it is found at roughly 4,264 ft (1,300 m) above sea level. It was first excavated in the 20th century, and many sacred offerings were found inside. In ancient times the entrance would have been surrounded by a dense forest. According to Greek myth, the infant Zeus was raised by the nymph Amaltheia, who lived in the woods. Demigods known as Kourites sang and danced at the entrance to the cave to conceal the noise of the baby crying, protecting him from his father.

By the 5th century CE Christianity was beginning to flourish on Crete and the cave fell into disuse. However, Mount Ida was still deemed sacred, and the Church of the Holy Cross was built on the summit. In recent times Christian Cretans have made the tough climb to the summit on September 13, in readiness for a special service in the church the next day, which is known as the Day of the Holy Cross. Visitors to Mount Ida may approach the summit from several different routes. The easiest and most popular is from Nida Plateau, where you can park your car before beginning the long trek up. Water, a hat, and sun-lotion are essential. Except in high summer, the peak itself is covered in snow.

The now-barren slopes of Mount Ida surrounding the Cave of Zeus were once covered in thick forests where demigods reputedly lived.

WALKESHWAR TEMPLE AND BANGANGA TANK

LOCATION	Mumbai, India
SPIRITUAL TRADITION	Hindu
ASSOCIATED DEITY	Shiva
DATE OF CONSTRUCTION	1127 CE
WHEN TO VISIT	Any time of year, but pilgrimages are especially popular at full and new moons

INDIA

The stunning Walkeshwar Temple and the peaceful Banganga Tank by its side are found near Malabar Hill at the highest point in the city of Mumbai, India. Dedicated to the great god Shiva, the temple and its sacred water tank are the site of many important Hindu ceremonies and celebrations.

According to Hindu mythology, the demon Ravana kidnapped Sita, wife of the god Ram, who set out in pursuit. Ram stopped at the site of the Walkeshwar Temple, where he fashioned a lingam from sand in order to worship Shiva. Becoming thirsty, Ram then shot an arrow into the River Ganges and pulled it back through the earth, creating the spring that fills the Banganga Tank.

In 1127 Lakshman Prabhu built the Walkeshwar Temple and nearby tank, but his temple—shaped like a great Shiva lingam—was destroyed in the 16th century by Portuguese colonialists. In 1715 Rama Kamath, a successful businessman from Mumbai, paid to have the temple rebuilt. Since then the temple complex has been extended and refurbished many times. Today, a number of sandy, stone-towered temples and simple shrines surround the tank, which is an important site of Shiva pilgrimage.

The tank is rectangular in shape and surrounded by steps on all sides to facilitate ease of entry. The water is said to come from the Ganges, the holiest Hindu river. Pilgrims believe not only that the water possesses magical healing powers, but also that it can speed up the karmic cycle of reincarnation, taking the devotee more quickly to God. Every January the Banganga Festival of Music attracts many thousands of pilgrims.

The Walkeshwar Temple and Banganga Tank in Mumbai are dedicated to the great Hindu god Shiva.

THE GIANT BUDDHA OF LESHAN

LOCATION	Szechuan province, China
SPIRITUAL TRADITION	Buddhist
ASSOCIATED DEITY	The Maitreya Buddha
DATE OF CONSTRUCTION	713–803 CE
WHEN TO VISIT	Any time of year

The Giant Buddha of Leshan is a monumental statue of the Buddha that rises impressively above the Min River near the city of Leshan in the Szechuan province of China. The great statue faces Mount Emei, a Buddhist sacred mountain, and attracts many pilgrims throughout the year. Carved from a huge rocky cliff, the Giant Buddha is the largest stone image of the Buddha in the world.

According to tradition, an evil spirit lived in the Min River at the point where it joined the Dadu and Quingyi rivers, making the waters overly choppy and endangering the lives of the local people. To calm the spirit, a devout Buddhist monk named Hai Tong began carving the statue of the Buddha in 713 CE. When money to complete the project ran out, Hai Tong is said to have gouged out his eyes. The sculpture languished, until many years later the governor

of the province provided sponsorship and work was completed in 803 CE. Soon afterward deaths in the river dramatically decreased. Some attributed this to the calming influence of the Giant Buddha; others to the effects of the mass of sandstone that was deposited in the river, which appears to have greatly reduced the water's turbulence.

The Giant Buddha is a depiction of the Maitreya Buddha—a future Buddha, as opposed to the more usual Shakyamuni Buddha, the most recent incarnation. Significantly, during the Tang dynasty when the Buddha was created, many Chinese Buddhists were anticipating the imminent arrival of the Maitreya Buddha. The finished statue stands more than 230 ft (70 m) tall, with shoulders almost 98 ft (30 m) wide.

The Maitraya Buddha is shown awaiting his forthcoming incarnation.

THE GOETHEANUM

LOCATION	Dornach, Switzerland
SPIRITUAL TRADITION	Anthroposophical
ASSOCIATED SAGE	Rudolph Steiner
DATE OF CONSTRUCTION	1923–28 CE
WHEN TO VISIT	Any time of year

The Goetheanum was designed by the spiritual teacher Rudolf Steiner, founder of the Anthroposophy movement in Europe. Located in the town of Dornach near the city of Basel, this exceptionally beautiful temple complex attracts pilgrims and spiritual seekers from around the globe.

Rudolf Steiner was one of the most influential spiritual thinkers of the late 19th and early 20th centuries. Inspired in part by the great German poet and dramatist Johann Wolfgang von Goethe, he spent most of his life working with artists, teachers, politicians, farmers, doctors, and the general public to promote a new spiritual philosophy based on scientific enquiry, which he called Anthroposophy. Between 1913 and 1919 he supervised the building of the First Goetheanum at Dornach, which was designed according to Anthroposophical principles. The space was used mainly for lectures by Steiner and to stage plays by Goethe, and as a meeting space for Steiner's followers, until it was destroyed through arson by right-wing fanaticists on New Year's Eve in 1922. Steiner immediately began constructing the Second Goetheanum, which was completed three years after his death and may still be enjoyed today.

The Goetheanum was constructed entirely from cast concrete, a pioneering development that led many to regard the building as an architectural masterpiece. Steiner wanted to do away with corners and straight lines to create a temple that was spiritually expressive, and concrete proved to be an excellent medium, enabling him to create the soft domes and gently curving walls that characterize this unique complex. The Goetheanum included two large performance halls for dance, music and theatre, a library, many lecture halls, and classrooms, and a research center. There was also a gallery housing Steiner's immense wooden sculpture,

SAGES, SAINTS, AND DEITIES

The Representative of Humanity, depicting the spiritual forces at work in a human being, which was miraculously undamaged during the fire that destroyed the First Goetheanum.

The Goetheanum was designed by Rudolph Steiner according to the principles of Anthroposophy.

THE SHRINE OF OUR LADY OF FATIMA

LOCATION	Fatima, Portugal
SPIRITUAL TRADITION	Christian
ASSOCIATED SAINT	The Virgin Mary
DATE OF CONSTRUCTION	1917 CE
WHEN TO VISIT	Any time of year, but appropriate covering attire must be worn

The Shrine of Our Lady of Fatima has become one of the most sacred sites for Marian pilgrimage anywhere in the world. Located in the small town of Fatima in central western Portugal, it was here that three young children had visions of the Blessed Virgin Mary in 1917. These visions captured the hearts and minds of the nation. Today, up to four million Christian pilgrims flock to Fatima every year.

According to Catholic tradition, on May 13, 1917 Jacinta and Francisco Marto and their cousin Lucia Santos were tending animals in a field outside Fatima when they beheld a spectacular vision of the Virgin Mary. She bade the children recite the Rosary every day, insisting that it would lead to world peace.

One month later, on June 13, the Virgin Mary reappeared to the children, foretelling of the imminent deaths of Jacinta and Francisco, both of whom died tragically of Spanish flu during the next two to three years. One month after the second apparition, on July 13, 1917, the Virgin Mary appeared again, sharing with the children three chilling prophecies concerning the fate of the world. One foretold of hell on Earth; another apparently of the Second World War and the end of Communism; and the third told of the murder of the Pope, a prophecy that was kept secret by the Church for another 80 years, for fear of how people might react.

Three months later, on October 13, more than 70,000 people gathered in the field to see if the Virgin Mary would appear again, and the assembled masses apparently witnessed an extraordinary

The Shrine at Fatima was built to commemorate the exact spot where visions of Mary occurred.

miracle. At the time rain was pouring from the heavens, when suddenly the dark clouds parted to reveal the sun, which magically changed color many times, before turning black and then falling from the sky. Practically everyone present claimed to witness this miracle—even non-believers who had shown up to cast derision on it—although only the three children saw the Holy Virgin herself.

In 1919 work began to erect a shrine at the site of the apparition, known as the Cova da Iria; this was followed in 1928 by the building of a much larger church, known as the Basilica of Our Lady of Fatima. This beautiful church is adorned by a graceful spire that rises to a height of 213 ft (65 m); it is flanked by stone colonnades, which spread out as if in a gesture of welcome to pilgrims. In 1932 a golden sculpture of Jesus preaching—known as the *Monument to the Sacred Heart of Jesus*—was erected in the vast open plaza in front of the church. It is said that a holy spring rises under this statue, which has caused many healing miracles. Inside the church are the tombs of Francisco and Jacinta, who died young, just as the Virgin Mary predicted; and above the high altar is a painting that depicts the children receiving the apparitions.

Pilgrimage to Fatima frequently coincides with the dates of the first and last apparitions on May 13 and October 13 respectively. After praying in the church, pilgrims usually visit the Chapel of Apparitions, where a marble pillar marks the exact spot where the visions were seen. There was once a tree here, under which the children had apparently waited for the Virgin to appear, but it seems to have been stolen by collectors. A replacement has been planted nearby. In 1967 Pope Paul VI made a pilgrimage to Fatima and prayed at the shrine with the only surviving child of the visions, Lucia Santos, who had since become a nun; a monument has been erected to commemorate his personal pilgrimage. In 1989 an enormous chunk of the Berlin Wall was given to the church as a gesture of thanks for the ending of Communism, which the Blessed Virgin had predicted, and it is proudly displayed in the grounds.

A holy statue of the Virgin Mary, who appeared to three local children in Fatima in 1917.

THE GREAT STUPA OF SANCHI

INDIA

LOCATION	Madhya Pradesh, India
SPIRITUAL TRADITION	Buddhist
ASSOCIATED DEITY	Gautama Buddha
DATE OF CONSTRUCTION	3rd century BCE–12th century CE
WHEN TO VISIT	Any time of year, but best from November through February; easiest from the nearby city of Bhopal

The Great Stupa is one of more than 50 ancient Buddhist stone monuments that sit on a hilltop in the small village of Sanchi in the state of Madhya Pradesh, India. Erected by the great Emperor Ashoka in the 3rd century BCE, the Great Stupa is said to protect the relics of Gautama, the last living Buddha (566–486 BCE), thus making the site an exceptionally sacred place that attracts pilgrims from all over India and beyond.

The Great Stupa is not a actually temple, but a sacred monument, here symbolizing the Buddha and his final release from life. Ashoka built many stupas at Sanchi, but this was by far his finest and greatest achievement. It is a perfectly shaped hemispherical dome, with a wide perimeter pathway for devotional circumlocutory walks. In the 1st century BCE the stupa was seriously vandalized, which led to a number of significant additions during the long process of repair. A flight of steps to a new paved terrace was added at ground level. In addition, four huge ornamental gateways were built, elaborately depicting symbols of the Buddha's teaching. At the time it was not thought appropriate to show the Buddha himself, so the sculptors depicted, among other scenes, the horse that the Buddha rode when he left his father's estate and saw suffering for the first time; the footprints that he left during his long quest for knowledge; and the bodhi tree under which he sat when he finally attained enlightenment.

During the next several hundred years Buddhism underwent many changes in India, and in around 450 CE four beautifully sculpted Buddha images were added, facing each gate.

The Great Stupa is said to house the relics of the last living Buddha, Gautama.

THE TOMB OF RUKN-E-ALAM

LOCATION	Punjab, Pakistan
SPIRITUAL TRADITION	Sufi Muslim
ASSOCIATED SAGE	Shah Rukn-e-Alam
DATE OF CONSTRUCTION	1320–24 CE
WHEN TO VISIT	Any time of year, but temperatures may reach as high as 120°F (49°C) in summer and as low as 34°F (1°C) in winter

The awe-inspiring Tomb of Rukn-e-Alam is found in Multan in the Punjab region in Pakistan. Built in the early 14th century, it houses the remains of Sheikh Rukn-ud-Din Abul Fath, a much-loved Sufi saint, widely known as Rukn-e-Alam, which means "pillar of the world." The building is regarded as a pre-Mogul architectural masterpiece.

According to tradition, the tomb was built by Ghias-ud-Din Tughlak for himself, but his son gave it away for use by Rukn-e-Alam's family shortly after Rukn-e-Alam's death in 1335. Rukn-e-Alam came from a long line of Sufi saints, and as he was the direct successor of his grandfather, Shaikh Baha-Ud-Din Zakariya (another great Sufi saint), he was initially buried in his grandfather's mausoleum. However, upon receipt of the gift of the fabulous tomb, Rukn-e-Alam's remains were relocated.

The mausoleum is octagonal in shape and crowned by a huge

hemispherical dome, which rises to a height of 98 ft (30 m) from the ground. Built entirely from red brick, the exterior walls are decorated with glazed blue-and-white tiles, which—in combination with the red of the bricks—create a stunning visual effect. Higher up, a narrow passageway circumvents the mausoleum just below the high dome, and is used by the muezzin to call worshippers to prayer.

The interior is likewise adorned with a stunning array of glazed tiles and intricate brickwork, and the fine workmanship is attributed to the Kashigars of Multan. Quotations from the Qur'an in fine calligraphy decorate the *mihrab* niche, where worshippers kneel to pray.

The large dome above the Tomb of Rukn-e-Alam is thought to be the second largest in the world. In the 1970's, the Punjab Government undertook a restoration program to restore the Tomb to its former glory.

As many as 100,000 Sufi pilgrims from all over India, Pakistan, Afghanistan, and beyond travel to the tomb every year to pay their respects to Rukn-e-Alam, who to this day holds a special place in their hearts.

The Tomb of Rukn-e-Alam is a much-revered sacred site and an architectural masterpiece.

THE SHRINE OF BAHA'U'LLAH

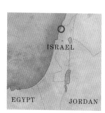

LOCATION	Near Acre, Israel
SPIRITUAL TRADITION	Baha'i
ASSOCIATED PROPHET	Baha'u'llah
DATE OF CONSTRUCTION	1892 CE
WHEN TO VISIT	Any time of year; the shrine is open Sunday through Friday

The Shrine of Baha'u'llah is located near Acre in northern Israel. A simple, but nonetheless exceptionally beautiful building, it is the most sacred site for followers of the Baha'i faith, for it houses the remains of their spiritual father, Baha'u'llah.

In 1892 Baha'u'llah passed away in the Mansion of Bahji, after a long and at times arduous life dedicated to uniting the world's religions. Just after sunset, his body was taken to a small square building in the grounds of the mansion, now known as the Shrine of Baha'u'llah, where he was formally laid to rest.

The shrine itself consists of a large central room, known to Baha'is as the Inner Sanctuary, which is adorned with trees and plants, with small rooms leading from it. Baha'u'llah's remains are kept in a small room in the far right-hand quarter, known to Baha'is as the Holy of Holies. The shrine is referred to by Baha'is as the Qiblih, meaning that it provides the direction to which Baha'is should face when saying their daily prayers. Ever since the passing of Baha'u'llah, followers of the Baha'i faith and many other religions and spiritual traditions have flocked to the shrine in huge numbers every year. Many report having profound spiritual experiences upon entering the shrine, while others find themselves unable to go inside, feeling too unworthy to enter such a sacred space.

The gardens around the shrine are some of the most spectacular in Israel. They are tended by volunteers from around the world, who view their work as spiritual service. They have created a beautiful and tranquil oasis for meditation and prayer.

In his will, Baha'u'llah appointed his son, Abdul Baha, as the new leader of the Baha'i faith. Following Abdul's death in 1922, another of Baha'u'llah's sons, Mirza Muhammad Ali, briefly occupied the shrine by force, claiming his right to be the new leader. The governor of Acre demanded that he leave, and the shrine was then entrusted to Shogi Effendi, who was universally regarded as the true guardian of the Baha'i faith.

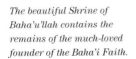

The beautiful Shrine of Baha'u'llah contains the remains of the much-loved founder of the Baha'i Faith.

ST. MARK'S COPTIC CATHEDRAL

LOCATION	Alexandria, Egypt
SPIRITUAL TRADITION	Coptic Christian
ASSOCIATED SAINT	St. Mark the Evangelist
DATE OF CONSTRUCTION	60 CE
WHEN TO VISIT	Any time of year

St. Mark's Coptic Cathedral is a profoundly beautiful modern church located in the city of Alexandria, the second-largest city in Egypt. Soaked in Christian myth and history, the church is said to have been built over the remains of Mark the Evangelist, author of the second gospel of the New Testament, thus making it an important site for Christian pilgrimage.

According to Christian tradition, St. Mark moved to Alexandria in around 60 CE, where he founded a church and evangelized for seven years, apparently performing many miracles and converting numerous unbelievers to Christianity. In one story, St. Mark and his father were journeying to Jordan when two lions approached them. St. Mark's father begged his son to flee, but St. Mark held his ground and prayed to Christ. The two lions immediately dropped dead, and his father converted to Christianity. In 68 CE, he was

martyred by the Roman authorities who had him dragged through the streets until he was dead. His followers took his body and buried it under his church, where it remained until 828 CE, when it was stolen by Venetians, who wanted to house his remains in the newly built Basilica di San Marco in Venice. According to the Coptic Church, they failed to take away St. Mark's head, which was subsequently displayed by every new Patriarch of Alexandria in his opening service, until the head was mysteriously lost, only to be rediscovered 250 years later. In 1968 the Catholic pope, Cyril VI, returned some of St. Mark's remains to the Coptic Church in an act of attempted reconciliation.

The site of St. Mark's Cathedral is of such enormous significance to Christians that many important events in the history of the Coptic Church have taken place there. Although the church was repeatedly destroyed as Egypt was overrun by foreign invaders, including Christian crusaders, it was always rebuilt by successive Coptic popes. The most recent church was erected by Pope Yusab II in 1952, and was later expanded by Pope Shenuda III in 1990. Today a beautiful many-domed church adorned with two graceful towers enshrines a peaceful interior, bedecked with splendid Byzantine art, which attracts Christian pilgrims from the around the world.

St. Mark's Coptic Chapel in Alexandria is said to have been built over the remains of Mark the Evangelist.

BASILICA DI SAN FRANCESCO

ITALY

LOCATION	Assisi, Italy
SPIRITUAL TRADITION	Christian
ASSOCIATED SAINT	St. Francis of Assisi, St. Clare
DATE OF CONSTRUCTION	13th century CE
WHEN TO VISIT	Any time of year

The picturesque town of Assisi in the Perugia region of central Italy was the birthplace in 1182 of St. Francis of Assisi, founder of the Franciscan order of friars and the patron saint of Italy. Ever since the 13th century vast numbers of Christian pilgrims have flocked to the town's main church, the Basilica di San Francesco, which not only houses holy relics of the revered saint, but also boasts beautiful frescoes depicting his life.

St. Francis is reputed to have been a gentle man, who devoted his whole life to God. It is said that he possessed a profound love of nature, and was so in touch with all of God's creation that he would even give sermons to the birds. He and the many friars who followed him took vows of poverty, chastity, and obedience to God. Then, as today, they wore dark-brown habits and depended on gifts from the community for their survival.

St. Francis was canonized by Pope Gregory IX in 1228, whereupon work immediately began on the Basilica di San Francesco, which comprises both a lower and an upper church, both of which contain exquisite frescoes depicting scenes from his life. Work on a Franciscan friary, il Sacra Convento, also commenced at the same time.

Assisi was also the birthplace in 1194 of St. Clare, who became one of St. Francis's most ardent followers after listening to him give a sermon in the town. She immediately devoted herself to Christ, took a vow of poverty, and founded the Order of Poor Ladies, which is today known as the Order of Poor Clares.

The beautiful Basilicia de San Francesco houses the relics of Saint Francis of Assisi.

OUR LADY OF GUADALUPE

LOCATION	Guadalupe, Spain
SPIRITUAL TRADITION	Christian
ASSOCIATED SAINT	The Virgin Mary
DATE OF CONSTRUCTION	1325 CE
WHEN TO VISIT	Any time of year

The ancient monastery of Guadalupe is located in the Extremadura region of western Spain. Rising above pretty whitewashed villas with red-tiled roofs, the old stone buildings rest peacefully in the sleepy hamlet, surrounded by mountainous hills. Inside the monastery is the Camarin Chapel, which is home to one of the most sacred relics in Christendom, a small black statue of the Virgin Mary, known locally as Our Lady of Silence.

According to Catholic tradition, the wooden icon of the Blessed Virgin was carved by Luke the Evangelist in the 1st century CE. The Black Madonna (or Dark Virgin) was greatly revered by the early Christian Church, and was kept first in Constantinople and then in Rome. In the late 6th century CE Pope Gregory I gave the precious statue to St. Leander of Seville. When Seville was conquered by the Moors in the early 8th century CE, the statue was entrusted to Catholic priests, who buried it in the hills of Extremadura.

Six hundred years later, in 1325, a shepherd named Gil had a vision of the Blessed Virgin, who told him to get the local priests to dig in the ground. The priests found the buried statue and built a shrine at the spot.

In 1326 the first pilgrims began to arrive to behold the sacred image, which was thought to possess magical powers. The Franciscan basilica was completed in the mid-15th century at Guadalupe, which by then had become the most-visited pilgrimage site in Spain. So powerful was the Black Madonna thought to be that Columbus had a replica made to accompany him on his voyages to the New World, as did subsequent Spanish conquistadors. Their veneration led in part to the widespread cult of the Madonna in Mexico, where a second shrine to Our Lady of Guadalupe was built in 1531, following her appearance near Mexico City. In recent years this second church has become the most-visited Catholic shrine in the world.

The basilica at Guadalupe houses a sacred statue of the Black Madonna, discovered following a miraculous apparition of the Virgin Mary.

TCHOGHA ZANBIL

LOCATION	Khuzestan province, Iran
SPIRITUAL TRADITION	Ancient Elamite
ASSOCIATED DEITY	Inshushinak
DATE OF CONSTRUCTION	1250 BCE
WHEN TO VISIT	Any time of year

Tchogha Zanbil was once the great holy city of the Kingdom of Elam, and is located in what is today southwestern Iran. Founded by King Untash-Napirisha in 1250 BCE, the city was structured around a great ziggurat—a stepped pyramidal temple—dedicated to the god Inshushinak, who was greatly revered by the Elamites. Historians believe that Untash-Napirisha built Tchogha Zanbil to create a new religious center that would unite all of the kingdom's disparate gods under a single roof.

Although it was a great city in size and scope, it seems unlikely that anyone actually lived permanently at Tchogha Zanbil, apart from priests and their servants. Instead the city functioned as a singular immense temple, where religious rites and ceremonies could be conducted away from the hustle and bustle of everyday

Tchogha Zanbil was built around a great ziggurat—the remains are seen here.

life. Significantly, there is no ready water supply near Tchogha Zanbil, which made it a very poor choice for an actual city, but also necessitated the building of a great canal many miles long to enable the city's religious functions to be maintained.

Much of the city was destroyed in 640 BCE, after which it gradually sank under desert sands. Excavations began in 1952 and again in 1962, revealing three concentric walls and the great ziggurat, which many believe to be the finest, best-preserved one in the world. Archeologists have determined that the concentric walls were built to demarcate the different zones of the city. The innermost wall surrounded the great ziggurat, which was built over an earlier temple; the middle wall enclosed 11 subsidiary temples dedicated to minor gods, while the outer wall enclosed several royal palaces and a crypt for royal burials. The city was not completed by the time it was sacked in 640 BCE.

191

THE CAVES OF THE PATRIARCHS

LOCATION	Hebron, West Bank
SPIRITUAL TRADITIONS	Jewish, Christian, Muslim
ASSOCIATED SAINTS	Abraham, Sarah, Isaac, Rebecca, Jacob, and Leah
DATE OF CONSTRUCTION	1000 BCE
WHEN TO VISIT	Direct access to the caves is not possible at present

The Caves of the Patriarchs comprise a holy shrine located in the city of Hebron on the West Bank. The shrine, which was built by King Herod in the 1st century BCE in caves that had been sacred since 1000 BCE, is deemed the most holy site in Judaism after Temple Mount in Jerusalem, and has been sacred to Jews for thousands of years. The site is also sacred to Christians and Muslims.

It is thought that King Herod erected the stone shrine in Hebron above the holy caves of Machpelah in order to win favor with his Jewish subjects, for according to the Jewish Tanakh, the caves house the remains of Abraham and his wife Sarah, along with their sons Isaac and Jacob and their wives, Rebecca and Leah. In Jewish, Christian, and Islamic scripture, it is written that Abraham entered into a holy covenant with God nearly 4,000 years ago, giving rise to the Jewish

religion, which explains the site's supreme spiritual significance. Herod's shrine is remarkably well preserved, with most of the outer structure still being visible today, divided into Islamic and Jewish quarters.

Christians began making pilgrimages to the shrine in the 4th century CE, and records indicate that they built a church next to the shrine. In the early 10th century the Fatimid empire took over Palestine and the shrine was converted into a mosque. Over the next 70 years many domes were added, and the shrine's inner walls were adorned with Islamic art. In 1100 the shrine was taken over by Christian crusaders, who renamed it the Castle of St. Abraham. In 1187 Saladin converted the shrine into a mosque.

The holy shrine, built over the Caves of the Patriarchs, is sacred to Jews, Christians, and Muslims.

PLACES OF
PILGRIMAGE

CATHEDRAL OF SANTIAGO DE COMPOSTELA

LOCATION	Santiago de Compostela, Spain
SPIRITUAL TRADITION	Christian
ASSOCIATED SAINT	St. James the Apostle
DATE OF CONSTRUCTION	9th century CE
LENGTH OF PILGRIMAGE	The full length is 560 miles (900 km) or 30 days' walking
WHEN TO MAKE THE PILGRIMAGE	Arriving during the festival of St. James on July 25 is considered especially auspicious

The Portico de Gloria of the cathedral dedicated to St. James marks the end of the pilgrimage.

The Cathedral of Santiago de Compostela is a stunning medieval church located in the beautifully preserved city of Santiago de Compostela in northern Spain. Believed to be the final resting place of the remains of St. James the Apostle, the church has been the destination point for the world-famous Camino de Santiago pilgrimage for more than a thousand years.

According to Christian tradition, St. James was an apostle who undertook early missionary work in Spain, before returning to Jerusalem in around 42 CE, only to be martyred by Herod Agrippa. His followers are said to have taken his body to the sea and placed it in a stone coffin, which was magically blown by heavenly winds all the way to Spain, where it was washed ashore near Cape Finisterre. Upon receiving news of this strange occurrence, the local queen ordered that a team of oxen pull the stone sarcophagus to a holy site inland, where it was placed inside a marble tomb; 800 years passed and St. James's tomb was all but forgotten when a local hermit, Pelayo, experienced a divine apparition—possibly a star—that encouraged him to dig at the site. The tomb was rediscovered, and the local bishop was summoned to authenticate the remains, which he did. The bishop informed the king, Alfonso II, who informed the pope and the Emperor

Charlemagne, who both concurred that the remains were genuine.

The pope then declared that a pilgrimage to Santiago—along with pilgrimage to the great Christian cities of Rome and Jerusalem—would lead to a complete expiation of all sins. Almost immediately pilgrims began flocking to Santiago de Compostela, which was no longer perceived as an ordinary city, but as a holy city that devout Christians had a spiritual duty to visit. Many miracles were reported, and soon afterward a number of key pilgrimage routes to Santiago opened up, the most popular and widely traveled one being known simply as the Camino de Santiago. This is at least a 30-day trek that begins in southern France and ends at Santiago de Compostela.

King Alfonso II built a small chapel at the site, and in 829 CE a church was built around this simple shrine, but

had to be replaced in 899 CE by a larger pre-Romanesque church, in order to accommodate the growing number of pilgrims. In 997 CE the Moors invaded Spain and completely destroyed this church; they forced their captives to carry the heavy gates and bells to Cordoba, to be used in the Aljama Mosque. In 1075 work on the present Romanesque church was begun—using mainly granite, it took the masons roughly 50 years to erect it.

The magnificent Cathedral of Santiago de Compostela in Northern Spain is the final resting place of the remains of St. James.

In the mid-18th century the stunning Obradoiro facade was added to the western front of the cathedral. Carved from granite, this spectacular structure is flanked by two enormous bell-towers and adorned with numerous beautiful sculptures of St. James. It is depicted on the reverse side of three modern Spanish coins. The interior of the church is decorated everywhere with exquisite sculpture. Under the altar, the remains of St. James lie in a silver coffin, which may be viewed from the crypt. A statue of St. James marks its precise location. Before it most pilgrims kneel down in reverence, and many of them go even further by hugging the sacred image.

In 1884 Pope Leo XII issued a Bull confirming the authenticity of the remains at Santiago de Compostela, which may explain why the Camino experienced an upsurge in popularity during the 20th century. Today, at least 100,000 pilgrims from Europe (and some from even further afield) undertake the great journey in honor of St. James the Apostle every year.

The consecration took place in 1128, a prestigious ceremony attended by many illustrious figures, including the king. Work continued on the cathedral for another 50 years, until the magnificent building we see today was completed.

CHARTRES CATHEDRAL

LOCATION	Chartres, France
SPIRITUAL TRADITION	Christian
ASSOCIATED SAINT	The Virgin Mary
DATE OF CONSTRUCTION	1194–1260 CE
WHEN TO MAKE THE PILGRIMAGE	Any time of year

FRANCE

Chartres Cathedral is a beautifully preserved medieval church located in the town of Chartres, roughly 31 miles (50 km) south of Paris. Not only is the cathedral an outstanding architectural monument, but it houses one of Christianity's most sacred relics for pilgrimage—the Sancta Camisia—a tunic believed to have worn by the Blessed Virgin Mary.

Tradition states the Sancta Camisia was given to Chartres Cathedral by the Emperor Charlemagne in 876 CE. Soon afterward pilgrims from all over the world came to Chartres to pray before this most holy relic. In 1020 Chartres Cathedral was destroyed by fire, and a Romanesque basilica with a massive crypt underneath was built in its place. In 1194 lightning struck, causing a great fire that destroyed everything but the facade of the church, its towers, and the crypt. For a while, everyone

The interior of Chartres Cathedral, which houses the famous Sancta Camisia.

believed that the Sancta Camisia had been consumed by the flames, but when the tunic was discovered unharmed three days later, the bishop declared it to be a sign from the Blessed Virgin herself that a magnificent cathedral should be built in her honor. Construction began immediately, with donations and offers to help haul stone from the local quarry flooding in. By 1220 the new structure of the cathedral had been completed, incorporating the old crypt, facade, and west towers. In 1260 the cathedral was finally consecrated—an event deemed so important that it was observed by King Louis IX and his family.

The new cathedral was so large that double flying buttresses were used for the very first time to support the high nave and the new clerestory adorned with beautiful stained-glass windows. Towers were added to the new transepts, which flanked stunning rose windows above three portals, making a grand total of nine towers.

CHURCH OF THE HOLY SEPULCHRE

LOCATION	Jerusalem
SPIRITUAL TRADITION	Christian
DATE OF CONSTRUCTION	325 CE
WHEN TO MAKE THE PILGRIMAGE	Any time of year, but Easter is especially sacred

The Church of the Holy Sepulchre is an immensely important site for Christian pilgrimage, located in the Old City of Jerusalem. Many Christians believe that it stands on the very spot where Christ was crucified and subsequently interred in 33 CE.

In 135 CE Hadrian began to rebuild Jerusalem following successive Jewish revolts, and a Temple of Aphrodite was constructed at the present site. In 325 CE Constantine ordered the temple to be demolished, and in 326 CE his mother, Helena, oversaw the construction of a basilica in its stead, apparently discovering the tomb of Christ—the sepulchre—while removing the old temple foundations. It is said that she also discovered the cross on which Christ was crucified, along with the crosses of the two thieves. The original church consisted of a rotunda above the tomb of Christ, a basilica and a large atrium, in a corner of which a large rock—the Golgotha stone—marked the exact spot of the crucifixion. The church immediately attracted pilgrims from all over the Mediterranean and Middle East, and continues to do so today.

In 638 CE the caliph Omar, a devout Muslim, took control of Jerusalem. He chose not to worship in the Church of the Holy Sepulchre, claiming that he wanted the church to remain a Christian temple. More than 400 years later, Pope Urban II called for the first crusade. He was keen to reclaim Jerusalem, along with the Church of the Holy Sepulchre, which was finally recaptured in 1099. During the next 50 years the crusaders restored and rebuilt the ruined church, adding a bell-tower and a new roof, thus bringing the Golgotha and the Sepulchre together in a single building. They also built a chapel to Helena. Since then, the church has been ruined and restored many times, with extensive renovations in 1555 by Franciscan friars, who built an antechamber for the tomb, known as the Chapel of the Angel, which is thought to hold a fragment of the stone used to seal Christ's tomb after he was taken down from the cross.

The Church of the Holy Sepulchre marks the place where Christ was crucified.

BASILICA OF OUR LADY OF COPACABANA

LOCATION	Copacabana, Bolivia
SPIRITUAL TRADITION	Christian
ASSOCIATED SAINT	The Virgin Mary
DATE OF CONSTRUCTION	1576 CE
WHEN TO MAKE THE PILGRIMAGE	Any time of year, but there are special festivals on February 2, May 25, and August 6

The town of Copacabana sits peacefully on the banks of Lake Titicaca in northern Bolivia, near the border with Peru. It is extremely famous throughout Bolivia for housing the Basilica of Our Lady of Copacabana, which contains the holy shrine of the Virgen de la Candelaria, otherwise known as the Dark Virgin. Copacabana is also where one catches a boat to the Isla del Sol and the Isla de la Luna, two sacred Inca islands.

According to local tradition, a group of Inca men were fishing on Lake Titicaca one day in 1576 when a violent storm erupted. Fearing for their lives, they prayed for help, and a vision of the Blessed Virgin Mary appeared and led them to safety. The grateful men immediately built a shrine to the Blessed Virgin and installed a wooden sculpture of the Madonna inside it.

In 1583 a chapel was built to house the Inca sculpture, known as the Dark Virgin. Standing a little over 3⅓ ft (1 m) tall, she is black in appearance. Her halo is made of gold, an indirect evocation of the Inca sun god, Inti; and a boat sailing by her feet is made of silver, evoking the Inca moon goddess, Mama Quilla. Almost immediately people began to speak of miracles brought about by the Madonna, and in 1619 the chapel was extended to cope with the increasing number of pilgrims from Bolivia and neighbouring Peru. In 1805 the present cathedral was completed; it is now the most popular site for Christian pilgrimage in Bolivia.

Today the Dark Virgin stands on a mechanical altar, so that she may be turned to face the huge congregations at weekends. During the week she faces a side chapel, where people light candles and pray.

Our Lady of Copacabana attracts pilgrims from all over Bolivia and Peru.

THE GARDEN OF GETHSEMANE

LOCATION	Jerusalem
SPIRITUAL TRADITION	Christian
DATE OF CONSTRUCTION	33 CE
WHEN TO MAKE THE PILGRIMAGE	Easter is the most popular time for pilgrimages

The Garden of Gethsemane is thought to be located at the foot of the Mount of Olives, which is separated from the eastern edge of the Old City of Jerusalem by the Kidron Valley. One of the most sacred places in the world for Christians, the site is home to the Basilica of the Agony (otherwise known as the Church of All Nations), and to the Russian Orthodox Church of St. Mary Magdalene.

According to Christian scripture, Jesus prayed in the Garden of Gethsemane on the night that he was betrayed by Judas Iscariot, which led to his crucifixion the following day. As a consequence, the Garden of Gethsemane became a supremely important site for Christian pilgrimage, with the first written accounts by pilgrims dating back as far as 4th

The Garden of Gethsemane has attracted Christian pilgrims since 4th century CE.

century CE. Around the same time, a Byzantine church was built to accommodate them, but this church was destroyed by an earthquake in 746 CE.

Turkish rule of Jerusalem came to an end in 1917, when the British captured the city. In 1924 the Basilica of the Agony was completed next to the Garden of Gethsemane, with funds being donated by 12 countries: Argentina, Brazil, Chile, Mexico, Italy, France, Spain, Britain, Belgium, Canada, Germany, and the United States. This beautiful international church is supported by six pillars, above which are 12 domed cupolas, one for each donor nation. In addition, Ireland, Hungary, and Poland donated mosaics for the church, and Australia donated a crown for the bedrock, which is believed to be the actual stone upon which Christ prayed during his last night on Earth.

MOUNT CROACH PATRICK

IRELAND

LOCATION	County Mayo, Ireland
SPIRITUAL TRADITIONS	Celtic pagan, Celtic Christian, Christian
ASSOCIATED DEITY/SAINT	Crom Dubh, St. Patrick
DATE	*c.* 3500 BCE
WHEN TO MAKE THE PILGRIMAGE	Any time of year; during the last Sunday in July, known as Reek, the mountain is thronged with pilgrims

Mount Croach Patrick is a holy mountain about 2,510 ft (765 m) high, overlooking Clew Bay in County Mayo, Ireland. This peaceful and beautifully shaped mountain was the ancient abode of the Celtic god Crom Dubh, who is said to come every year with his scythe to help with the harvest. In the 5th century CE St. Patrick is said to have climbed Mount Croach to rid the mountains of its demons, and it has been an important site for Christian pilgrimage ever since.

It is not known how long Mount Croach Patrick has been a sacred site, although a rocky outcrop known as St. Patrick's Chair (and as the Bodeh Stone) is decorated with Stone Age carvings of circles and other geometric shapes that may be 5,000 years old. It is known that when St. Patrick arrived in 441 CE the mountain had long been a holy site for pagan ritual and worship. Recently a stone oratory

dating back to the 5th century CE has been discovered on the summit.

According to Christian tradition, St. Patrick travelled to Ireland with the express purpose of converting the Celts to Christianity. It is perhaps not surprising then that he chose to visit Mount Croach—a revered pagan monument—where he stayed for 40 days and nights. It is said that he prayed and fasted on the summit until he had succeeded in banishing all the pagan gods from Ireland, after which the people gave themselves to Christ. Today, it is estimated that as many as one million Christian pilgrims come to Mount Croach every year, with 40,000 making the climb during the festival of Reek, which takes place on the last Sunday in July. Many walk barefoot, and some travel on their knees.

A view of Mount Croach Patrick from Clew Bay in County Mayo.

THE SANCTUARY OF CHIMAYO

LOCATION	New Mexico, USA
SPIRITUAL TRADITION	Christian
DATE OF CONSTRUCTION	1810 CE
WHEN TO MAKE THE PILGRIMAGE	Any time of year

The Sanctuary of Chimayo in the state of New Mexico is widely regarded as the most significant site for Catholic pilgrimage in the United States. Roughly 31 miles (50 km) north of the city of Santa Fe, this peaceful sanctuary is visited by almost 300,000 pilgrims ever year, and is reputed to be the source of many miracles.

According to local tradition, one Good Friday in the early 19th century Don Bernardo Abeyta was praying in the El Potrero Hills when he saw a bright white light rising from the ground. He rushed there and began digging with his hands, whereupon he found a crucifix. Abeyta informed the local priest, Sebastian Alvarez, who traveled to Chimayo to collect it and bring it back to his church in Santa Cruz, where he proudly displayed it next to the altar. But, to his dismay, the next morning it had disappeared. The crucifix was later found in its original spot in Chimayo, whereupon Alvarez tried once more to restore it to his church, only for it to disappear again. After three attempts Alvarez gave up and conceded that the crucifix belonged in Chimayo.

In the year 1810 records show that Abeyta built a small chapel on the site. Pilgrims began to arrive, and in 1816 a larger church was built for them. It is said that most would eat a small amount of holy dirt, and many pilgrims claimed miraculous cures.

Today, pilgrims enter the adobe church with two bell-towers via a pretty walled courtyard. Inside the church a small room houses a pit of holy dirt. Pilgrims take a handful before praying at the altar. Most pilgrims later wash themselves with the holy dirt, hoping for miraculous cures.

Pilgrims enter the adobe church via a courtyard to gain access to the holy dirt.

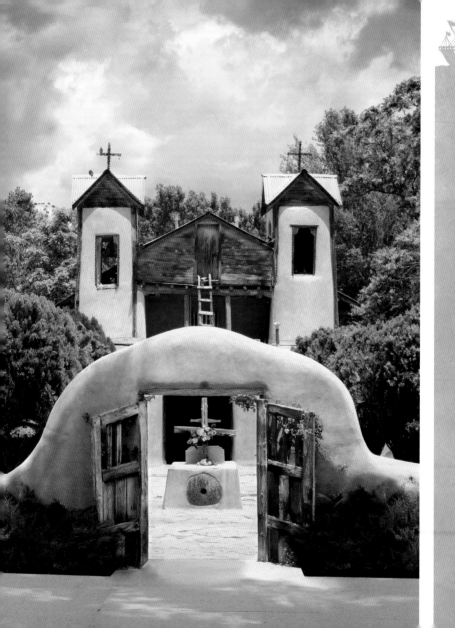

Prayer-flags adorn the golden spire of the Swayambhunath Stupa.

SWAYAMBHUNATH STUPA

LOCATION	Kathmandu, Nepal
SPIRITUAL TRADITIONS	Buddhist, Hindu
ASSOCIATED DEITIES	Manjushri, Shiva
DATE OF CONSTRUCTION	5th century CE or earlier
WHEN TO MAKE THE PILGRIMAGE	Any time of year

Kathmandu boasts a great many beautiful temples and shrines, but almost certainly the most important of these is the Swayambhunath Stupa, whose golden spire sitting on top of a wooded hill may be seen from almost anywhere in the valley. According to an ancient Buddhist legend, Kathmandu was once submerged under a lake, when the god Manjushri spied a magical lotus—Swayambhunath—floating on the water, emanating a brilliant light. The bodhisattva cut a big hole in the ground, draining all the water out to make the land habitable and accessible to pilgrims. The magical lotus became the hill where the Swayambhunath Stupa was built. Interestingly, geologists believe that the site of Kathmandu was indeed once a lake, and that Swayambhunath was once an island within it.

Although the city of Kathmandu was purportedly founded in 723 CE, there is archeological evidence that the site of the Swayambhunath Stupa was an important pilgrimage site for Buddhists at least as early as the 5th century CE. Many Buddhists believe that pilgrims have been visiting the site for much longer.

Today the stupa may be reached by climbing more than 350 stairs, which were built by King Pratap Malla in the 17th century. At the foot of the hill there is a large prayer wheel some 13 ft (4 m) tall, which strikes a bell as it turns. There is also a mysterious stone footprint, which some people believe was left by the Buddha himself.

At the top of the hill two temples have been built on either side of the majestic golden stupa, which comprises a large domed base, upon which sits a cube engraved with the four eyes of the Buddha, looking out in all directions. A number of other temples have been constructed on the Swayambhunath hill, one of which is dedicated to the Hindu goddesses Ganga and Yamuna.

NIDAROS CATHEDRAL

LOCATION	Trondheim, Norway
SPIRITUAL TRADITION	Christian
ASSOCIATED SAINT	St. Olav
DATE OF CONSTRUCTION	1031 CE
LENGTH OF PILGRIMAGE	The full length is 400 miles (643 km) or 25 days' walking
WHEN TO MAKE THE PILGRIMAGE	Any time of year; a huge festival takes place on 29 July

The city of Trondheim on the western coast of Norway was once the most popular site for Christian pilgrimage in northern Europe. It is now home to a stunning Gothic cathedral, which houses the relics of St. Olav, the patron saint of Norway.

Historians believe that Olav Haraldsson was born in 995 CE. A proud Viking warrior, he was fighting in France when he was converted to Christianity at the age of 18. He immediately began a pilgrimage to the Holy Land, but enroute he is said to have heard a voice telling him to return to Norway to become King. He arrived in Trondheim (then known as Nidaros), the capital of Norway, in 1015 and duly became monarch. He ruled for 13 years, during which time he made strenuous efforts to convert all of Norway to Christianity. However, many powerful pagan warlords rose up to oppose him, and in 1028 he found himself too far extended militarily and

was defeated by King Canute of England. Olav fled to Russia, where he is said to have heard another voice telling him to reclaim his throne and continue his missionary work. He returned to Norway, only to be fatally wounded in the Battle of Stiklestad on July 29, 1030. His body was taken to Trondheim and buried.

In 1031 the bishop exhumed Olav's body and declared him a saint, much to the approval of the Norwegian people. They erected a wooden church over his grave, which attracted pilgrims from all over the country. Tales of miraculous healings connected with his shrine began to spread, and by 1300 a great Gothic cathedral had been built to accommodate the massive flow of pilgrims. This building was destroyed by fire on five separate occasions, and each time the people built an even greater church than before, until Nidaros Cathedral was the largest medieval building in Norway. After the Reformation in 1537, pilgrimage to Nidaros ceased, but in recent decades it has recommenced, and today thousands of pilgrims trek from Oslo to Trondheim along the old pilgrimage trails that have been carefully restored.

The stunning Gothic facade of Nidaros Cathedral was once the finest medieval building in Norway.

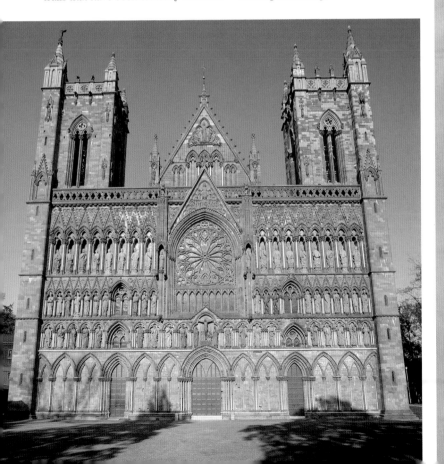

THE JOKHANG TEMPLE

LOCATION	Tibet, China
SPIRITUAL TRADITION	Tibetan Buddhist
ASSOCIATED DEITY	The Buddha
DATE OF CONSTRUCTION	7th century CE
WHEN TO MAKE THE PILGRIMAGE	Any time of year; special permits must be obtained from the Chinese Government

The Jokhang Temple is located in the city of Lhasa—sometimes referred to as the Forbidden City—in southern Tibet. Overlooked by Mount Gephel, it is the most sacred site in Tibetan Buddhism. It is home to the highly revered Joyo Sakyamuni statue, and is where the initiation ceremonies for the Dalai Lama take place.

The city of Lhasa has been sacred to Buddhists since the 7th century CE, when King Songtsen Gampo married twice, each time to practicing Buddhists. His first wife was Brikhuti Devi of Nepal, and his second was Princess Wencheng from China, who brought with her two sacred statues of the Buddha, the Akshobya Vajra and the Joyo Sakyamuni. According to tradition, the latter was fashioned during the Buddha's lifetime by Vishvakarman, who was directed by the god Indra, and is the most sacred

The Joyo Sakyamuni statue attracts thousands of pilgrims every day.

image of the Buddha for Tibetans. The King built the Rimoche Temple to house the Joyo Sakyamuni, but when he died in 649 CE, Queen Wencheng hid the Joyo Sakyamuni in the Rasa Trulnang Tsuglag Khang Temple, which had been built for the other statue, fearing that it might be stolen by the invading Chinese. In 710 CE the danger was deemed to have passed and the Joyo Sakyamuni was uncovered. The temple was renamed Jokhang after the most sacred statue.

Today, the Jokhang Temple is a massive four-story building, largely because of the major extensions undertaken by the 5th Dalai Lama during the 17th century, when a number of chapels were added. In the 18th and 19th centuries many fine murals appeared on the walls, but these were damaged during the Cultural Revolution that followed the Chinese invasion in 1959. The Joyo Sakyamuni is currently on display on the first floor.

217

THE JASNA GORA MONASTERY

POLAND

LOCATION	Czestochowa, Poland
SPIRITUAL TRADITION	Christian
ASSOCIATED SAINT	The Virgin Mary
DATE OF CONSTRUCTION	1382–86 CE
WHEN TO MAKE THE PILGRIMAGE	Any time of year

The Jasna Gora Monastery is the most sacred site for Christian pilgrimage in Poland, and the third most important site for Marian pilgrimage in the world. Located in the city of Czestochowa on the Warta River, this beautiful monastery houses the Black Madonna of Czestochowa, which is reputed to have caused many miracles.

According to Christian tradition, the Black Madonna was discovered by the Roman Emperor Constantine's mother, Helena, in the 4th century CE on a trip to the Holy Land. It was said that the holy relic had been painted by Luke the Evangelist, one of the four Apostles, on a table constructed by Christ. Helen took the icon to Constantinople for permanent safe-keeping, but it was given away in 803 CE by the Byzantine Emperor as a wedding gift. The Black Madonna then lived in the Ukraine for almost 600 years, until it was finally brought to Poland in 1382 after the Polish army sacked the city of Belz.

The King of Poland entrusted the sacred relic to a group of Hungarian monks, who built the Jasna Gora Monastery at Czestochowa in 1382–86. In 1430 invading proto-Protestants from Czechoslovakia sacked Jasna Gora and desecrated the Black Madonna by slashing her face with a sword. They left her in a pool of blood and mud, but apparently a spring arose in the ground where she lay, which the monks used to clean her. The gash is still visible today.

In 1655 the Swedish army was amassing on the Polish border, when a squad of Polish soldiers prayed to the Black Madonna for assistance. Miraculously the Swedes retreated, and Jasna Gora instantly became the major site for Christian pilgrimage in Poland. In 1920 the Soviet Red Army was about to invade Poland, so the people again prayed to the Black Madonna, which reputedly caused the Miracle of Vistula—many battles during which the Russians were defeated.

The Black Madonna of Czestochowa, said to be painted by Luke the Evangelist.

THE GREAT MOSQUE OF KAIROUAN

LOCATION	Kairouan, Tunisia
SPIRITUAL TRADITION	Muslim
DATE OF CONSTRUCTION	670 CE
WHEN TO MAKE THE PILGRIMAGE	Any time of year

The Great Mosque of Kairouan is located in the historical city of Kairouan in Tunisia. It is universally regarded as one of the finest buildings of the ancient Islamic world and the mosque boasts the oldest-known minaret ever built. It has three stories which soar to a majestic height of 98 ft (30 m).

According to legend, the Arab general Uqba ibn Nafi and his followers were riding across the desert when they found a golden goblet buried in the sand. A Muslim warrior recognized the goblet as one that had mysteriously gone missing from Mecca. He pulled it up, whereupon a spring magically appeared. Another warrior tasted the water, and declared that it was from the same source as filled the holy well in Mecca. In response to these miracles, a decision was made to found a desert city and build a great mosque.

Whatever the credentials of this particular story, it is known that Uqba ibn Nafi founded the desert city of Kairouan around 670 CE. There he built a mosque, using slabs of stone taken from cities that he would subsequently conquer, notably Carthage. As the city of Kairouan grew in importance, the first mosque was replaced by a larger one, a process that recurred many times, until the great mosque that still stands today was finally completed by the end of the 9th century CE.

The mosque consists of a vast prayer hall, a courtyard, and the enormous minaret. It is supported by a total of 414 columns, which for a long time no one was allowed to count—the punishment for doing so was being blinding, although whether by God or his followers is unclear. The interior design of the mosque is exquisitely beautiful, decorated with fine paintings and carvings in wood, marble, and stone, along with the very best Islamic calligraphy.

By the 11th century Kairouan was fading as a center of economic and military power, but the great mosque ensured that it remained a most important holy site for Islamic pilgrimage. Seven trips to Kairouan are said to be the equivalent of one trip to Mecca.

The Great Mosque of Kairouan is supported by 414 stone columns, and the courtyard is overlooked by an enormous minaret.

KUSHINARA

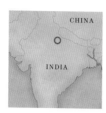

LOCATION	Uttar Pradesh, India
SPIRITUAL TRADITION	Buddhist
ASSOCIATED DEITY	Gautama Buddha
DATE OF CONSTRUCTION	3rd century BCE
WHEN TO MAKE THE PILGRIMAGE	Any time of year

Kushinara—also known as Kushinagar—is a supremely sacred Buddhist site by the Hiranyavati River near the town of Kasia in the state of Uttar Pradesh in northern India. Universally regarded as the place of the Buddha's death, it is one of the four holy sites for pilgrimage that were identified by the Buddha himself.

According to Buddhist tradition, at the age of 80 the Buddha became severely sick, so he traveled to the north of India to die. He took a bath in the Hiranyavati River, before making a rope bed that he hung between sal trees. He then reclined, placing his left hand over his body and his right hand behind his head—the posture associated with all images of the reclining Buddha. Shortly afterward a disciple named Subhadda approached the Buddha, but was prevented from speaking with him by Ananda, the Buddha's cousin. The Buddha called out to Subhadda to come closer, and then gave what is known as the "last sermon." He told Subhadda not to be sad at his passing, but instead to recognize that he would still be present in his teachings. He urged Subhadda to work for his own liberation, and reminded him that everything in creation is impermanent. Then the Buddha sank deeper and deeper into meditation, before finally entering the blissful void known as Nirvana. The Buddha's disciples cremated his body at Makutabandhana on the night of the full moon in the month of May 483 BCE.

In the 3rd century BCE the Buddhist Emperor Ashoka helped to build many temples at Kushinara, which flourished until about the 5th century CE. But by the 13th century the site had been abandoned and Kushinara was all but forgotten. In the 18th century excavations began and many ancient stupas were unearthed. The most important of these was the Mahaparinirvana Temple, which marks the spot of the Buddha's death, and which was rebuilt in 1956. It houses a reclining image of the Buddha dating from the 5th century CE; lovingly carved from sandstone, this is a beautiful statue more than 19 ft (6 m) long.

Buddhist monks ceremonially dress the huge statue of Buddha, depicted at the moment of his death.

LALIBELA

LOCATION	Lalibela, Ethiopia
SPIRITUAL TRADITION	Ethiopian Orthodox Christian
ASSOCIATED SAINT	St. George of Ethiopia
DATE OF CONSTRUCTION	12th century CE
WHEN TO MAKE THE PILGRIMAGE	Any time of year

The city of Lalibela is considered by Ethiopian Orthodox Christians to be the second most holy city in Ethiopia after Axum. Named after King Lalibela, it is home to an extraordinary collection of 12th- and 13th-century rock-hewn churches, which serve as a major site for Christian pilgrimage.

According to legend, a swarm of bees gathered around Prince Lalibela during his birth, which his mother interpreted as representing the soldiers who would one day serve her son as King. She named him Lalibela, which means "the bees behold his sovereignty." Lalibela's older brother grew jealous of his mother's untiring devotion and poisoned him. A host of angels gathered up Lalibela's body and took him to heaven, where God told him to build a New Jerusalem replete with 12 special churches. After three days Lalibela returned to Earth, where he reconciled with and then deposed his elder brother, to become King of Ethiopia in 1189, two years after the old Jerusalem had been taken by Islam. The brothers traveled together to the city of Roha where they met the Archangel Gabriel, who helped them build the churches in 25 years. Upon his death, King Lalibela was canonized and the city renamed in his honor.

The churches that King Lalibela created are quite unlike any others in the world. Each structure has been wholly carved from rock, either directly from a cliff-face or from the ground, and they exist as separate buildings, some of which are linked by underground tunnels. The churches are still in use today, and they are decorated with beautiful murals.

The most impressive church is dedicated to St. George, the patron saint of Ethiopia, who is said to have appeared to King Lalibela riding a white horse during the period of construction. Built in the shape of a cross, the church sits in a deep cave carved from the ground. The roof is decorated by three Greek crosses.

Three Greek crosses are carved into the roof of the church dedicated to St. George.

THE SHRINE OF THE HOLY HOUSE

LOCATION	Loreto, Italy
SPIRITUAL TRADITION	Christian
ASSOCIATED SAINT	The Virgin Mary
DATE OF CONSTRUCTION	1294 CE
WHEN TO MAKE THE PILGRIMAGE	Any time of year, but the feast day of Our Lady of Loreto is on December 10

The sacred Shrine of the Holy House is located in the city of Loreto, just off the central Marche coast of eastern Italy. A seemingly insignificant, small stone building, it is widely considered to be the most important site for Marian pilgrimage anywhere in the world, attracting up to four million pilgrims every year.

In the New Testament it is written that Jesus lived as a boy with his parents in a humble dwelling in the town of Nazareth near Jerusalem. According to Catholic tradition, the Roman Emperor Constantine built a church over this sacred site in the 4th century CE, dedicating it to Jesus' mother, Mary. In 1291 angels are said to have magically transported the Holy House under the church to a field in Croatia, apparently fearing that it was about to be destroyed. Then, in 1294, a threatened Muslim invasion caused the angels to fly the Holy House to

Recanti in Italy, before moving it again to Loreto, where it was deemed safe.

In 1469 the Catholic Church erected a fortress-like basilica over the Holy House, which is still standing, although it has undergone much inner and outer change. In 1507 an elaborately carved marble wall was erected to protect the Holy House. In 1510 the site was declared an official destination for Christian pilgrimage.

The Holy House is a small rectangular building, about 13 ft (4 m) wide by 33 ft (10 m) deep. The inner walls are decorated with faded medieval drawings, and at the end of its single cavernous room there is a small medieval statue of the Virgin Mary above an altar, which bears the inscription "Here the Word was made flesh" in Latin.

Scientists have analysed the Holy House and concluded that the side walls date from the 1st century CE.

The magnificent interior of the church above the Shrine of the Holy House.

SANCTUARY OF OUR LADY OF LOURDES

LOCATION	Hautes-Pyrénées, France
SPIRITUAL TRADITION	Christian
ASSOCIATED SAINT	The Virgin Mary
DATE OF CONSTRUCTION	1858 CE
WHEN TO MAKE THE PILGRIMAGE	Any time of year, but August 15 is the main pilgrimage festival

Lourdes is a small town in south-western France that has been a major site for Christian pilgrimage ever since a girl had visions of the Virgin Mary there in the mid-19th century. Perched in the foothills of the Pyrenees, Lourdes is today home to the spectacular Sanctuary of Our Lady of Lourdes, known locally as "the Domain," where rises a sacred spring that has attracted pilgrims from all over the world.

On February 11, 1858 a 14-year-old peasant girl, Bernadette Soubirous, entered a grotto on the banks of the River Gave de Pau and had the first of many visions of a lady dressed in a white gown. On March 25 Bernadette had her 16th vision of the mysterious lady, who revealed herself to be the Virgin Mary. It is said that Bernadette fell to her knees, then began digging in the earth around her until she found water, which became the sacred spring for which Lourdes is now famous. The last vision took place a few months later on July 16. Although others accompanied the girl into the grotto, apparently only Bernadette saw and heard the Blessed Virgin.

Initially no one knew what to make of this strange event, but three years later the local bishop, Monsignor Bertrand-Severe Mascarou Laurence, bought the grotto and surrounding land and, together with the local priest, began to build the first church at the site. The following year he commissioned a sculptor to create an image of the Blessed Virgin, which remains in the grotto to this day and has become a focal point for Marian worship. It is estimated that more than 200 million pilgrims have since visited Lourdes.

The Sanctuary of Our Lady of Lourdes has attracted 200 million pilgrims.

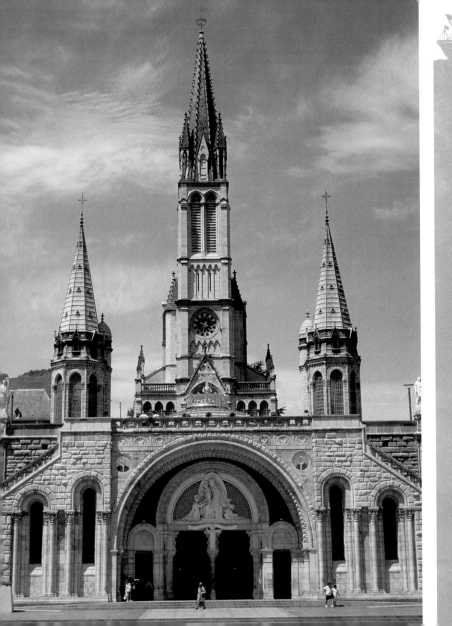

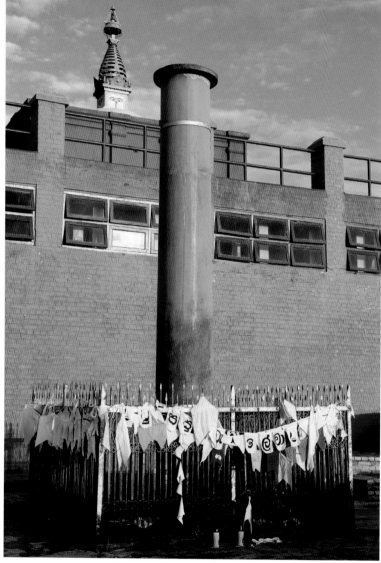

The great Ashoka pillar at the Buddha's birthplace in Lumbini.

LUMBINI

LOCATION	Kapilavastu district, Nepal
SPIRITUAL TRADITION	Buddhist
ASSOCIATED DEITY/ DIGNITARY	Gautama Buddha, Queen Mayadevi
DATE OF CONSTRUCTION	6th century BCE
WHEN TO MAKE THE PILGRIMAGE	Any time of year

Lumbini is a small town in the foothills of the Himalayas in southern Nepal near the border with India. Buddhists believe it is the birthplace of Siddhartha Gautama, the last incarnation of the Buddha, making it one of the four most sacred sites for Buddhist pilgrimage in the world. The others are Bodhgaya (see pages 266–267), the place of the Buddha's enlightenment; Sarnath (see pages 238–239), the place of his first sermon; and Kushinara (see pages 222–223), the site of his death.

According to Buddhist scripture, Prince Siddhartha Gautama was born in Lumbini to Queen Mayadevi in 563 BCE. Here he lived happily until the age of 29, when against his father's wishes he left the royal palace and beheld human suffering for the first time, thus beginning the long journey to his eventual enlightenment.

The exact spot of the Buddha's birth is marked by the Temple of Mayadevi, a small white structure that —astonishingly—lay forgotten for centuries until it was rediscovered in 1895 by a German archeologist. It houses an ancient bas-relief, which depicts Queen Mayadevi supporting herself on the branch of a sal tree having just given birth to the Buddha, who stands unaided on a lotus. This temple is thought to stand on the foundations of a much older temple dating back to the 3rd century BCE. A huge pillar was also unearthed, supposedly one of four erected by the Buddhist King Ashoka in 249 BCE. Outside the temple is the sacred birthing pool known as Puskarini, where Queen Mayadevi is believed to have taken a bath just before giving birth to the Buddha.

Today, Lumbini is bordered by a large monastic zone used exclusively for Buddhist worship, divided into eastern and western zones. The eastern zone is for Theravada Buddhists and the western zone for Mahayana and Vajrayana Buddhists.

MASJID AL-HARAM

LOCATION	Mecca, Saudi Arabia
SPIRITUAL TRADITION	Muslim
ASSOCIATED PROPHET	Muhammad
DATE OF CONSTRUCTION	570 CE
WHEN TO MAKE THE PILGRIMAGE	From the 7th to 13th day of Dhu al-Hijah (the 12th month in the Islamic calendar)—the date changes every year; non-Muslims are forbidden

Mecca is the capital of Saudi Arabia and the birthplace of the Prophet Muhammad, making it the holiest city in Islam. Located roughly 43 miles (70 km) from the Red Sea in a narrow valley, Mecca houses the great Masjid al-Haram, the largest mosque in the world. At the center of the mosque is the sacred Kaaba stone, which attracts millions of pilgrims every year.

Mecca features in many pre-Islamic myths, where it is described as the site of a holy shrine given to Adam, the first man. In one Arabian story, Noah's Ark circumnavigated Adam's shrine seven times, before journeying on to find dry land further north. Islamic writings make no mention of this ancient biblical connection; however, they do describe Mecca as the home of Sarah and her son Ishmael, and they relate how her husband, Abraham, was a regular visitor. According to Islamic scripture, upon Sarah's death, Allah commanded Abraham to build a temple at the site of her home. When Abraham's work was complete, the Angel Gabriel appeared and gave him a sacred stone, the Kaaba, to place inside the temple. Gabriel then instructed Abraham and Ishmael to walk round the stone seven times. Today, many millions of Muslim pilgrims travel to Mecca to perform this selfsame rite—a sacred duty that all Muslims are expected to fulfil at least once during their lifetime, if health and money permit.

In 570 CE the Prophet Muhammad was born in what was then the pagan city of Mecca. In 630 CE Muhammad returned to Mecca from the holy city of Medina (see pages 236–237) with an army and converted the people to Islam. He declared Mecca to be sacred only to Allah, and told his followers that it was the holy site for Islamic pilgrimage. Muhammad then traveled through the city and destroyed all the pagan idols, apart from those depicting Jesus and the Virgin Mary, which he considered sacred. At that time an image of the moon god Hubal was sitting on top of the sacred Kaaba stone, and Muhammad instructed his cousin, Ali, to stand upon his shoulders to topple it. Muhammad told his followers that he had come to restore the ancient rites initiated by Abraham and Ishmael, and that all Muslims were expected to show their devotion in this way, thus paving the way for the instigation of the Hajj

Pilgrims on their way to the Kaaba Stone inside the Masjid al-Haram.

pilgrimage to Mecca, which is widely referred to as the "fifth pillar of Islam."

In recent years more than two-and-a-half million pilgrims have made the holy pilgrimage to Mecca during the annual Muslim festival of Eid. According to tradition, when pilgrims are roughly 6 miles (10 km) from the Masjid al-Haram, they must change into specially tailored white tunics, whereupon they enter a spiritual state known as *Ihram*. Pilgrims then journey to the Masjid al-Haram. Once inside, they walk round the great Kaaba stone in a counterclockwise direction seven times, as instructed by Muhammad 13 centuries ago. Pilgrims then kiss the sacred black stone, which is mounted in a silver frame more than 3½ ft (1 m) above the ground. Afterwards pilgrims travel to a number of other sacred sites in and around Mecca, including a mass congregation on the plain of Arafat where Muhammad received the last verses of the Qur'an, before they return to the Masjid al-Haram one last time. When the pilgrims return home, men customarily add the suffix al-Hajji to their names, and women the suffix al-Hajjiyah. Many pilgrims make a painting of the Kaaba stone, which they display prominently at home.

Hundreds of thousands of Muslim pilgrims assemble in the courtyard of the Masjid al-Haram.

THE MOSQUE OF THE PROPHET

LOCATION	Medina, Saudi Arabia
SPIRITUAL TRADITION	Muslim
ASSOCIATED PROPHET	Muhammad
DATE OF CONSTRUCTION	622 CE
WHEN TO MAKE THE PILGRIMAGE	Any time of year, but many Muslims make the pilgrimage after going on pilgrimage to Mecca; much of Medina is only accessible to Muslims

The sacred city of Medina is 210 miles (340 km) north of Mecca in western Saudi Arabia, and is nearly 125 miles (200 km) from the Red Sea. Located in a fertile green valley surrounded by mountains, Medina is the second most holy city in Islam after Mecca (see pages 232–235).

According to Islamic tradition, the people of Medina gave refuge to Muhammad in 622 CE, and there he remained until he had succeeded in uniting the warring tribes under Islam. After conquering Mecca in 630 CE, Muhammad returned to Medina, where he died in 632 CE. In accordance with his wishes, he was buried at the site of his old house, where his followers erected the Mosque of the Prophet.

Today, the Mosque of the Prophet is a hundred times bigger than the original mosque. During the 13th century a large lead-lined dome (since painted green—the Green Dome) was added, marking the exact spot of the Prophet's tomb underneath. Later the Ottoman sultans who ruled for 400 years made significant additions to the mosque, but the most important enlargements have been made since the formation of the Kingdom of Saudi Arabia in 1932, largely to accommodate the growing number of pilgrims who visit every year. As a result, the Mosque of the Prophet is now the second-largest mosque in the world, able to hold half a million worshippers at once. It is a stunning sight to behold: 24 beautiful domes adorn a great temple flanked by graceful minarets.

During the annual pilgrimage to Saudi Arabia, vast numbers of pilgrims come to the Tomb of the Prophet, and most of them want to get as close to the tomb as they can in order to pray. A small area to the south of the tomb has been dedicated for this purpose, but the sheer volume of pilgrims means that it is not possible for everyone to gain access. This is unfortunate, for tradition decrees that one prayer here is equivalent to a thousand prayers at any other mosque and, furthermore, that no prayer made here goes unheeded.

The Mosque of the Prophet in Medina was built above the Tomb of the Prophet Muhammad himself.

SARNATH

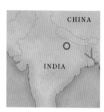

LOCATION	Uttar Pradesh, India
SPIRITUAL TRADITIONS	Buddhist, Jain
ASSOCIATED DEITY/SAGE	Gautama Buddha, Shreyansanath
DATE OF CONSTRUCTION	6th century BCE
WHEN TO MAKE THE PILGRIMAGE	Any time of year

The sacred Buddhist city of Sarnath is located just 8 miles (13 km) north of the holy Hindu city of Varanasi (see pages 284–287) in the Indian state of Uttar Pradesh. It is said to be where the Buddha gave his first sermon, and is one of the four sacred sites to which the Buddha explicitly directed Buddhists to make holy pilgrimage, should they feel the need to do so. It is also the birthplace of Shreyansanath, the 11th Jain Tirthankara (enlightened being), thus making it an important site for Jain pilgrimage as well.

According to Buddhist tradition, in the 6th century BCE the Buddha traveled to Sarnath after his complete enlightenment at Bodhgaya (see pages 266–267). Having no money, he was unable to pay the toll to cross the Ganges, so he flew over the holy river. The Buddha arrived in Sarnath and found his five former traveling companions in the deer park, and he proceeded to teach them his wisdom, known as the Dharma, until they too

were enlightened. These five men became the very first Buddhist monks and formed the first Buddhist community, known as the Sangha. In time, the community grew to 60 in number, at which point the Buddha instructed all the monks to leave Sarnath to teach the Dharma to the people. The monks set out in all directions, spreading the word of the Buddha across India and beyond.

Today, the Dharmekh Stupa marks the spot where the Buddha gave his first sermon. This beautifully carved stone edifice is more than 130 ft (40 m) tall and nearly 98 ft (30 m) wide. It dates from the 5th century CE, having replaced a 2nd-century BCE structure.

The magnificent stone stupa marks the place where the Buddha first taught.

ST. CATHERINE'S MONASTERY

LOCATION	Mount Sinai, Egypt
SPIRITUAL TRADITIONS	Jewish, Christian, Muslim
DATE OF CONSTRUCTION	527 CE
WHEN TO MAKE THE PILGRIMAGE	Any time of year

St. Catherine's Monastery sits at the foot of Mount Sinai on the Sinai peninsula in Egypt, which borders the Gaza Strip and Israel. According to Jewish, Christian, and Muslim theology, Mount Sinai is the place where Moses received the Ten Commandments from God, and where he was instructed to lead the Jews out of Egypt during the miracle of the burning bush, thus making it a supremely important site for pilgrimage.

Evidence of monastic life on Mount Sinai dates back to the 3rd century CE, and early in the 4th century St. Helena of Constantinople came to Sinai and built the Chapel of the Burning Bush at the precise place where God is believed to have appeared to Moses.

In the early 5th century CE the Byzantine Emperor Justinian erected sturdy granite walls up to 230 ft (70 m) high to protect the chapel, before

The monastery at the foot of Mount Sinai where Moses received the commandments.

going on to build the Church of the Transfiguration around the chapel before his death in 565 CE. The church was later named St. Catherine's Monastery in honor of St. Catherine of Alexandria, whose dismembered body was reputedly brought by angels to Mount Sinai after her gruesome martyrdom in the 3rd century CE. In around 800 CE monks apparently found her remains at the site, and they are stored to this day in a marble container in the basilica. The massive walls that surround the monastery have enabled it to survive intact, despite numerous assaults over the last 1,400 years.

St. Catherine's is presently run by the Eastern Orthodox Church, and some say that it is the oldest functioning Christian monastery in the world. The main attraction is the shrub that grows in the chapel, an ancient rose bush native to Sinai, which many believe to be the actual burning bush in which God appeared to Moses.

THE TEMPLE MOUNT

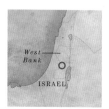

LOCATION	Jerusalem
SPIRITUAL TRADITIONS	Jewish, Muslim, Christian
DATE OF CONSTRUCTION	10th century BCE
WHEN TO MAKE THE PILGRIMAGE	Any time of year; modest dress is required and religious activity is forbidden

The Temple Mount—known as the Noble Sanctuary to Muslims—is an elevated plateau spanning 35 acres (14 hectares) in the Old City of Jerusalem. It is one of the most important and contested sacred sites in the world, for it is where Jews believe Jehovah created Adam; and where Muslims believe Muhammad began his divine ascension; it is also where Christians believe Christ preached his famous Sermon on the Mount. Although it is in Israel, the Temple Mount is managed by the Muslim Religious Council, who ask that non-Muslim visitors refrain from prayer—a ban that is enforced by the Israeli government.

The Temple Mount is believed to be the site of King Solomon's Temple (957 BCE), which housed the original Jewish Ark of the Covenant. In the 6th century BCE the Jews were forced into exile: the Ark was stolen and the temple completely destroyed. Today, it is not clear exactly where the temple stood, but devout Jews refrain from entering the Temple Mount in case they should accidentally stand on the original site of the Ark.

In 19 BCE King Herod greatly extended the Temple Mount for the

A view of the Temple Mount from the Western Wall showing the Golden Dome of the Rock alongside the al-Aqsa Mosque.

Jewish people. He built a great temple on a raised platform supported by a huge wall, parts of which are still visible today. This is thought to be the temple from which Christ banished Jewish money-lenders in the gospel stories of the New Testament. In 70 CE a war erupted between the Romans and the Jews, and the Romans destroyed the Temple of Herod. Over the next 70 years skirmishes regularly broke out between Romans and Jews, resulting in the Jews being banned completely from Jerusalem. It was not until the early 4th century CE, when Constantine became the first Christian Roman emperor, that Jews were allowed back into Jerusalem—and then only once a year, when they would assemble at the one remaining wall of Herod's temple and mourn its loss and their eviction from the Holy Land. This stretch of wall almost 200 ft (60 m) long is known as the Western Wall, or the Wailing Wall, and is the most sacred site in Judaism.

In 325 CE Constantine's mother, Helena, is believed to have built the Church of St. Cyrus and St. John on the Temple Mount, almost certainly siting the building directly over the Roman Temple of Jupiter. A hundred years later the Jewish people petitioned to be allowed back into Jerusalem and to worship at the wall. Permission was granted, and for the next two hundred years Christians

worshipped in the Church of St. Cyrus and St. John, while Jews prayed at the Western Wall.

In 637 CE Caliph Omar took control of Jerusalem and the Christian church was destroyed. In 691 CE Muslims chose the same spot to erect the Dome of the Rock, a stunning building

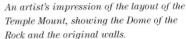

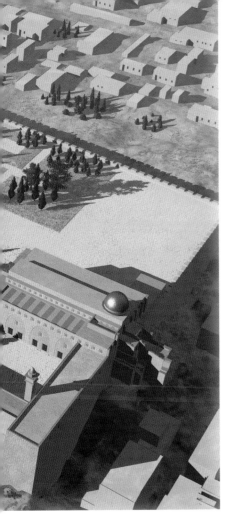

An artist's impression of the layout of the Temple Mount, showing the Dome of the Rock and the original walls.

house the very rock upon which Muhammad stood when he ascended to heaven. In 720 CE the beautiful al-Aqsa Mosque was built near the entrance of the Noble Sanctuary and is widely considered the third most holy site in Islam. Muhammad initially instructed Muslims to pray in the direction of this mosque, before later settling upon Mecca.

In 1099 Christian crusaders conquered Jerusalem, after which they committed a terrible massacre of Jews and Muslims. They destroyed the Jewish synagogue and converted the al-Aqsa Mosque into a Christian church. In 1187 Saladin retook Jerusalem. The al-Aqsa Mosque was restored and the Jews were invited back into Jerusalem, where they continued to pray at the Western Wall. It was not until 1928 that the serious violence between Muslims and Jews, which has been the source of conflict ever since, erupted at the Western Wall. In 1967 Israel took control of the Western Wall by force, turning it into the most major site of Jewish pilgrimage. The future of the Temple Mount seems to be extremely uncertain.

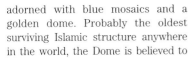

adorned with blue mosaics and a golden dome. Probably the oldest surviving Islamic structure anywhere in the world, the Dome is believed to

245

THE VATICAN: ST. PETER'S BASILICA AND THE SISTINE CHAPEL

LOCATION	Rome, Italy
SPIRITUAL TRADITION	Christian
ASSOCIATED SAINT	St. Peter the Apostle
DATE OF CONSTRUCTION	324 CE–late 17th century
WHEN TO MAKE THE PILGRIMAGE	Any time of year, but knees and shoulders must be covered

St. Peter's Basilica and the Sistine Chapel are located within Vatican City, a walled enclave that functions as a separate country in the center of Rome. Until recently St. Peter's Basilica was the largest church in Christendom, and it is undoubtedly one of the most important sites for Christian pilgrimage in the world. The Vatican is home to literally thousands of exemplary artefacts and relics, as well as many exquisite works of art.

According to Catholic tradition, St. Peter's church was founded by Constantine in 324 CE on the site where St. Peter was crucified by Emperor Nero in 64 CE. St. Peter is widely considered to be the first pope of the Catholic Church, and his remains are said to rest under the basilica, along with the remains of countless other popes who succeeded

him. For visiting Christians, the shrine of St. Peter is usually the main focus of their pilgrimage.

In the late 15th century Pope Sixtus IV commissioned the celebrated Sistine Chapel next to the old church, and in the early 16th century Pope Julius II decided to completely rebuild St. Peter's Basilica, transforming it into the stunning complex that we see today. Numerous talented artists and architects were employed, including the venerated Michelangelo, who designed the great dome that rises majestically above the basilica. He also painted the massive ceiling of the Sistine Chapel and his masterpiece *The Last Judgment*, which are widely considered to be his crowning artistic achievements.

In the late 17th century, St. Peter's Square was completed to front the immense basilica. It is surrounded by a monumental colonnade which is adorned with fine sculptures of more than 140 Christian saints. It also features a stunning ancient Egyptian obelisk that once belonged to Emperor Nero, along with two beautiful fountains that delight tourists and pilgrims alike.

The magnificent St. Peter's Basilica in the heart of Vatican city.

THE TIRTHANKARA STATUES AT SHATRUNJAY

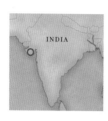

INDIA

LOCATION	Gujarat, India
SPIRITUAL TRADITION	Jain
ASSOCIATED DEITY	Adinath
DATE OF CONSTRUCTION	11th–20th century CE
WHEN TO MAKE THE PILGRIMAGE	Any time of year; elevators are available to those unable to climb up the flight of 3,764 steps to the top of the hill

Shatrunjay hill in the western Indian state of Gujarat is home to a stunning collection of Jain temples that have been a focal point for spiritual pilgrimage for thousands of years. In Jainism, enlightened beings are known as Tirthankaras, and in these sacred temples they are depicted in the form of exquisite statues that embody their divine and peaceful presence.

According to Jain legend, the first ever Tirthankara, Adinath, attained enlightenment on Shatrunjay hill, as did most of the other Tirthankaras who followed him. In recognition of the supreme sacredness of the site, a Jain monk and his disciple founded the first temples at Shatrunjay hill. Legend has it that the monk could fly and also that he could create gold, which explains the presence of many riches that adorn these stunning hilltop temples today.

There are nearly 900 temples on the holy hill, each one housing a unique sacred treasure. The largest and most important temple is the Shri Adishwar. It is said this temple was built in 1618 by a rich merchant in an attempt to redeem his soul. The sacred image of Adinath is carved from marble and is shown with four faces pointing in the four directions of the compass. All day long, devout monks make offerings to the enlightened being, ringing bells and chanting prayers. They take great care not to harm any insects as they worship, for Jains are committed to not harming any living beings.

Every year during the late autumn a great full-moon festival takes place on Shatrunjay hill, which attracts Jain pilgrims from all over India and beyond. The pilgrims carry huge pictures of the sacred hill through the streets of the nearby town of Palitana.

A Jain worshipper walks through the sacred temple of Shri Adishwar.

YAMUNOTRI

LOCATION	Uttarakhand state, India
SPIRITUAL TRADITION	Hindu
ASSOCIATED DEITY	Yamuna
DATE OF CONSTRUCTION	1923 CE
LENGTH OF PILGRIMAGE	3¾ miles (6 km)
WHEN TO MAKE THE PILGRIMAGE	Best in summer when the weather is least harsh

Yamunotri is located at high altitude in the Himalayas in the northern Indian state of Uttarakhand. Widely regarded as the source of the Yamuna River—the second most holy river in Hinduism after the Ganges, into which it flows—Yamunotri is home to a small Hindu temple that serves as one of the four main destinations of the Chota Char Dham pilgrimage, the most important pilgrimage tour in the Himalayas for Hindu pilgrims.

The first temple at Yamunotri was not built until the 19th century, but the extreme weather conditions, including earthquakes, meant that it did not last long. In 1923 a new temple was built, which has only just survived until the present day. Dedicated to the goddess Yamuna, it houses a small silver statue in her image, adorned with garlands.

Yamunotri is at least one day's walk from the nearest town, which means that the pilgrimage consists of a spectacular, if arduous walk through glacial mountains lined with soothing waterfalls. The old and the infirm are forced to make this pilgrimage on ponies or horses, which are available for rent, or are carried up by other people. Upon arriving, pilgrims are able to bathe in a hot spring, and to eat rice that is cooked in another hot spring, which is ritually prepared by the temple priests. The waters that create these thermal springs arise from the melting of the Yamuna glacier, and for that reason they are especially sacred. In Hindu mythology, Yamuna is the daughter of the sun god Surya, and the twin of the god Yama, whose role is to pull the soul from the corpse. Yamuna is traditionally associated with purity, meaning that pilgrims who bathe in her waters are able to cleanse themselves of their sins and thus speed up the karmic cycle of rebirth and death, leading more quickly to their ultimate liberation.

An older pilgrim is carried to the sacred site of Yamunotri.

ALLAHABAD/PRAYAG

LOCATION	Uttar Pradesh, India
SPIRITUAL TRADITION	Hindu
DATE OF CONSTRUCTION	1575 CE
WHEN TO MAKE THE PILGRIMAGE	October through February (summer can be very hot and winter very cold)

Allahabad—also known as Prayag—is a city sacred to Hindus in the northern Indian state of Uttar Pradesh. Generally regarded as the most important of the four sites of the Kumbh Mela pilgrimage (a mass Hindu river pilgrimage that has been observed for at least 1,400 years), it can attract up to 75 million pilgrims during a festival year.

According to Hindu scripture, when Brahmin instructed Lord Brahma to create the world, he chose Prayag because it is located at the confluence of three holy rivers: the Ganges, the Yamuna, and the invisible Sarasvati. It is said that during creation a few drops of nectar dropped into the sacred rivers where they join, giving the waters magical powers.

In 1575 the Mughal Emperor Akbar founded the city of Prayag on the site of the ancient city of Agra, erecting a majestic fort which is flanked by high towers on the banks of the Yamuna River near the place

where it meets the River Ganges. Inside the fort is the underground Patalpuri Temple, which is dedicated to Shiva and houses an immortal tree known as the Akshayavat. The fort is also home to the huge Ashoka Pillar, which is made from polished sandstone and stands nearly 36 ft (11 m) high. This pillar is reputed to be more than 2,000 years old.

Just along from the fort is the Saraswati Ghat, where pilgrims come to bathe in the sacred waters; and a little further along is the Mankameshwar Mandir, another beautiful temple devoted to Shiva. Of even greater interest is the small but busy Hanuman temple, built on the confluence side of the fort and open to non-Hindus. Hanuman is the clever monkey god devoted to Lord Rama, and in this temple a huge idol of him is depicted in the reclining posture. It is unlike those in any other temple in northern India, where he is always shown standing. It is claimed that every year the Ganges floods until it reaches the temple and submerges the sleeping Hanuman's feet, after which he wakes and the river recedes.

Pilgrims gather in boats beneath the majestic fort, which was built by Emperor Akbar on the banks of the Yamuna River.

KEDARNATH TEMPLE

LOCATION	Uttarakhand state, India
SPIRITUAL TRADITION	Hindu
ASSOCIATED DEITY	Shiva
DATE OF CONSTRUCTION	8th century CE
LENGTH OF PILGRIMAGE	The pilgrimage to Kedarnath is a 9 mile (14 km) uphill walk from Gaurikund
WHEN TO MAKE THE PILGRIMAGE	This is only possible from April to October because of the extreme cold weather

Kedarnath Temple is located in the city of Kedarnath in the northern state of Uttarakhand, high on a mountain range in the Himalayas and close to the Mandakini River. It is a most sacred site of holy pilgrimage for Hindus who are devoted to Shiva.

According to Hindu tradition, the five Pandava brothers—whose lives are described in the Mahabharata—gave up their kingdom and their riches to worship Lord Shiva in the Himalayas. At one point they glimpsed him in the form of a buffalo and chased him. Shiva ran all the way to Kedarnath, where he suddenly thrust himself into the ground. But before he completely disappeared, one of the brothers managed to get hold of his rear-end, whereupon the protruding hind turned into a stone Shiva Lingam, which the brothers promptly worshipped. Pleased with their

devotion, Shiva told them he would grant them a wish. They asked that he remain permanently in Kedarnath, so that the local people could worship him and always be happy. Shiva obliged, and the stone Shiva Lingam—meaning "sign of Shiva"—is still worshipped in the temple at Kedarnath today.

The present temple is thought to have been built by Adi Shankara, who was a highly important Advaitic philosopher (one believing in non-duality: no separation between God and the true self), in the 8th century CE, although no one is sure. It is constructed from large granite stone slabs. There is a main inner hall adorned with statues of Hindu deities, and an inner sanctum, which houses the great Shiva Lingam.

The arduous uphill pilgrimage from Gaurikund to the temple can only be made during the summer months, on account of the extreme cold weather at high altitude in the Himalayas. The town of Gaurikund is named after the goddess Gauri, Shiva's consort. Here there is a beautiful shrine dedicated to her and a lovely hot-water spring where pilgrims may take a bath. Older pilgrims who will find the mountain walk difficult may ride on ponies.

Hindu pilgrims enter the Kedarnath Temple, which houses a highly revered stone Shiva Lingam.

THE MOSQUE OF IMAM ALI

LOCATION	Najaf, Iraq
SPIRITUAL TRADITION	Shia Muslim
ASSOCIATED SAINT	Imam Ali
DATE OF CONSTRUCTION	691 CE
WHEN TO MAKE THE PILGRIMAGE	The recent war in Iraq has made Najaf an extremely difficult and dangerous place to visit

Najaf is a holy Muslim city in southern Iraq, roughly 93 miles (150 km) south of Baghdad. It is the final resting place of Imam Ali—the founder of the Shia tradition in Islam—making it the third most important site for Shia pilgrimage in the world, after Mecca and Medina.

Shortly after the Prophet Muhammad's death in 632 CE, Islam divided into two separate traditions known as Sunni and Shia. The Sunnis wanted to elect a new leader, whereas the Shia argued that the new leader should be one of Muhammad's relatives. Both sides parted company, and Imam Ali—Muhammad's cousin, son-in-law, and closest living relative—became the new leader of Islam for the Shia. During the fighting that followed, Ali was martyred in Najaf in 661 CE. The city of Najaf was founded on the site of a village in 691 CE.

It is believed that Ali's tomb was discovered in the city in 750 CE. The tomb quickly became a focus for Shia pilgrimage, and the first of many great shrines was built over it. In around 1500 the present mosque—the Mosque of Imam Ali—was constructed.

The Mosque of Imam Ali is a truly magnificent temple, its great dome and towering minarets lavishly adorned with thousands upon thousands of gleaming gold tiles, resplendent in the hot desert sun. Inside, the arched ceilings are stunningly lit by thousands of tiny lights, which glitter on the great swathes of hammered silver that lavishly adorn the beautiful walls.

Many Shia Muslims bring their dead to the tomb of Ali. Family members carry the coffin around the crypt before taking it to Wadi-as-Salam, a cemetery north of the mosque. This cemetery is possibly the largest burial site in the world. It is said the remains of Adam and Noah are buried here.

Shia Muslim pilgrims entering the golden Mosque of Imam Ali to say prayers.

Hindu pilgrims approach the temple to pay homage to Krishna and Radha.

VRINDAVAN

LOCATION	Uttar Pradesh, India
SPIRITUAL TRADITION	Hindu
ASSOCIATED DEITIES	Krishna, Radha
DATE OF CONSTRUCTION	3228 BCE
WHEN TO MAKE THE PILGRIMAGE	Any time of year; the main pilgrimage takes place in August or September

Vrindavan is a holy town in the Mathura district of Uttar Pradesh in northern India. Home to thousands of stunning temples and shrines, it has been a focus for Krishna and Radha worship for thousands of years. Today, Vrindavan is one of the most important sites for Krishna pilgrimage in India, attracting millions every year.

According to Hindu tradition, more than 5,000 years ago Lord Krishna was born in the forests of Vrindavan, where he grew up as a playful trickster, stealing butter and dancing with local girls, including the beautiful Radharani —also known as Radha—who would later become his devotee and consort. For her worshippers, Radharani is the supreme goddess, more important even than Krishna, for she offers a direct pathway to God.

Today, devotees of Radha flock in their thousands to the Shree Radha Ras Bihari Ashta Sakhi Temple in Vrindavan. Built hundreds of years ago, this temple is believed to be the first devoted to Krishna, Radha, and her eight female companions, the Ashta Sakhi, who play a key role in helping Krishna and Radha enjoy each other's love. According to tradition, Krishna actually visits this temple to perform the Rasa Lila, his sacred love-dance with Radha, and on those nights worshippers are said to hear the sound of the eight girls' anklets tinkling as they dance. This dance is re-enacted at many temples in Vrindavan, the role of Krishna being played by a 13-year-old boy. At the end of the dance the girls lay garlands at the boy's feet, and for a moment he is said to be transformed into Krishna himself, enabling the audience to pay direct homage.

The other main pilgrimage shrines in Vrindavan are the Banke Bihari Temple, the Rangnathji Temple, the Shri Krishna Balaram Temple, and the Radharaman Temple. These temples welcome pilgrims during the Janmashtani festival associated with Krishna's birthday.

BADRINATH TEMPLE

LOCATION	Uttarakhand state, India
SPIRITUAL TRADITION	Hindu
ASSOCIATED DEITY	Vishnu
DATE OF CONSTRUCTION	16th century CE
WHEN TO MAKE THE PILGRIMAGE	Late April to early November

Badrinath Temple is located in the town of Badrinath on the banks of the Alaknanda River in the Himalayan region of India. It is sacred to the Hindu god Vishnu, and is the main site of the highly important Char Dham pilgrimage. It is open for only six months of the year because of the harsh weather conditions in this elevated region of India.

The present-day temple was built in the 16th century, although Badrinath has been a pilgrimage site since at least the 9th century CE, and mention of the town can be found in ancient Vedic texts. The temple stands roughly 49 ft (15 m) tall and is crowned with a beautiful cupola adorned with gold. Unlike other Hindu temples in the area, Badrinath is painted in bold, striking colors, leading some to believe that it was at one point run by Buddhist monks.

A wide stone stairway leads up to the main entrance, which opens into an intricately decorated hall supported by pillars. This beautiful space leads to the main shrine, where a black stone statue of Lord Vishnu meditating under a bodhi tree is housed. This is by far the most important sacred image at Badrinath, and many Hindus believe that it was not carved by human hands, but was manifested by the creator god himself. It is said that the statue was found by Adi Shankara in the 9th century CE in the nearby Alaknanda River. Shankara made a shrine for the statue in a cave near the Tapt Kund hot springs, which rise just below the temple's site today. In the 16th century the statue was moved to the temple, and when the temple shuts down in November, it is taken to the town of Jyotirmath for safe-keeping.

There are many other sacred images at Badrinath, including Lakshmi —Vishnu's consort—Garuda and Ganesha, the elephant-headed god. Most visiting pilgrims bathe in the hot springs in an act of ritual purification before entering the temple.

The Badrinath Temple is bedecked with gold and painted in vibrant colors.

THE TEMPLES OF MADURAI

LOCATION	Tamil Nadu, India
SPIRITUAL TRADITION	Hindu
ASSOCIATED DEITIES	Shiva, Parvati
DATE OF CONSTRUCTION	500 BCE
WHEN TO MAKE THE PILGRIMAGE	Any time of year

The captivating city of Madurai on the banks of the Vaigai River in the southern Indian state of Tamil Nadu is widely known as "Temple city." Home to a vast array of exquisite Hindu temples and shrines, Madurai has a thriving festival and pilgrimage tradition that stretches back for thousands of years.

According to Hindu tradition, King Kalusakarar—a ruler of the once-great Pandyan dynasty—dedicated a holy temple to Lord Shiva and built a city in the shape of a lotus around it. As the King sought a name for his new city, Shiva appeared and blessed it by drenching it with *madhu* ("nectar" in Sanskrit), which poured from his hair. Hence the name Madurai was chosen for the sacred city, which has long been famous for its sweet-smelling jasmine flowers that grow everywhere.

Over time, Kalusakarar's temple became the Meenakshi Sundareswarar Temple, a vast temple complex that is the focal point of the city today. Major extensions and renovations took place in the 16th and 17th centuries, which resulted in four monumental gateways being built around the two main temple shrines. In the larger one, Shiva is worshipped in his incarnation as Sundareswarar; and in the smaller one, his consort Parvati is worshipped as the fish-eyed Meenakshi. Facing Shiva's shrine is the elaborately ornamented Pudu Mandapam, which is delightfully adorned with sculpted images of Shiva in his many manifestations. Parvati's temple has 11 towers, one of which rises to a height of 230 ft (70 m) and is adorned with hundreds of sculpted images of Hindu mythological creatures. Within the temple are eight sculpted Shakti goddesses—manifestations of the divine feminine principle that Parvati embodies. Once a year devotees of Shiva and Shakti come to the temple for the great Bhramhotsavam festival.

The Meenakshi Sundareswarar Temple complex with its monumental stone gates.

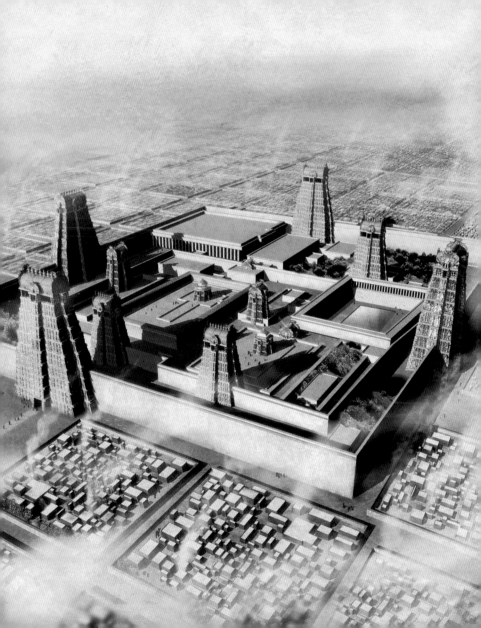

THE VAISHNO DEVI TEMPLE

LOCATION	Jammu and Kashmir, India
SPIRITUAL TRADITION	Hindu
ASSOCIATED DEITY	Ma Vaishno Devi (Shakti)
DATE OF CONSTRUCTION	2000 BCE
LENGTH OF PILGRIMAGE	7½ miles (12 km)
WHEN TO MAKE THE PILGRIMAGE	Any time of year, although access is difficult in winter because of the snow

The Vaishno Devi Temple is a cave temple located at high altitude near the town of Katra in the state of Jammu and Kashmir in northern India. Dedicated to the great Mother Goddess, Ma Vaishno Devi, this unique temple receives millions of Hindu pilgrims every year.

According to Hindu tradition, Ma Vaishno Devi was born to human parents, who called her Trikuta. At the age of nine she was granted permission by her father to pray to Rama, an avatar of Lord Vishnu. When Rama acknowledged Trikuta for her penance, she offered herself in marriage. Rama wanted to accept, but had promised that he would always be faithful to Sita. He told Trikuta that he would reincarnate in Kaliyuga (one of the four stages that the world goes through) as Kalki and would then marry her. Trikuta retreated to a cave where she meditated upon Rama's victory over Ravana, as described in the Ramayana. In thanks, Rama promised that the whole world would worship Trikuta as Ma Vaishno, or Shakti, and also that she would be immortal.

In one very important myth, Ma Vaishno's meditation was cut short by Bhairav, who tried to kill her as she prayed. She took the form of Maha Kali and beheaded him, at the same time offering him forgiveness for his sins. Bhairav's skull landed at a place near her cave, now known as Bhairav Ghati, and Ma Vaishno declared that all pilgrims seeking salvation must pay homage there, as well as making *darshan* (beholding the image and then worshipping it) at her cave. She then assumed the shape of a three-headed rock in order to complete her meditation, and has remained that way ever since.

Today, pilgrims must climb to the entrance of the cave after the long walk from Katra, where they are met by a narrow tunnel which is flooded by a stream. They must wade through the cold water to enter the grotto, where they are greeted by the three-headed stone of Ma Vaishno Devi. They leave by a different route, to pay homage to Bhairav.

The Vaishno Devi Temple is a cave shrine approached by a long mountain trek.

BODHGAYA

LOCATION	Bihar state, India
SPIRITUAL TRADITION	Buddhist
ASSOCIATED DEITY	Gautama Buddha
DATE OF CONSTRUCTION	3rd century BCE
WHEN TO MAKE THE PILGRIMAGE	Best in the cooler months of December through March

Bodhgaya (or Bodh Gaya) is a sacred city in the state of Bihar in eastern India, universally regarded to be the place where the Buddha attained enlightenment. As such, it is one of the most important sites for Buddhist pilgrimage anywhere in the world.

According to Buddhist tradition, in the 6th century BCE Prince Siddhartha Gautama left his spiritual companions to travel to the village of Senami in search of ultimate self-realization. He sat under a pipal tree facing east, and resolved not to rise until he was fully enlightened. Many days or possibly weeks later Prince Siddhartha stood up, this time as the Buddha.

About 250 years after the Buddha's enlightenment, Emperor Ashoka made a pilgrimage to Senami and founded the Bohimanda-vihara, now the Mahabodhi Temple and the focal point for Buddhist pilgrimage at Bodhgaya today.

Buddhist pilgrims gather before the Mahabodhi Temple in Bodhgaya.

At some point during or before the 5th century CE the present Mahabodhi Temple was built, either replacing or extending earlier ones. The main temple building consists of a large, intricately carved, tapering brick pyramid, which rises from a platform roughly 49 ft (15 m) square. Flanked by four ornate towers, this beautiful structure stands more than 164 ft (50 m) tall. Inside is a colossal image of the Buddha, who is shown facing east in the touching-the-ground pose, to portray his enlightenment under the pipal or bodhi tree.

At the back of the Mahabodhi Temple, securely growing behind protective railings is an ancient pipal tree, known as the Sri Maha Bodhi. According to Buddhist tradition, this tree was grown from a sapling that was taken from the actual tree under which the Buddha attained enlightenment. The pipal tree is a type of fig tree with heart-shaped leaves and can live for more than 3,000 years.

THE CHURCH OF THE NATIVITY

LOCATION	Bethlehem, West Bank
SPIRITUAL TRADITIONS	Christian, Muslim
DATE OF CONSTRUCTION	339 CE
WHEN TO MAKE THE PILGRIMAGE	Any time of year, but Christmas is especially popular

The Church of the Nativity was founded in the city of Bethlehem, allegedly at the precise place where Christ was born. One of the oldest churches in continuous use in the world, it is sacred to both Christians and Muslims.

In 339 CE the Emperor Constantine dedicated a church at the present site above a cave where he believed Christ was born. The floor of this church had a large hole in the center, so that it was possible to look directly down into the cave, now known as the Grotto of the Nativity. Parts of this tiled floor have survived to this day. From 527 to 565 CE the Byzantine Emperor Justinian built a much larger church in place of the old one, using many of the church's original pillars and adding an octagonal baptismal font, which can still be seen today.

In 614 CE invading Persians decided not to destroy the church, apparently

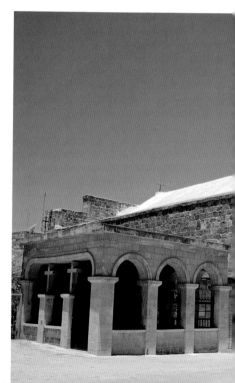

because they were so impressed by its artwork. In 1009 Hakim bi-Amr Allah decreed that all Christian monuments were to be destroyed, but again the Church of the Nativity was spared, this time by local Muslims, who had worshipped in the south transept for nearly 400 years.

In 1099 the First Crusade took control of Jerusalem, and on Christmas Day the following year Baldwin I was crowned the first King of Jerusalem in the Church of the Nativity; 50 years later the French crusaders and Byzantines joined forces to completely refurbish the interior of the church, and much of their work can still be seen, including many beautiful wall mosaics. Unfortunately, much of the marble they used was stolen during the Ottoman period to furnish the Temple Mount (see pages 242–245) in Jerusalem.

In the mid-19th century the cave was badly damaged, first by an earthquake and then by fire, but the Church of the Nativity once again survived, as if a divine hand was at work, watching over this most sacred place. Today, the Grotto of the Nativity is looked after by the Greek Orthodox Church.

The Church of the Nativity was built over a cave where Christ is thought to have been born.

THE DAKSHINESWAR TEMPLE OF KALI

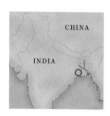

LOCATION	West Bengal, India
SPIRITUAL TRADITION	Hindu
ASSOCIATED DEITIES	Kali, Shiva
DATE OF CONSTRUCTION	1855 CE
WHEN TO MAKE THE PILGRIMAGE	Any time of year

The Dakshineswar Temple of Kali was built in the mid-19th century in West Bengal on the banks of the River Ganges, the most holy river in Hinduism. It is revered as the home of the great goddess Kali—the Divine Mother—who attracts millions of pilgrims every year, making this temple one of the most sacred sites in India.

The Dakshineswar Temple has nine exquisite turrets in shining white marble rising from the two-tiered roof. Four of the turrets rise from the corners of the first tier, four more from the corners of the second tier, and a larger dome-shaped turret rises majestically from the center. Beyond the main temple are 12 smaller two-tiered temples to Shiva, Kali's consort. The complex also includes a Vishnu temple, which is home to icons of Krishna and his consort Radha.

The Dakshineswar Temple is the legacy of the widow Rani Rasmani, who was planning to make a holy pilgrimage to Varanasi (see pages 284–287) in 1847 to show her devotion

to the Divine Mother when the goddess appeared to her in a dream. Rani was told that she must build a temple on the banks of the Ganges and install a statue of Kali, with the promise that the goddess would manifest to pilgrims who came there to worship. Rani cancelled her trip, bought land and commissioned an architect to design a suitable shrine. Work on the temple was soon under way, and shortly before completion an artist was hired to fashion a beautiful image of Kali in black basalt. In 1855 Kali was installed and her temple consecrated.

In 1886 Sre Ramakrishna Paramahamsa was appointed priest of the temple, with dramatic repercussions. After spending long hours worshipping before Kali's statue, he was so overcome with *maha-bava* —a rare form of ecstatic love for the deity—that he was no longer able to function normally. He was relieved of his duties, but continued to live and worship in the compound, over time merging completely with Shiva, Kali, Krishna, Christ, and Muhammad.

The Dakshineswar Temple of Kali is surrounded by smaller Shiva temples.

AACHEN CATHEDRAL

LOCATION	Aachen, Germany
SPIRITUAL TRADITION	Christian
DATE OF CONSTRUCTION	792 CE
WHEN TO MAKE THE PILGRIMAGE	Any time of year

Aachen Cathedral is a Catholic church located in the city of Aachen in the North Rhine-Westphalia region of Germany. It is the oldest surviving cathedral in northern Europe. In the Middle Ages it was known as the "Royal Church of St Mary at Aachen," and in recent times as the "Imperial Cathedral." It is a major site for Christian pilgrimage.

The great Emperor Charlemagne instituted the first work on Aachen Cathedral as early as 792 CE, with the construction of the Palatine Chapel. Since then the cathedral has played a key role in German history, being the site of the coronation of 30 kings and 12 queens. Upon his death in 814 CE, Charlemagne was buried in a vault under the chapel, seated on a throne with the Gospels open on his lap, a scepter in his hand and a crown on his head. His throne is still on display in the cathedral today.

In 1215 Frederick II built a splendid golden shrine for Charlemagne in the chapel, into which the bones of the revered leader were placed. During the early 12th century the shrine of the Virgin Mary was added to the choir of the church. It is adorned with paintings of Jesus, Mary and the 12 disciples, Charlemagne and Pope Leo III. In the 14th century a large choir hall was built to accommodate the ever-growing congregation.

Charlemagne spent his life collecting holy relics, many of which are today kept in the shrine of the Virgin Mary. Among the most significant are the swaddling clothes of the baby Jesus, the loincloth worn by Jesus during his crucifixion, a cloak worn by the Virgin Mary, and the cloth onto which the decapitated head of John the Baptist was apparently placed. Pilgrims from all over the world have come to worship at the site of these sacred keepsakes for more than a thousand years.

Aachen Cathedral is home to some of Christianity's most sacred relics.

TRIER CATHEDRAL AND ST. MATTHIAS ABBEY CHURCH

LOCATION	Trier, Germany
SPIRITUAL TRADITION	Christian
ASSOCIATED SAINTS	St. Peter, St. Matthias
DATE OF CONSTRUCTION	326 CE
WHEN TO MAKE THE PILGRIMAGE	Any time of year, but the Festival of the Holy Robe takes place on April 28 and the Feast Day of St. Matthias on May 14

Trier sits on the banks of the Moselle River, near to the border of Germany with Luxembourg. It is home to the magnificent Trier Cathedral—thought to be the oldest church in Germany—and to the St. Matthias Abbey Church, containing the Tomb of the Apostle.

In 326 CE the Roman Emperor Constantine built a colossal cathedral in Trier dedicated to St. Peter to celebrate the 20th anniversary of his reign, and parts of it can be seen today. Shortly afterward Constantine's mother, Helena, is said to have made a gift to the church of the Holy Robe of Christ, allegedly the tunic that Christ wore during his crucifixion, although no written records of this event predate the 12th century.

In 1512 an excavation was carried out under the high altar and the Holy Robe was miraculously found, along with a nail that had been used during Christ's crucifixion. The Holy Robe was proudly displayed to the public, and more than 100,000 pilgrims visited within 23 days. Ever since, the Holy Robe has been intermittently exhibited to enormous crowds in the Cathedral Square, usually for a period of a few weeks at a time. The last public showing took place in 1933—an event that drew more than two million pilgrims to Trier; it is not known when the Holy Robe will be displayed again.

Also in Trier is the beautiful St. Matthias Abbey Church, dedicated to Matthias the Apostle, who witnessed Christ's resurrection and replaced Judas Iscariot. According to tradition, Matthias was martyred in Turkey and his remains were stored in Jerusalem. They were taken back to Europe by Helena, who shared them between the

Abbey Church at Trier and the Basilica of St. Mary Major in Rome. In 882 CE the Abbey Church was destroyed, but was rebuilt in the 12th century. Pilgrims still flock to the church today to worship at the Tomb of the Apostle.

Millions of Christians have made pilgrimage to Trier Cathedral to see the Holy Robe—the tunic "worn by Christ during his crucifixion."

THE BASILICA OF THE HOLY BLOOD

LOCATION	Bruges, Belgium
SPIRITUAL TRADITION	Christian
ASSOCIATED SAINT	St. Basil the Great
DATE OF CONSTRUCTION	1134–57 CE
WHEN TO MAKE THE PILGRIMAGE	Any time of year, but the procession of the Holy Blood takes place on Ascension Day every year

The Basilica of the Holy Blood is an astonishing 12th-century church located in Bruges in Belgium. Formerly the chapel of residence for the Court of Flanders, this minor basilica is world-famous for housing one of the world's most sacred Christian relics: a vial of Holy Blood. It also houses the relics of St. Basil the Great, a venerated 4th-century bishop, who was highly instrumental in bringing Christianity to Europe.

In 1134 Thierry of Alsace, a devout Catholic, commissioned the building of a double chapel in the Romanesque style in the town's Burg Square for private worship. In 1147 Thierry left Bruges to join his brother Baldwin on the second of two major crusades to the Holy Land. According to tradition, he returned in 1150 with a vial containing a cloth dipped in the blood of Jesus Christ, which had been preserved by Joseph of Arimathea, whom Matthew records as having tended Christ's body after his crucifixion. In 1310 Pope Clement V issued a decree granting indulgences to all who came to witness the vial, thereby ensuring that the Basilica of the Holy Blood became an important site for Catholic pilgrimage.

The upper chapel containing the vial of Holy Blood was rebuilt in the Gothic style toward the end of the 15th century, and was renovated again in the early 19th century. Today, only the curved arches leading into the side chapel remain from the original structure. By contrast, the dark lower chapel—which is dedicated to St. Basil —has changed little; it is considered to be one of the finest and best-preserved examples of the Romanesque style in Belgium.

According to tradition, Count Robert II of Flounders—later known as Robert of Jerusalem—brought back the relics of St. Basil to Bruges after the First Crusade in 1095–99. These were stored in the lower chapel and have remained there ever since, attracting pilgrims from around the world.

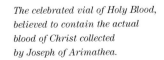

The celebrated vial of Holy Blood, believed to contain the actual blood of Christ collected by Joseph of Arimathea.

CANTERBURY CATHEDRAL

LOCATION	Kent, England
SPIRITUAL TRADITION	Christian
ASSOCIATED SAINT	St. Thomas à Becket
DATE OF CONSTRUCTION	602 CE
WHEN TO MAKE THE PILGRIMAGE	Any time of year

Canterbury Cathedral is a magnificent Christian church located in the city of Canterbury in Kent, southern England. It is the seat of the Archbishop of Canterbury, who is generally regarded as the spiritual leader of the worldwide Anglican communion.

In 597 CE Pope Gregory the Great sent St. Augustine of Rome (not to be confused with St. Augustine of Hippo) to heathen England as a missionary. After making a favorable impression on the king, Augustine founded Canterbury Cathedral in 602 CE, becoming its first archbishop. Since then the cathedral has been rebuilt and extended many times.

In 1066 the French conquered England, and in 1070 they appointed Lanfranc as the first Norman archbishop. He completely rebuilt the badly damaged cathedral in the style of his old abbey at Caen. In 1170

The glorious nave built in the Perpendicular style of English gothic.

Archbishop Thomas à Becket so infuriated Henry II that four of his knights traveled to Canterbury and murdered him in the transept of the cathedral. Becket was subsequently canonized by Pope Alexander III, ensuring Canterbury's place as an important site for holy pilgrimage, as recorded by Geoffrey Chaucer in his famous *Canterbury Tales*. In 1174 a fire wrought terrible damage at Canterbury, occasioning a great deal of rebuilding. The French architect William of Sens designed a beautiful new choir at the eastern end with flying buttresses, high-pointed arches and rib vaulting, all of which are in evidence today. His work was completed by William the Englishman, who added the Trinity Chapel as a shrine for St. Thomas the Martyr. At the far end of the chapel he erected the Corona Tower to house the crown of St. Thomas's head, which had been carefully preserved after it was sliced off during his brutal murder.

THE SHRINE OF OUR LADY OF KNOCK

LOCATION	County Mayo, Ireland
SPIRITUAL TRADITION	Christian
ASSOCIATED SAINT	The Virgin Mary
DATE OF CONSTRUCTION	1879 CE
WHEN TO MAKE THE PILGRIMAGE	Any time of year

The small town of Knock in County Mayo, Ireland, achieved nationwide fame in 1879 when it was the site of a series of divine apparitions at the parish church, which included visions of the Virgin Mary, her husband Joseph, John the Evangelist, and the Lamb of God surrounded by angels, which was taken to represent Jesus Christ. Today, the Shrine of Our Lady of Knock attracts more than one-and-a-half million pilgrims every year.

According to Catholic tradition and eyewitness testimony, the middle-aged housekeeper of Archdeacon Kavanagh was the first to see the divine figures around the south gable of the church, and they were later seen by her friend as they locked up the church together. The friend alerted her brother, who alerted the rest of his family and their neighbors, so that within hours a large number of people (ranging in age from 6 to 75) had assembled by the church to witness the divine vision. Two other people also saw the figures as they walked past the church, but thought that they must have been statues placed there by the archdeacon, so they paid no particular attention. About ½ mile (1 km) away, on the same evening, a farmer reported seeing a brilliant bright light in the air above the church, which he likened to a globe of golden beer.

Almost immediately pilgrims from all over Ireland began visiting Knock. In response, the Catholic Church launched an investigation, which confirmed the eyewitness accounts. A second investigation was carried out in 1936, which again confirmed the trustworthiness of the accounts given by the surviving eyewitnesses. In the 1970s a basilica was built next to the church to accommodate the huge number of pilgrims. In 1979 Pope John Paul II, a self-proclaimed Marian devotee, made a pilgrimage to Knock, as did Mother Teresa in 1993.

Pope John Paul II and Mother Teresa visited The Shrine of Our Lady of Knock.

EPHESUS

TURKEY

LOCATION	Anatolia, Turkey
SPIRITUAL TRADITIONS	Greek mystery, Roman pagan, Christian
ASSOCIATED DEITY/SAINTS	Artemis, the Virgin Mary, John the Apostle, St. Paul
DATE OF CONSTRUCTION	10th century BCE
WHEN TO MAKE THE PILGRIMAGE	Any time of year

The city of Ephesus, located near the town of Selcuk in modern-day Turkey, was once the most important center for commerce and trade in the ancient world. Founded in the 10th century BCE, Ephesus is not only home to quite exceptional Greek and Roman ruins, but is a major pilgrimage site for Christians, who believe that it was the last home of Mary, mother of Jesus, and the place where the Gospel of John was written.

Ephesus gained early fame for its celebrated Temple of Artemis (550 BCE), reputedly the largest and most sacred building in the ancient world. According to legend, the temple was built by the god Ephesus, who was the son of the local river god, Caystrus, in tandem with another god, Cresus. Today, only a single pillar of the great temple remains, rising majestically from a swamp; however, two fabulous 1st- and 2nd-century Roman statues of Artemis, the many-breasted fertility goddess, have survived. These may be seen in the Ephesus Museum, along with other extraordinary Greek and Roman artefacts.

After long periods of occupation and liberation, Ephesus came under Roman influence during the 2nd century BCE. The Emperor Augustus made Ephesus the capital of Asia in 27 BCE, and before long the city was expanding rapidly. The great Temple of Hadrian, a massive open air theatre, and the spectacular facade of the Library of Celsus were built, all of which may be admired today.

Soon after Christ's resurrection in 33 CE his mother, Mary, is thought to have been taken to Ephesus by John the Evangelist, who wrote his New Testament gospel while he was living there. A 6th-century CE chapel built over a much older dwelling is said to mark her home, while the Basilica of St. John is said to house his remains. In 52–54 CE it is thought that the

Apostle Paul also lived in Ephesus, writing his first letter to the Corinthians; and in 62 CE Paul wrote his famed letter to the Ephesians from a prison cell in Rome.

The entrance to the Temple of Hadrian (c. 130 CE) is supported by four Corinthian columns.

VARANASI

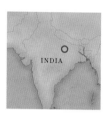

INDIA

LOCATION	Uttar Pradesh, India
SPIRITUAL TRADITIONS	Hindu, Buddhist, Jain
ASSOCIATED DEITY	Shiva
DATE OF CONSTRUCTION	3000 BCE or older
WHEN TO MAKE THE PILGRIMAGE	Any time of year, although summer can be brutally hot

Varanasi—also known as Benares—is located on the west bank of the River Ganges in the state of Uttar Pradesh in northern India. Universally regarded as the most sacred of all Hindu cities, Varanasi is revered by all denominations. The city is mentioned in numerous Hindu scriptures, including the Rig Veda, the Puranas, the Ramayana, and the Mahabharata, which suggests that the city is more than 5,000 years old. Varanasi is also sacred to Buddhists, being just 7½ miles (12 km) from Sarnath (see pages 238–239), where the Buddha is believed to have given his first sermon. There are many beautiful Buddhist stupas in the city. And Jains, too, view Varanasi as sacred, for it is the birthplace of Parshvanatha, the 23rd Tirthankara. Varanasi attracts more than a million pilgrims every year. It is the proud home of numerous gurus, saints, philosophers, artists, and poets, and continues to be one of the most important cultural hubs in India.

The River Ganges is the most sacred river in Hinduism and plays a central role in the religious life of the city. Hindus believe that bathing in the water can help speed up the process of liberation from the karmic cycle of rebirth, which has led to the creation of many great temples and ghats— steps that lead down to the water— along the west bank. One of the most important river temples at Varanasi is the shrine of the Kashi Viswanath. This stunning temple with its great golden spire is generally regarded as the holiest of the 12 sacred Jyortirlingas in

Hindus believe that bathing in the sacred River Ganges can help speed up liberation from the karmic cycle of rebirth.

India: places where Hindus of an advanced level of spiritual attainment can see columns of fire piercing through the earth up into the sky. Hindus of all persuasions are encouraged to make a pilgrimage here at least once in their life to pay homage to Lord Shiva, and follow by a swim in the Ganges. Some Hindus still place the half-burnt bodies of their loved ones in the waters, in an attempt to deliver them from karma, and the corpses can be seen floating downriver past the pilgrims. In recent years the Indian government has banned cremation on the river ghats in attempt to limit this practice, because it is deemed to be damaging the river.

Just along from the temple is the magnificent Dashashwamedh Ghat, where every night Hindu priests perform a form of fire worship, called Agni Pooja, in dedication to Lord Shiva. It is said that this ghat was created by Lord Brahma to welcome Shiva to Varanasi. According to one Hindu myth, long ago Lord Brahma performed a ritual sacrifice of ten horses at this spot.

Further along the west bank is the Manikarnika Ghat, where Hindu pilgrims gather all day long and participate in religious ceremonies after dark, as they have done for thousands of years. According to Hindu mythology, Shiva's consort, Parvati, wished to keep him from his devotees with whom he was spending too much time, so she hid her earrings and told him she had lost them on the banks of the Ganges. Her hope was that Shiva would never tire of looking for the earrings, and would thus stay near her for ever. Because of Parvati's cunning ploy, it is said that Shiva is always at the Manikarnika Ghat, searching for the lost earrings, and whenever someone is cremated at this ghat, it is believed that Shiva asks them if they have seen the earrings. In another Hindu myth, Shiva's consort was torn to pieces by Lord Vishnu's *sudarshana chakra*—a sharp disc that spins through the air—and her earrings fell into the water. Her devotees built the great domed Vishalakshi Temple by the river in her honor, which is one of the highlights for both pilgrims and tourists of a visit to Varanasi.

Another favorite with Hindu pilgrims is the Durga Temple, known locally as the Monkey Temple because so many monkeys live there. It contains a celebrated statue of the Goddess Durga, a manifestation of Shakti, which is believed to have appeared in the 18th century without human intervention. Tourists may enter the courtyard; only Hindu pilgrims can enter the inner-sanctum.

Pilgrims wash in the sacred water of the Ganges at one of the many river ghats.

कर्पात्री

कदार घाट

TEMPLES, CHURCHES,
AND CATHEDRALS

THE TEMPLES OF BAGAN

LOCATION	Mandalay division, Burma
SPIRITUAL TRADITION	Theravada Buddhist
DATE OF CONSTRUCTION	1057–1287 CE
WHEN TO VISIT	Any time of year; Burma is considered a difficult country to visit, but determined travelers invariably conclude that the trip was worthwhile

The ruined temples of Bagan offer one of the most striking and awe-inspiring sacred sights to be found anywhere in the world. Occupying an area that exceeds 40 sq miles (103 sq km), thousands of temples and shrines rise from a dusty plain, in open view from the distant hills.

The first kingdom of Bagan dates from the 2nd century CE, but it was not until 1057 that the massive spree of temple building began, after the city had been captured and subdued by King Anawrahta, a convert to Theravada Buddhism. During the following one hundred years, more than 13,000 temples and pagodas were built, of which only a small proportion are standing today.

The golden era of Bagan came to an end in 1287, when the city was overrun by the armies of Kublai Khan. Since then, various wars and natural disasters have reduced many temples to rubble, and one whole third of the city has been washed away by the encroaching waters of the Irrawaddy River. Nevertheless, there are many exceptional temples still standing in Bagan. One of the best preserved is the striking Ananda Temple, which was cloaked in gold and fully restored in 1990 after a fire in 1975. Built in 1091, it is a veritable masterpiece of Mon architecture, allegedly modeled on the famous Nandamula Cave Temple in the Himalayas. Wonderfully cool and spacious inside, the temple is home to the four sacred images of the Buddha: Kakusanda to the north, Konagamana to the east, Kassapa to the south, and Gautama—the most recent incarnation of the Buddha—to the west.

Another fascinating temple is Mahabodhi, which was constructed as an exact replica of the world-famous Mahabodhi Tree Temple in Bodhgaya (see pages 266–267) in the Indian state of Bihar, situated at the very site where the Buddha attained enlightenment. It has a sitting image of the Buddha on the lower floor and a standing one on the upper floor; 465 sculpted images of the Buddha adorn the spire.

The Mahabodhi Temple in the foreground, with the Gawdawpalin and Ananda Temples in the distance.

The huge Kalyan Minaret, built in 1127, dominates the skyline of Bukhara.

BUKHARA

LOCATION	Bukhara province, Uzbekistan
SPIRITUAL TRADITION	Muslim
DATE OF CONSTRUCTION	500 BCE–1550 CE
WHEN TO VISIT	Any time of year

KAZAKHSTAN
UZBEKISTAN
TURKMENISTAN
AFGHANISTAN

Bukhara is an astonishingly well-preserved holy city built on the banks of the Zervshan River in Uzbekistan. During the 9th and 10th centuries CE Bukhara experienced a golden age, becoming the intellectual and spiritual focus of central Asia, if not the world. During this time, many madrasas—Islamic spiritual schools—were formed and hundreds of beautiful mosques were built, many of which can still be seen today.

Located on the historic Silk Road, Bukhara has been an important focal point for traders for thousands of years. Formerly a significant city of the great Persian empire, Bukhara (founded in 500 BCE) was vigorously contested for many centuries until it was irrevocably conquered by the Arabs in 751 CE. From then on, Islam took permanent hold, and during the following centuries Bukhara flowered, thanks in no small part to the many Sufi philosophers, poets, and scientists who lived there.

Dominating the present-day skyline is the Kalyan (Great) Minaret. Built in 1127, it rises in a flawless and majestic fashion to a height of more than 148 ft (45 m). Just beneath its top is a large gallery, where the muezzin stood to sing out the call to worship. It later became known as the Tower of Death, because criminals were regularly thrown from the top.

The Ismail Samani Mausoleum was erected in the 10th century to store the remains of the founder of the Samanid dynasty, along with his closest relatives. The 6½ ft (2 m)-thick walls are covered with intricate terracotta stonework, creating one of the most aesthetically pleasing monuments in all of central Asia.

By contrast, the nearby Chashma-Ayub Mausoleum is hardly ornamented. Built in the 12th century, its beauty comes from its lack of ostentation and its simple forms. Job alledgedly visited there and made a still-functioning well by smiting the ground with his staff.

ROSSLYN CHAPEL

LOCATION	Roslin, Scotland
SPIRITUAL TRADITION	Christian
ASSOCIATED SAINT	St. Matthew
DATE OF CONSTRUCTION	15th century CE
WHEN TO VISIT	Any time of year

Rosslyn Chapel, formally referred to as the Collegiate Chapel of St. Matthew, is a small Catholic church on a hillock overlooking Roslin Glen near the Scottish city of Edinburgh. Founded in 1446 by the Earl of Caithness, Sir William St. Clair, the chapel has long been associated with the Knights Templar and the Holy Grail.

In its early years the chapel was used for traditional Catholic services for members of the St. Clair family and for religious study, but the Scottish Reformation of 1560 brought Catholic worship to an end. The chapel closed and remained so until 1861, when it reopened as a Scottish Episcopal church. Today, tourists flock to this exquisitely ornate church, some to admire the intricate carvings, but most lured by its appearance in *The Da Vinci Code*, Dan Brown's best-selling novel about the Knights Templar.

The most striking feature of Rosslyn Chapel is that its whole surface area is completely adorned with arresting stone carvings, many depicting important figures and scenes from religious mythology and history. The finest is generally considered to be the Apprentice Pillar—a stone masterpiece that is thought to be a synthesis of the Christian Tree of Life and the Yggdrasil tree of ancient Nordic mythology. The eight dragons of Neifelheim who guard the Nordic hell can be seen gnawing at the tree's roots, while the leaves that form its crown are believed to rise up to Valhalla, the Nordic heaven.

In addition to the Nordic references, the carvings depict traditional Jewish and Christian themes, and others that are decidedly pagan—for example, the more than 100 exquisite carvings of men's faces bedecked by leaves, known as "green men." This wealth of religious imagery makes for an exceptionally beautiful church.

The walls and pillars of the churh are adorned with intricate stone carvings.

CHIANG MAI TEMPLES

LOCATION	Chiang Mai province, Thailand
SPIRITUAL TRADITION	Buddhist
DATE OF CONSTRUCTION	13th century CE
WHEN TO VISIT	Any time of year, but October and November after the rainy season has ended are especially good

Chiang Mai is a city in northern Thailand, overlooked by the stately mountain of Doi Suthep and built on the banks of the River Ping. The city is famous for its more than 300 Buddhist temples, known locally as "Wats."

The most famous temple is Wat Phrathat Doi Suthep, which was constructed on the slopes of Doi Suthep in 1383. It is said the precise location was chosen because a roaming elephant carrying a relic of the Buddha stopped here, circled, trumpeted, then knelt down and died—apparently an extremely auspicious sign. Ever since, this ornate and beautifully constructed temple has been an important site for Buddhist pilgrimage.

The oldest temple is Wat Chiang Man. Built in the 13th century, it was initially home to King Mengrai, who was mainly responsible for building the city. The temple has two exceptional Buddhas: the Phra Sila statue, made of marble, and the Phra Satang Man statue, made of crystal.

Perched in the foothills of Doi Suthep, west of Chiang Mai, is the 700-year-old Wat Umong, which literally translates as "tunnel temple." This extraordinary Wat is hidden inside a large artificial mound of earth, which is adorned with a beautiful pointed *chedi* (or stupa). After the rainy season in September, the mound is bedecked with luscious green vines and is a wonderful site to behold. The temple itself can only be entered via one of the many stone tunnels, which were built at the same time as the temple in the 14th century.

A popular temple with tourists is Wat Phra Singh, a seemingly ordinary building that houses the exquisite Phra Singh Buddha, its centerpiece and focus of worship. Wat Ram Poeng is a meditation retreat for Thais and visitors alike. Monks and students practice Vipassana meditation here.

The beautifully ornate Wat Phrathat Doi Suthep overlooks the city of Chiang Mai.

THIEN MU PAGODA

LOCATION	Hue, Vietnam
SPIRITUAL TRADITION	Buddhist
DATE OF CONSTRUCTION	1601 CE
WHEN TO VISIT	Any time of year

The grand Thien Mu Pagoda is located on Ha Khe hill, overlooking the Perfume River in the ancient city of Hue in Vietnam. Built during the powerful Nguyen dynasty, the stupa of the great temple rises an imposing seven stories high, and for many it symbolizes the majesty and splendour of imperial Vietnam. The temple houses exceptional sculptures and holy relics, and a huge bell, which can be heard from great distances away.

According to tradition, in 1601 Nguyen Hoang, the governor of the province of Hue, was traveling in the area when he came upon Ha Khe hill. He heard an old lady with mysterious powers, Thien Mu, had prophesied that a great lord would visit the hill and build an important pagoda on it, ensuring the good fortune of the people. Hoang ordered a temple to be built, and he named it after her.

The seven-storied Thien Mu Pagoda houses many sacred Buddhist treasures.

In 1695 Thich Dai San, a Buddhist master from China, arrived and settled at the pagoda, where he oversaw the development of a sangha, or Buddhist community. The following year Dai San returned to China, but not before conferring bodhisattva vows on the reigning lord of the province, Nguyen Phuc Chu, who became a devout Buddhist and patron of the pagoda. In 1710 Phuc Chu had a enormous bell cast, which is still audible 6 miles (10 km) away. In 1714 Phuc Chu paid for grand gates to be erected, as well additional shrines, bell-towers, prayer halls, libraries, and living quarters for the monks. He later sent monks on an expedition to China to bring back sacred scriptures, and organized the annual Vassana retreat, which is still practiced by the monks today.

In 1844 the grand seven-storyed tower was built by Emperor Thieu Tri, each level reputedly dedicated to a different manifestation of the Buddha. The monastery is still active today.

THE SHAOLIN TEMPLE

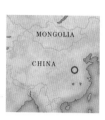

LOCATION	Henan province, China
SPIRITUAL TRADITION	Zen Buddhist
ASSOCIATED DEITY	Bodhidharma
DATE OF CONSTRUCTION	5th century CE
WHEN TO VISIT	Any time of year

The Shaolin Temple is a complex of ancient Buddhist monasteries on the Song Shan sacred mountain in the Henan province of China. It is famous for its long association with the martial art of kung fu, making it a pilgrimage site for martial-arts enthusiasts from around the world.

The first Shaolin Temple was founded in the 5th century CE. According to tradition, around this time an ascetic monk from southern India, Bodhidharma, took up residence in a nearby cave. For nine years he meditated in the cave without speaking, gradually formulating the principles of Zen Buddhism. He then left the cave and entered the Shaolin Temple, where he found a collection of physically degenerate monks. Bodhidharma encouraged them to study and emulate the movements of animals, thereby restoring their bodies to good health. Over time, the practices evolved into the martial art of kung fu, which became an important

form of self-defence, for the monastery was often attacked by bandits. When Bodhidharma died, the monks are said to have buried him in his cave behind the temple, a place that attracts pilgrims to this day.

In the 7th century CE the monks used their fighting skills to save the life of the future emperor, Li Shimin. In gratitude, he enlarged the monastery and supported their training. By the 14th and 15th centuries the monks had gained full military status, and were employed to help quell rebellions and repel invasions, but in 1647 invading Manchus destroyed the temple and killed the monks. It was not until 1800 that the temples were rebuilt, only to be burned down by the warlord Shi Yousan in 1928. The temples were restored, only to be sacked again during the Cultural Revolution. The temple re-opened in the 1980s.

A view of the impressive "Pagoda forest" at the Shaolin Temple.

THE SANCTUARY OF ELEUSIS

LOCATION	Saronic Gulf, Greece
SPIRITUAL TRADITION	Ancient Greek mystery
ASSOCIATED DEITIES	Demeter, Persephone
DATE OF CONSTRUCTION	1600 BCE
WHEN TO VISIT	Any time of year

Eleusis, 12½ miles (20 km) north of Athens, was one of the most sacred sites of the ancient Greek world. Devotees of the earth goddess Demeter and her daughter Persephone would travel here to be initiated in secret ceremonies known as the Mysteries. Only remnants remain, but these are inscribed with pagan scriptures that attest to its former importance.

Little is known of the rites themselves (the penalty for revealing what took place during the Mysteries was death), which began as early as 1600 BCE and lasted roughly 2,000 years. According to Homer (7th century BCE), Demeter came upon Eleusis during her search for Persephone, who had been taken to the underworld by Hades. Here, Demeter asked that a temple be built in her honor, where she could lock herself away and pine for her daughter. She forbade all plants to grow until she was reunited with Persephone, so Zeus himself was forced to intervene. He declared that Persephone would spend two-thirds of the year with her mother and one-third of the year with Hades. Demeter then taught the people secret rites to commemorate the coming and going of Persephone, which are thought to be associated with the planting and harvesting of crops, for in the myth Persephone is forced to return to the underworld every winter.

Some historians believe the rites included the use of psychotropic power-plants. Although only a minority of the ancients were initiated at Eleusis, knowledge of the Mysteries was widespread; those who had tasted them were said to be eternally happy.

A reconstruction of the sanctuary where the secret mystery rites were enacted.

PERSEPOLIS

IRAN

SAUDI ARABIA

LOCATION	Fars province, Iran
SPIRITUAL TRADITION	Zoroastrian
DATE OF CONSTRUCTION	518 BCE
WHEN TO VISIT	Any time of year; the site can be extremely hot during the day and very cold at night

Persepolis—which means "City of the Persians" in Greek—is a World Heritage site in modern-day Iran, 43 miles (70 km) north of Shiraz. Founded by Darius I in 518 BCE on mountainous and largely inaccessible land, it was an unlikely setting for a new capital city, but flourished nonetheless. Today, Persepolis is uninhabited, and the site consists of a vast collection of well-preserved ruins that attracts tourists from all over the world.

Persepolis sits on an enormous terrace, which is in part a natural formation and in part constructed by tremendous human effort. It is approached by a magnificent double stairway made from 111 stone steps. On the terrace itself, the ruins of many great buildings can be seen, the grey limestone from which they are all made being hewn from a nearby mountain. Even though no mortar was used, a great many of the stone slabs are still perfectly in place, a testament to the craftsmanship of the builders. The most significant building is the Palace of Apadana, which was built by Darius I for official Persian business and completed by his son, Xerxes I, who famously conquered Athens in 480 BCE. The great meeting hall was a staggering 197 ft (60 m) long and supported by 72 columns almost 65 ft (20 m) high, the tops of which were sculpted in the shapes of animals; 13 of these great pillars are standing today. Archeologists believe that Persepolis was only used at certain times of the year, probably for important ceremonies such as royal coronations and funerals, as well as for significant religious rituals.

In 1933 an excavation beneath the great hall revealed an extraordinary collection of gold and silver plates dating back to the 6th century BCE. On the south wall an inscription attributed to Darius was found, which read in part: "I built it secure and beautiful and adequate, just as I was intending to."

An artist's reconstruction of the magnificent city of Persepolis, which was built by Darius I and Xerxes I.

TEMPLE OF APHRODITE

LOCATION	Aphrodisias, Turkey
SPIRITUAL TRADITIONS	Ancient Greek pagan, Roman pagan
ASSOCIATED DEITY	Aphrodite
DATE OF CONSTRUCTION	2nd century BCE–2nd century CE
WHEN TO VISIT	Any time of year

The Temple of Aphrodite is located in the ancient town of Aphrodisias just over 124 miles (200 km) from the city of Izmir in Turkey. Initially the site was used to worship Aphrodite, the Greek goddess of love and fertility, but later a second temple was built to worship her Roman equivalent, Venus, which was converted to a Christian church. In recent years much of the temple has been restored to its former glory.

Archeological evidence suggests that people have practiced fertility rites at Aphrodisias for nearly 8,000 years. In the 2nd century BCE the site became specifically associated with Aphrodite, and her devotees built a shrine to perform their sacred rites.

In the 1st century CE the Romans defeated the Greco-Persian king, Mithridates VI, and Aphrodisias came under their influence. Significantly, the Roman emperors Sulla, Julius Caesar,

The remains of a columned temple, built to enclose the shrine of Aphrodite.

and Augustus all belonged to the cult of Venus, with the result that Aphrodisias prospered greatly during their reigns. An impressive columned temple was built around the shrine, and a large theatre, a stadium, a bathhouse, and many other stone structures were added, parts of which are still in evidence today. The cult flourished until Christianity became the official religion of Rome.

According to Greek mythology, Aphrodite was born when Uranos was castrated by his son Cronus and his genitals were dropped into the sea. The waters foamed and out sprung beautiful Aphrodite, fully formed. Zeus was so concerned that her exceptional charms would lead to fighting between the gods that he quickly married her to the steady Hephaestus. He lavished great gifts upon her, but that did not stop her straying with other gods. Even though she was reputedly fickle in her affections, she was much loved by Greek and Roman men.

TEMPLE OF APOLLO

GREECE

LOCATION	Delphi, Greece
SPIRITUAL TRADITION	Ancient Greek pagan
ASSOCIATED DEITY	Apollo
DATE OF CONSTRUCTION	7th century BCE
WHEN TO VISIT	Any time of year

The Temple of Apollo lies on the southern slopes of Mount Parnassos by the town of Delphi, some 112 miles (180 km) north-east of Athens. The Temple was first built around the 7th century BCE, and the Doric columns that still delight visitors today date from the 4th century BCE.

The son of Zeus and Leto, Apollo was the Greek god of the sun, one of the most important deities in the Olympian pantheon. He was loved by his followers for his musicality and revered for his prophecies, which were given at this temple for nearly a thousand years. His devotees would travel great distances from all over the ancient world to ask important questions of the Pythia, the priestess of the temple, who would go into a trance and channel a response from Apollo's spirit. The words spoken by the priestess were taken extremely seriously, for Apollo was traditionally associated with spiritual purity and moral rectitude; failing to heed his counsel could have grave consequences both in this life and the next.

Such was the importance of the Delphic oracle to Greek society as a whole that it was rebuilt after a fire in the 6th century BCE, and then again after an earthquake in the 4th century BCE. The Athenian architects who designed the original temple of the ruins visible today, modeled it upon earlier versions, giving it a peristasis (porch) of six columns across the front and 15 columns down the sides. To all who visited it must have been a truly spectacular sight, the beautiful stone structure being set against a backdrop of jutting mountain rock under a vast blue sky.

Little is known of the interior layout, or of the nature of the secret ceremonies that were conducted inside, but on the exterior forecourt was clearly inscribed the famous ancient philosopher's epithet: "Know Thyself!" To those initiated into the Mystery tradition of the ancient Greeks, this instruction meant much more than simply acknowledging one's strengths and weaknesses, but was a call to experience one's spiritual essence. As such, the temple and its surroundings were viewed as a profoundly sacred site, and to this day many people claim that they feel spiritually moved when they visit, as if Apollo's spirit lives on.

The surviving doric columns of the Temple of Apollo on the slopes of Mount Parnassos.

ANURADHAPURA

LOCATION	North Central Province, Sri Lanka
SPIRITUAL TRADITION	Buddhist
ASSOCIATED DEITY	The Buddha
DATE OF CONSTRUCTION	3rd century BCE
WHEN TO VISIT	Any time of year

The beautiful city of Anuradhapura is an important site for Buddhist pilgrimage in central Sri Lanka. Formerly the capital of the ancient Lankan civilization, Anuradhapura contains quite exceptional ruins and is today home to many active Buddhist monasteries.

According to Buddhist tradition, Princess Sanghamitta traveled from India to Sri Lanka in the 3rd century BCE with a branch of the sacred bodhi tree under which the Buddha himself had become enlightened. She stopped in Anuradhapura, where she founded an order of nuns. Soon afterward many splendid temples and monasteries were built in Anuradhapura, and the city became the thriving capital of the mighty Lankan civilization.

In 993 CE the Chola Emperor Rajaraja invaded Sri Lanka and took control of Anuradhapura. In 1017 his son Rajendra toppled him and sacked the great city. Anuradhapura was abandoned and became overgrown by jungle, where it lay hidden until the British took control of the country in the 19th century and cleared the jungle.

Excavations began and fantastic ruins were uncovered, including many Buddhist temples with large bell-shaped stupas made from sun-dried bricks. One of the most notable is Ruwanwelisaya: a magnificent stupa erected in a beautiful compound supported by stone elephants. Another great temple is Thuparamaya, the first to be built in Anuradhapura after the introduction of Buddhism to Sri Lanka, and which reputedly housed the Buddha's collarbone.

In the 1870s people began to resettle Anuradhapura, and once again it became an important site for Buddhist pilgrimage. Without doubt the most significant site today is the bodhi tree—referred to as the Sri Maha Bodhiya—which Sanghamitta is believed to have brought with her to Anurahadpura more than 2,000 years

ago. Planted on high ground and surrounded by protective railings, the tree has been dated to approximately 250 BCE, making it probably the oldest living tree in the world. It is universally admired by tourists and pilgrims alike, who flock to see it all year round.

The magnificent Ruwanwelisaya Stupa, whose huge courtyard is supported by stone elephants.

THE BONE CHURCH OF SEDLEC

LOCATION	Kutna Hora, Czech Republic
SPIRITUAL TRADITION	Christian
DATE OF CONSTRUCTION	1278 CE
WHEN TO VISIT	Any time of year

The Sedlec Ossuary, also known as the Bone Church, is a small chapel built beneath the Church of All Saints in Sedlec, a suburb of Kutna Hora east of Prague. This extraordinary chapel houses the skeletons of more than 40,000 people, whose bones have been used to decorate its roof and walls, creating a stunning effect.

According to tradition, when the great Bohemian King Ottakar II was fighting a losing war with Rudolph of Habsburg in 1278, he dispatched Abbot Henry of the monastery in Sedlec to the Holy Land on a diplomatic mission. When Henry arrived at the Golgotha in Jerusalem (the site of Christ's crucifixion) he picked up a handful of earth, which be brought back to Sedlec and sprinkled around the cemetery beside his monastery. The cemetery became an extremely popular burial site for Christians from central Europe.

Sometime around 1400 a large vaulted church was built in the middle of the cemetery, which had by then grown greatly in size, in no small measure because of the Black Plague that had swept through Europe.

In the early 18th century the upper church was substantially rebuilt, and in the 19th century a woodcarver named Rint was employed to tidy up the mass of bones in the lower chapel. In the event, Rint surpassed himself. He created a great chandelier made entirely from human bones, which he hung from the nave as the centerpiece. He tied human skulls together like daisy-chains and hung them from the vaults. He made a coat of arms from bones, and even signed his macabre handiwork with a bone signature by the entrance.

The great chandelier is constructed entirely from human bones.

The Church of the Holy Ghost in front of the huge domed Assumption Cathedral.

TRINITY-SERGIUS MONASTERY

RUSSIA

UKRAINE

LOCATION	Sergiyev Posad, Russia
SPIRITUAL TRADITION	Eastern Orthodox Christian
ASSOCIATED SAINT	St. Sergius of Radonezh
DATE OF CONSTRUCTION	1345 CE
WHEN TO VISIT	Any time of year

The historic Trinity-Sergius Monastery, also known as the Holy Trinity Lavra, is located in the city of Sergiyev Posad, roughly 50 miles (80 km) from Moscow. Universally regarded as the most sacred monastic site in Russia, the complex is staffed by more than 300 Eastern Orthodox monks.

The Holy Trinity Lavra was founded in 1345 by a hermit known as Sergius, who is said to have built a small wooden church in a forest for Christian worship. Ten years later Sergius introduced a charter of regulations to govern the lives of the many monks who had come to worship with him. This charter proved so successful that monasteries all over Russia soon copied it, and Sergius achieved national fame. In 1380 he blessed Prince Dmitri Donskoi before the pivotal Battle of Kulikovo against the Tatars, which the people believed contributed to Donskoi's success.

In 1392 Sergius died at the age of 70. Thirty years later he was made patron saint of Russia, and a group of Sergian monks built a stone cathedral on the site of his monastery to honor him. In 1476 the beautiful Church of the Holy Ghost was constructed at the site, a rare example of a Russian church with bell-tower. Many of Sergius's disciples were later buried here. In 1585 the mighty Assumption Cathedral was completed at the site. Commissioned by Ivan the Terrible in 1559, it is topped by five beautiful Russian domes that are modeled on the Kremlin in Moscow.

The Holy Trinity Lavra continued to grow until the Russian Revolution in 1917, when the monastery was closed. However, at the end of the Second World War in 1945, Stalin, an atheist, albeit one who had attended Eastern Orthodox seminary school, returned the monastery to the Church.

NOTRE-DAME BASILICA, MONTREAL

LOCATION	Montreal, Canada
SPIRITUAL TRADITION	Christian
DATE OF CONSTRUCTION	1824–88 CE
WHEN TO VISIT	Any time of year, but the Christmas recital of Handel's *Messiah* is especially popular

The Notre-Dame Basilica is a stunning neo-Gothic church located on the east side of the island of Montreal. Constructed in the mid-19th century, it was for a long time the largest and most splendid church anywhere in North America, with the capacity to hold more than 4,000 worshippers. The interior is widely regarded as one of the most beautiful in the world.

The basilica was designed by the architect James O'Donnell, who is said to have been so moved by the finished church that he converted to Catholicism prior to his death. In recognition of his great contribution, his remains were buried in the crypt; he is the only person to have been honored in this way.

The church has two great bell-towers; in the east tower there is a carillon of ten bells, and in the west tower a single massive bell weighing more than 12 tons, which is only rung on special occasions, such as the funeral of the head of state. A smaller chapel—the Chapelle Sacré-Coeur—sits at the back of the church and provides a more intimate place for worship.

The interior of the church is predominantly fashioned from wood, which has been carved and stained in the most exquisite detail. The ceiling is blue and adorned with golden stars, and the walls are variously gold, silver, azure, and red, all carefully coordinated to create a visually stunning and inspiring effect. Towards the back of the church there is a monumental Casavant Frères pipe organ, which with four keyboards and nearly 7,000 pipes plays a key role in recitals and church services, such as Céline Dion's marriage to René Angélil in 1994.

The interior is carved from wood and stained in exquisite detail.

SALT LAKE TEMPLE

LOCATION	Salt Lake City, USA
SPIRITUAL TRADITION	Christian (Mormon)
ASSOCIATED DEITY	Moroni
DATE OF CONSTRUCTION	1853–93 CE
WHEN TO VISIT	It is not possible to enter the temple without a recommendation from a practicing Mormon, although visitors are welcome to explore the grounds

The Salt Lake Temple is a magnificent Mormon church in the heart of Salt Lake City, Utah. Not only does it play a key role in the Mormon religion, but its location is central to the whole layout of the city, because streets are numbered according to their proximity to the temple. This is widely regarded as the most sacred site for Mormons, thus making the temple an important site for spiritual pilgrimage.

The site of the temple was chosen in 1847 by Brigham Young, an early leader of the Mormon religion (otherwise known as the Church of Jesus Christ of Latter-Day Saints).

Work on the great temple began in 1853, with the colossal granite exterior finally being completed in 1892; the interior was completed the following year, exactly 40 years to the day after building work began. The temple was inspired by the Temple of Solomon in Jerusalem, and was designed to point in the direction of the holy city. Six Gothic spires rise above the elegantly carved walls, each one topped by an all-seeing eye, representing the eye of God. The central spire is adorned by a beautiful sculpture of the angel Moroni, which is said to have appeared and spoken to Joseph Smith, the founder of the Mormon religion, in the early 19th century. Smith claimed that Moroni was the guardian of the golden plates, the original source material for the Book of Mormon, the primary scripture for Mormons. At the foot of each buttress are earth-stones, moon-stones, and then sun-stones, and high above these are cloud-stones, and higher still star-stones—the overall progression thought to represent the human being's spiritual journey from Earth to the heavens.

The central spire is adorned with a sculpture of the angel Moroni.

ST. PAUL'S CATHEDRAL

ENGLAND

LOCATION	London, England
SPIRITUAL TRADITION	Christian
ASSOCIATED SAINT	St. Paul
DATE OF CONSTRUCTION	1675 CE
WHEN TO VISIT	Any time of year

St. Paul's Cathedral is an iconic British landmark and a much-loved London church. Designed by Christopher Wren in the 17th century, this architectural masterpiece has witnessed many major events in the history of the British monarchy, including the marriage of Prince Charles to Princess Diana, which was watched on television by approximately 750 million people around the globe.

The first cathedral at the site was built in wood and dedicated to St. Paul in 604 CE. Like many early churches, it was built over the ruins of a pagan Roman temple. In the 10th century it was sacked by Viking invaders, and a stone church was built to replace it. In 1087 this church was destroyed by fire, and a grand new cathedral boasting Europe's tallest spire was erected, with work continuing for more than 200 years. In 1666 this church was destroyed by the Great Fire of London, paving the way for the present cathedral.

Adorned with a beautiful dome modeled on St. Peter's Basilica in Rome, Wren's magnum opus opened in 1708. The pillared facade is adorned with two elegant towers, which frame the spire bedecked by a golden cross rising from the central dome.

Inside, the great dome toward the end of the nave creates a serene and sacred space, ideally suited for services commemorating the many joyful and sad events that St. Paul's has witnessed over the centuries. As well as the jubilee celebrations of kings and queens, the funerals of Lord Nelson, the Duke of Wellington, and Winston Churchill all took place here.

St. Paul's Cathedral was targeted during the Blitz and suffered extensive damage. It was thus a fitting site as a venue for the nation's Christian service held to mark the end of the Second World War.

A golden cross rises from the great dome, modeled on St. Peter's Basilica in Rome.

THE TEMPLE CHURCH

LOCATION	London, England
SPIRITUAL TRADITION	Christian
ASSOCIATED ORDER	The Knights Templar
DATE OF CONSTRUCTION	1185 CE
WHEN TO VISIT	Any time of year

The Temple Church was built in London in the 12th century, between Fleet Street and the River Thames as the main headquarters of the Knights Templar order. A beautiful round church, it houses numerous stone effigies of its various patrons.

The Knights Templar were formed in 1118 as a military order of the Christian Church. They played a crucial role in the crusades to the Holy Land, receiving endorsement from the Catholic Church in 1129. By the end of the 12th century they were extremely powerful, and a non-military wing evolved to finance the building and protection of Christian churches globally, which in turn led to an early form of banking. At first housed in High Holborn, the Knights Templar built this church to accommodate their rapidly growing congregation. In 1185 the Temple Church was consecrated to

The church houses stone effigies of key patrons and the Knights Templar.

the Virgin Mary by Heraclius, Patriarch of Jerusalem, with Henry II in attendance. His son, Richard I, would go on to play a pivotal role in the subsequent crusades.

When the Holy Lands were finally lost to Islam, the Templars' high regard in Europe began to fade. Philip IV of France, who owed the order a great deal of money, persuaded the pope to disband them. The church was seized by Edward II and the order collapsed, but it was rumored that this immensely wealthy and powerful group simply went to ground, and continued to meet in secret. Some believe that an offshoot of the Knights Templar is playing a major role in running the world today.

The church's round design is modeled on the Church of the Holy Sepulchre in Jerusalem (see pages 202–203), first seen by the knights during their crusades to the Holy Land. It is decorated with heads and stone effigies of patrons and knights.

TEMPLE OF ISIS AT PHILAE

EGYPT

LOCATION	The island of Philae, Egypt
SPIRITUAL TRADITION	Ancient Egyptian
ASSOCIATED DEITIES	Isis, Hathor, Horus, Osiris
DATE OF CONSTRUCTION	380 BCE
WHEN TO VISIT	Any time of year; by boat

The Egyptian island of Philae in the River Nile is located about 31 miles (50 km) upriver from the city of Aswan in southern Egypt. Philae was once home to the beautiful Temple of Isis, until it was carefully moved to the neighboring island of Agilkai, when the extension of the Aswan Dam in the 1970s threatened to submerge the temple completely.

The first temple on Philae was the Temple of Hathor, built by Egyptian kings of the 30th dynasty (380–343 BCE). During the later Greco-Egyptian Ptolemaic dynasty (305–30 BCE) the magnificent Temple of Isis replaced it, along with another temple to the goddess Hathor, who shares many attributes with Isis. As a consequence, the island of Philae became a major site of pilgrimage for devotees of Isis and remained a pagan sacred site until the 6th century CE, when the Roman Christian Emperor Justinian finally discovered it and closed it down. A church dedicated to the Virgin Mary was quickly built, but it was destroyed by Muslim invaders within a hundred years.

The Temple of Isis sits deep within the temple complex. Visitors have to pass through a courtyard and two towered monumental gates decorated with images of Isis, Hathor, and Horus before they reach the holy temple, which consists of a number of rooms leading to the revered inner sanctuary. This is where the sacred image of Isis was kept, and where her many pilgrims came to pay homage. The walls bear testament to this fact, being awash with reliefs of kings and emperors such as Philadelphus, Euergetes II, Augustus, and Tiberius, making offerings to the all-forgiving and all-giving goddess of love.

According to Egyptian mythology, Isis had a husband, Osiris, with whom she conceived their son, Horus. When Osiris was killed by Seth, Isis wept so much that the Nile flooded. She picked up the pieces of his body and magically restored him to life—an event that would have been ritually re-enacted in her temple during sacred rites.

The magnificent temple is surrounded by a vast courtyard which is approached through monumental gates.

TEMPLE OF KARNAK

EGYPT

LOCATION	Luxor, Egypt
SPIRITUAL TRADITION	Ancient Egyptian
ASSOCIATED DEITY	Amun
DATE OF CONSTRUCTION	2000 BCE
WHEN TO VISIT	Any time of year; at present, only the Great Temple of Amun may be visited

The ancient city of Thebes near Luxor in modern Egypt is home to a vast complex of temples and other sacred monuments known simply as Karnak. Construction began almost 4,000 years ago and continued for more than a thousand years, spanning the reign of nearly 30 pharaohs. As a consequence, a breathtaking array of ruined temples, impressive gateways and other sacred monuments—all bearing extraordinary hieroglyphs and quite exquisite ornamentation—now covers an area of roughly 2 sq miles (5 sq km).

By far the most impressive monument at Karnak is the Great Temple of Amun, built in 1391–1351 BCE to honor the supreme god Amun, generally identified with creation and the breath of life. The temple was once approached along the Avenue of the Sphinxes, originally consisting of more than 2,000 sphinxes that stretched all the way from Luxor, 2 miles (3.2 km) away. A much shorter avenue leading to a big monumental gateway, or pylon, is still in evidence. The surviving sphinxes protect ancient kings between their paws, and are shown with rams' heads to signify Amun.

Through the first great gateway is a large courtyard, which contains a major triple-chambered temple made of granite and sandstone, built by Seti II. The left chapel is dedicated to Amun's consort, Mut; the center chapel to Amun; and the right chapel to Kohnsu, Amun's son. A small sphinx stands opposite this great temple; curiously, its face has the features of Tutankhamun. In the center of the courtyard is the kiosk of Taharqa, although only one great column and a huge block of Egyptian alabaster remain; and leading off to the right is the small but beautiful Temple of Rameses III. At the end of the courtyard, a second gateway leads to the magnificent Hypostyle Hall.

The stone pillars of the Hypostyle Hall with hieroglyphic decorations.

CATHEDRAL OF OUR LADY OF AMIENS

LOCATION	Picardy, France
SPIRITUAL TRADITION	Christian
DATE OF CONSTRUCTION	1220 CE
WHEN TO VISIT	Any time of year, but at Christmas and New Year the cathedral facade is specially lit to re-create its original medieval appearance

FRANCE

The Cathedral of Our Lady of Amiens is located in the city of Amiens in Picardy, 62 miles (100 km) north of Paris. The tallest completed cathedral in France, its founding stone was laid in 1220 on the site of an earlier Romanesque cathedral, which was likewise built on the site of many earlier churches dating back as far as the 4th century CE.

In 1206 the head of John the Baptist was reputedly taken from Constantinople to Amiens by Wallon de Sarton, who had fought in the Fourth Crusade. This, coupled with a great fire that seriously damaged the Romanesque cathedral, is thought to have provided the stimulus for building such a grand cathedral at Amiens. The building was officially completed in 1266, although additional works continued long after that.

The front exterior of the cathedral is formed by two ornate stone towers flanking and rising high above a beautiful rose window, which sits above a gallery of 22 sculpted kings. Below are three enormous portals, which house exceptional sculptures of important local saints, including Domitius, Ulphia, and Fermin, and also foreign saints, such as Victoricus and Fuscian, Christian missionaries from Rome who were reputedly martyred near Amiens in the 3rd century. In medieval times these were painted in bright colors, bringing the whole cathedral facade to life.

The roof of the cathedral is supported by 126 very tall pillars, giving it the largest interior space of any medieval cathedral in Europe. Enormous stained-glass windows create a light and airy feel, highly conducive to worship and prayer.

The ornate facade comprises a rose window flanked by stone towers.

ANGKOR WAT

LOCATION	Angkor, Cambodia
SPIRITUAL TRADITIONS	Hindu, Buddhist
ASSOCIATED DEITIES	Vishnu, Avalokitesvara
DATE OF CONSTRUCTION	12th century CE
WHEN TO VISIT	From November through January, after the monsoon season, and before the hottest weather begins

Angkor Wat is part of a stunning complex of temples located at Angkor near Siam Reap in north-western Cambodia. One of the largest and most-admired religious monuments in the world, Angkor Wat was built by King Suryavarman II, ruler of the Khmer empire from 1113 to 1150 CE, who dedicated the temple to the Hindu god Vishnu.

Like many Hindu temples, the design of Angkor Wat is inspired by Hindu mythology. The five exquisite stone towers that rise majestically above the temple represent the five peaks of Mount Meru, the mythical home of the Hindu gods. The lavish temple is surrounded by a huge wall, which represents the Earth's mountains, and beyond the wall an enormous moat represents the world's

oceans and rivers. The individual temple walls are adorned with extensive bas-reliefs, which depict guardian spirits and scenes from Hindu myths. The most famous is *The Churning of the Sea of Milk*, which depicts a fantastic and much-loved Hindu creation myth. At the center of the huge carving, which is almost 164 ft (50 m) long, a sacred snake known as Vasuki is coiled around Mount Mandara, allowing his front half to be pulled by demons—known as *asuras*—and his rear half to be pulled by devas, or gods. Lord Vishnu holds the sacred mountain in place, creating a pivot for the mythical tug of war between demons and gods, which has the effect of churning the world's oceans to produce *amrita*, the elixir of immortality.

Visitors to Angkor Wat approach the western gate of the great temple along a causeway lined with carvings of sacred snakes, which in Hinduism are symbols of rebirth, for snakes shed

A view of the main temple with its five stone towers from across the moat.

331

their skin to be "reborn." The main temple is raised on a vast terrace known as a Jagati. The temple itself is formed by three tiered galleries, the highest one being crowned by the central tower, which marks the site of the main shrine underneath. In the early days a sacred image of Vishnu was housed in this shrine.

In 1177 Angkor was overrun by the Cham people, and Angkor Wat was sacked. The future king Jayavarman VII organized the Cambodian people into a rebellion and succeeded in retaking Angkor in 1181, which led to him being crowned King of the Khmer empire the same year. Jayavarman was married to an extremely devout Buddhist princess named Jayarajadevi, who appears to have had a major influence on the king during his early reign. Instead of reinstating Angkor Wat as the state temple, he built a new Mahayana Buddhist temple known as the Bayon a few miles to the north. This stunning stone temple was dedicated to the bodhisattva Avalokitesvara, who is noted for his compassion for the world, and is today one of the main attractions at Angkor.

Jayavarman's son was also a Buddhist, but the Khmer king after him was Jayavarman VIII, a Hindu, which meant that Angkor Wat began to flourish once more, and the Bayon was modified to include Hindu beliefs. But at the tail end of the 13th century a

new ruler, Srindravarman, came to power, who had trained as a Buddhist monk in Sri Lanka many years before. Srindravarman immediately changed the state religion from Hinduism to Theravada Buddhism. The statue of Vishnu in the main shrine at Angkor Wat was walled up, and Buddhist stupas were erected. Ever since Angkor Wat has been a Buddhist temple, although its Hindu roots are plain for all to see. Under the temple's southern tower is a superb statue of Vishnu, known as Ta Reach, which many believe was originally housed in the main shrine. Today, Angkor Wat is still greatly loved by the people of Cambodia, who placed its image on their flag at the birth of their nation in 1863.

In recent years, a number of astonishing facts have been discovered pertaining to the exact geographical location of Angkor Wat. It has been shown, for example, that the placement of the main buildings replicated the position of the stars in the constellation of Draco at the Spring Equinox in 10,500 BCE, and that the temple lies 72 degrees longitude East of the Great Pyramid of Giza.

A reconstruction showing the monumental size of the terrace upon which the great temple was built.

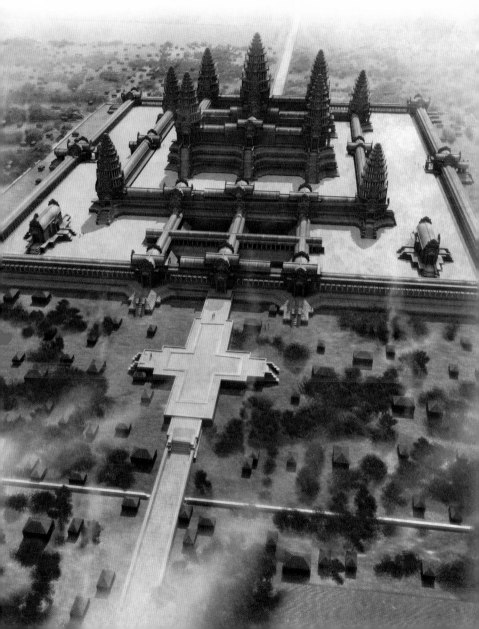

THE BADSHAHI MOSQUE

LOCATION	Lahore, Pakistan
SPIRITUAL TRADITION	Muslim
DATE OF CONSTRUCTION	1673 CE
WHEN TO VISIT	Any time of year

The Badshahi Mosque is a stunning Mughal temple in Lahore, Pakistan. Crowned by three beautiful domes and bordered by four enormous minars (large minarets), the exterior is lavishly adorned with white marble on red sandstone, making it a spectacular site to behold.

The devout Muslim emperor, Aurangzeb—also known as Alamgir I—ordered the building of this great mosque opposite the Lahore Fort in 1671 CE. When the mosque was completed in 1673 it was the largest in the world, and remained so until 1986. The light and airy prayer hall is simply vast, built to accommodate up to 100,000 worshippers at the same time. Its majestic walls and curved ceilings are adorned with marble and stone, and intricately decorated with fine Islamic calligraphy.

In 1799 Ranjit Singh, the first Maharaja of the Sikh empire, conquered Lahore. During his subsequent reign Muslims were not allowed to enter the mosque, and the inside fell into disrepair, allegedly being used as a stable for horses.

In 1849 the British took control of Lahore and used the mosque for military training. Aware of the hatred felt by local Muslims, they demolished large parts of the walls of the mosque so that it could not be turned into any kind of fort during a possible insurgency. However, in 1852 the British abandoned the mosque, returning it to the Muslim community in an effort to improve relations between them. They set up the Badshahi Mosque Authority, which was able to undertake minor repairs. When the period of British rule moved closer to its end in 1939 with the onset of the Second World War, restoration work greatly accelerated. Four years after the formation of the Islamic Republic of Pakistan in 1960, the mosque was fully restored.

In 1974, 39 heads of Muslim states jointly offered Friday prayers in the

Badshahi Mosque, emphasizing its place as one of the most important sacred sites for Muslims anywhere in the world.

Tens of thousands of worshippers gather in the courtyard of the beautiful three-domed mosque.

THE BAHA'I HOUSE OF WORSHIP

LOCATION	Upolu Island, Samoa
SPIRITUAL TRADITION	Baha'i
ASSOCIATED PROPHET	Baha'u'llah
DATE OF CONSTRUCTION	1984 CE
WHEN TO VISIT	Any time of year; Baha'i services are on Sundays

The Baha'i House of Worship was dedicated by His Highness Susuga King Malietoa Tanumafili II in the city of Apia on Upolu Island in Samoa in 1984. It is an exquisitely designed and understatedly beautiful temple, open to followers of all faiths and spiritual traditions.

The House of Worship is set within stunning landscaped gardens, where worshippers are encouraged to sit or walk as they meditate and contemplate God. The building itself has nine sides—a feature of all Baha'i temples—and is topped by a huge white dome, almost 98 ft (30 m) high. It has the overall shape and appearance of a *fale*, a circular thatch-roofed home found everywhere in Samoa, where Baha'i is the most widely practiced religion.

Inside, huge windows underpin the temple's massive white dome, making the interior space bright, light, and airy. Between the windows are many wooden panels engraved with Baha'i scripture in Samoan and English. At the center of the dome, the name Baha'u'llah—that of the 19th-century founder of the Baha'i faith—is written next to a nine-pointed star, a sacred symbol for Bahai's. Significantly, it was nine years after the Bab (the founder of Babism) announced the coming of the chosen one that Baha'u'llah received notice of his divine mission to found the Baha'i faith. The number nine is also the greatest single digit possible, suggesting completeness, a central idea in the Baha'i faith, which is committed to working toward bringing together all peoples and all religions under one spiritual roof.

In 1967 an Italian, Dr. Ugo Giachery, gave a book of Baha'u'llah's writings to King Malietoa Tanumafili II, who read them and subsequently became a Baha'i, leading to a rise in popularity of the Baha'i faith in Samoa. Dr. Giachery is still remembered fondly in Samoa, and his grave in the House of Worship gardens is a popular site where visiting Baha'is stop and pay their respects.

The Baha'i House of Worship is surrounded by tranquil gardens where visitors are encouraged to meditate.

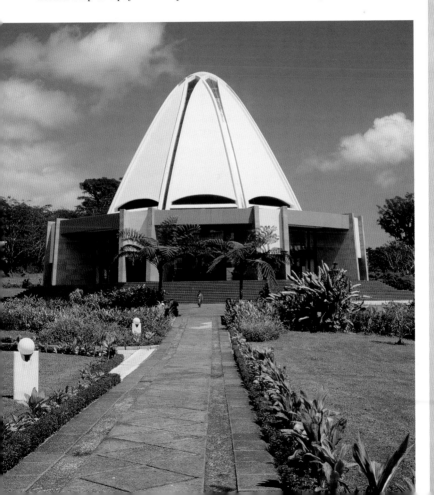

BARCELONA CATHEDRAL

LOCATION	Barcelona, Spain
SPIRITUAL TRADITION	Christian
ASSOCIATED SAINT	St. Eulalia
DATE OF CONSTRUCTION	1298–1460 CE
WHEN TO VISIT	Any time of year

Barcelona Cathedral, also known as "La Seu" and the Cathedral of St. Eulalia, is a stunning Catalan-style Gothic cathedral, in the old Gothic quarter of Barcelona on an ancient Roman burial site. Construction began in 1298 and was completed in 1379, although many additions and alterations were subsequently made, leading some people to give 1460 as the final date of completion.

The cathedral boasts imposing bell-towers decorated with striking neo-Gothic pinnacles, huge Gothic arches set with beautifully painted stained-glass windows, and a number of chapels with richly adorned altars. There is also a finely sculpted choir and a cloister, overlooking a garden with citrus and palm trees and a pond.

For many people, part of the attraction of the Catalan Gothic style is its simplicity. Typically, large surfaces

The flat stone pillars reach up high to the stunning Gothic arches.

consist only of unadorned flat stone bordered by relentless straight lines. This austere style is not to everyone's liking, and in the 19th century a neo-Gothic facade was added to the front of the church, providing sumptuous ornamentation and fine detail.

The patroness of Barcelona's great cathedral is St. Eulalia, who was allegedly burned at the stake by pagan Romans in 304 CE for refusing to renounce her Christian faith. One story says she was exhibited naked in public, and a sudden flurry of snow fell to protect her modesty. Her enraged tormentors then put her in a barrel filled with long knives pushed through to its inside, and rolled her down a hill. Whatever the truth is, her alabaster sarcophagus rests under the high altar, and visitors may drop coins in a slot to illuminate the exposed crypt. Interestingly, 13 white geese have lived in the cloister for centuries, and legend has it that they have stayed to symbolize St. Eulalia's virginity.

ST. MARK'S BASILICA

LOCATION	Venice, Italy
SPIRITUAL TRADITION	Christian
ASSOCIATED SAINT	St. Mark the Evangelist
DATE OF CONSTRUCTION	1063 CE
WHEN TO VISIT	Any time of year

The Basilica di San Marco—nicknamed the "Church of Gold"—overlooks St. Mark's Square just off the Grand Canal in Venice. Originally it was an opulent chapel for the city's wealthy rulers, and was not the city's cathedral; however, in 1807 it became the official seat of the Archbishop of Venice and assumed its cathedral status.

In 828 CE Venetian merchants are said to have stolen the remains of the Christian apostle, Mark the Evangelist, from Alexandria and brought them to Venice, where they were stored at the site of San Marco for the next 250 years. In 1063 construction work began on the present church, but by 1094 the remains of St. Mark could no longer be found. It was then, according to Catholic tradition, that the saint revealed himself by extending an arm from a pillar, to point to where his remains lay hidden. These were placed in a sarcophagus in a crypt under the newly built basilica, which was consecrated the very same year.

Over the next two hundred years the basilica was greatly enhanced. During the 13th century a new entrance was added to the foot of the nave, and a new facade was constructed to make the building

The roof of the basilica is dominated by five domes; the walls are adorned with marble and fine sculpture.

blend more successfully with its surroundings. Around the same time, most of the church's stunning Byzantine interior mosaics were completed, and the great domes atop the church were first raised in wood and then set with lead. During the following century many wealthy merchants returning to Venice after successful trips abroad made great gifts to the church, and before long almost all of the exterior brickwork was covered with exquisite carvings and marble sculpture, while the interior floors were lavishly decorated with beautiful mosaics, the walls covered with marble and the ceilings adorned with intricately patterned gold.

The retable behind the high altar is known as the Golden Pall. First commissioned roughly a thousand years ago, it is a work of astonishing Byzantine craftsmanship. The lower part depicts the life of St. Mark in a series of enamels, while the upper part is dominated by an image of the archangel Michael. The piece is set with many precious stones, some of which were plundered by Napoleon in the late 18th century.

In 1968 Pope Paul VI is believed to have given a small bone taken from the crypt at St. Mark's to Pope Cyril VI of Alexandria as recompense for the original theft of St. Mark's remains.

BOROBUDUR

LOCATION	Java, Indonesia
SPIRITUAL TRADITION	Mahayana Buddhist
ASSOCIATED DEITY	The Buddha
DATE OF CONSTRUCTION	9th century CE
WHEN TO VISIT	Any time of year

Borobudur is a stupendous Buddhist monument located in Magelang in central Java, Indonesia. The land around the monument is known as the Garden of Java, for it is both beautiful and fertile, overlooked by two volcanoes and enclosed by two rivers.

It is believed that Borobudur was built as a shrine to the Buddha in the 9th century CE. The walls of this colossal monument are adorned with thousands of relief panels and more than 500 statues of the Buddha. The structure itself is crowned with a great dome, which is mysteriously empty, and which is surrounded by yet another 72 statues of the Buddha seated inside an enormous perforated stupa.

Borobudur was for many hundreds of years a major sacred site for Buddhist pilgrimage. Pilgrims would walk from the base of the monument up and along the myriad corridors and stairways that lead to the dome at the summit, meanwhile meditating upon the extensive sacred art on the walls, which was designed in narrative fashion to guide the pilgrim along a path to enlightenment.

Historians believe that Borobudur fell into disuse in the 14th century when the majority of the people of Java converted to Islam. However, since the major restoration projects of the late 20th century, Borobudur has once again become a major site for holy pilgrimage. Many Indonesian Buddhists now travel there to celebrate the annual festival of Vesak, one of the holiest days in Buddhism, for it commemorates the birth, death and enlightenment of the Buddha.

An interesting theory about Borobudur is that it once floated in water and was designed by its builders to depict a giant lotus. This idea has been given credence by the initial archeological discovery of an underground lake, and by a later geological study which found that Borobudur would have been situated on the banks of the lake in the 13th to 14th centuries. Curiously, the structure of the monument as a whole resembles a giant lotus.

One of the 72 seated statues of the Buddha on the top platform dominated by perforated stupas.

343

THE CAO DAI TEMPLE

LOCATION	Tay Nihn, Vietnam
SPIRITUAL TRADITIONS	Taoist, Buddhist, Confucian, Christian
DATE OF CONSTRUCTION	1933–55 CE
WHEN TO VISIT	Any time of year

The Cao Dai Temple—also known as the Great Temple or Holy See—is located 60 miles (96 km) north-west of Ho Chi Minh City, the capital of Vietnam. This colorful and richly decorated temple symbolizes the sacred heart of the Cao Dai religion, which blends Buddhism, Taoism, Confucianism, and Christianity into a highly unique spiritual tradition.

Work on the Cao Dai Temple began in 1933 and finished in 1955. The overall structure is modeled on a Christian church, with an altar, apse, and ambulatory at the end of a long central nave bordered by aisles on either side. The ornamentation, both inside and out, however, could not be more different. The 28 columns that extend the length of the nave are shaped like dragons, and the surrounding walls are painted red, blue, and yellow, beautifully depicting a diverse selection of sacred images and holy saints, including Jesus Christ, the Buddha, Victor Hugo, and Lao Tzu.

The centerpiece of the temple is large sphere painted with a giant third-eye. This sacred symbol is found in all Cao Dai temples and in the homes of worshippers. It is always the left eye, which in Eastern religions traditionally represents nirvana, or God; the right eye is a representation of samsara, or the physical world. Inside the pupil of the divine eye is the famous yin-yang symbol, a Taoist representation of the fundamental polarity of all things.

Lay worshippers typically dress in long, flowing white robes, with the men sitting on the floor on the right side of the nave and the women on the left. At 6 a.m. every morning a mesmerizing chanting ceremony begins, led by ten musicians and 20 young singers. This is followed by further ceremonies at noon, 6 p.m., and midnight. The Cao Dai Temple is constantly in use for spiritual worship. Visitors are always welcome, although they must remove their shoes and cover their knees before entering.

The facade embodies a blend of Eastern and Western spiritual traditions.

NOTRE-DAME CATHEDRAL, PARIS

LOCATION	Paris, France
SPIRITUAL TRADITION	Christian
DATE OF CONSTRUCTION	1163 CE
WHEN TO VISIT	Any time of year

Notre-Dame Cathedral is a magnificent Gothic church located in the 4th arrondissement of Paris. Work on this great cathedral began in 1163. It was badly damaged during the French Revolution in the late 18th century, restored in the 19th century, and is today the seat of the Catholic Archbishop of Paris. Notre-Dame attained worldwide fame in the 20th century on account of the many films and musicals inspired by Victor Hugo's seminal novel, *The Hunchback of Notre Dame* (1831).

The basic structure of the church dates to the late 12th and early 13th centuries, when the stone transepts, choir, nave, towers, western facade, and spectacular rose window above the north transept were completed. The flying buttresses that support the exterior walls were not part of the original design, but an innovation to support the towering walls. The great portals that lead into the church are adorned with stunning sculptures depicting the infant Jesus, the Virgin Mary, and a collection of important French saints. The whole building is set with beautiful stained-glass windows, which are more naturalistic than stylized in execution, a consistent feature of French Gothic art.

Notre-Dame has five massive bells. The largest, known as Emmanuel, resides in the south tower and weighs more than 13 tons. It chimes every hour on the hour to mark the time, as well being rung during important services. The other four bells are located in the north tower, and these are only ever rung during special services. On August 24, 1944, Emmanuel began to ring, heralding the end of Nazi occupation.

The stunning Gothic facade with sculpted figures, including Jesus, Mary, and saints.

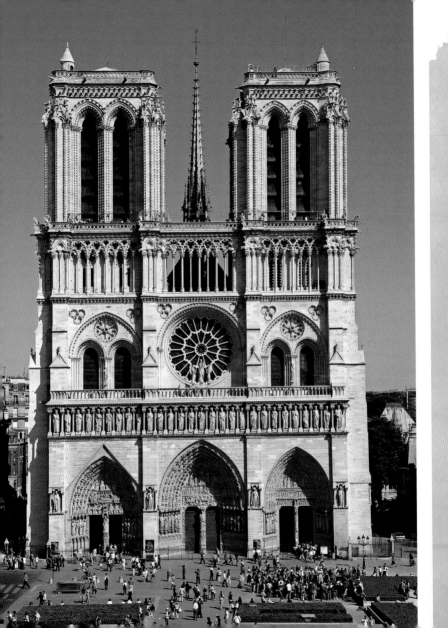

THE FAISAL MOSQUE

PAKISTAN

INDIA

LOCATION	Islamabad, Pakistan
SPIRITUAL TRADITION	Muslim
ASSOCIATED DIGNITARY	King Faisal
DATE OF CONSTRUCTION	1976–1986 CE
WHEN TO VISIT	Any time of year; the mosque is open to non-Muslims, who should follow local customs regarding dress

The Faisal Mosque in Islamabad was, until recently, the largest mosque in the world. Dedicated to the late King Faisal of Saudi Arabia—who financed its construction—this stunning mosque is the National Mosque of Pakistan, a devoutly Islamic republic.

Work commenced on the building of the great mosque in 1976, one year after the assassination of King Faisal.

Initially, traditional Muslims were disturbed by news that the new mosque would have no dome, but their concerns were assuaged when they saw the completed mosque ten years later. Set against a backdrop of the beautiful Margalla hills at the foot of the Himalayas, the mosque is flanked by four slender white minarets, rising to a monumental 262 ft (80 m) high, as if shielding the delicate tent-like core.

Traditionally, the place where one enters a mosque points towards Mecca —the same direction in which Muslims kneel to pray. For this reason, the entrance to the Faisal Mosque and its magnificent prayer hall is from the east. The prayer hall—which can house up to 10,000 worshippers—is an eight-sided chamber reminiscent of both a Bedouin tent and the Kaaba stone in Mecca (see pages 232–235), the principal sacred site for Islamic pilgrimage. An enormous chandelier hangs from the interior roof, which is completely clad in stunning white marble. The walls are adorned with intricate Islamic mosaics and a calligraphic rendition of the Kalimah, which Muslims affirm daily as a main pillar of their faith.

Visitors to the mosque are expected to leave their shoes at the door. Everyone is expected to conform to local customs regarding dress, meaning that men should cover their bodies apart from their hands, and women should do the same, as well as wearing a scarf that covers their hair. Inside the mosque complex are a library, a museum, the Islamic

Research Center, a lecture hall, and the offices of the faculty of the Islamic University, which was until recently based at the mosque.

The slender pointed minarets rise up as if to shield the delicate tent-like core of the mosque.

THE GOLDEN TEMPLE

LOCATION	Amritsar, India
SPIRITUAL TRADITION	Sikh
ASSOCIATED DEITY	Guru Nanak
DATE OF CONSTRUCTION	1581–1606 CE
WHEN TO VISIT	Any time of year

Nestled on land in the middle of a peaceful lake in the city of Amritsar, the Golden Temple is the most sacred site in the Sikh religion. It is a stupendous structure, beautifully adorned with gilding and marble sculptures, and its various rooms are inlaid with precious stones.

According to tradition, Guru Nanak, the founder of Sikhism, frequently visited the site to meditate and grow closer to God. After his death in 1539 his disciples made a shrine at the lake, and during the leadership of Guru Arjan Dev Ji (the 5th Guru of Sikhism), from 1581 to 1606, the Golden Temple was built. According to Sikh tradition, Guru Arjan invited his good friend Hazrat Mian Mir, a highly revered Sufi saint, to lay the cornerstone in 1588. Apparently a workman moved the stone slightly to ensure it was correctly positioned, which greatly

The Golden Temple sits peacefully on a sacred lake in Amritsar.

displeased Guru Arjan, who thought it a grave mistake to undo the work of a holy man. During the next two hundred years (up to 1786) the temple was destroyed numerous times by invading armies, which many Sikhs attributed to the workman interfering with Hazrat Mian Mir's original placing of the cornerstone. However, despite these setbacks, the Golden Temple was always rebuilt by devoted Sikhs in ever more beautiful fashion, aided by many generous donations from Sikhism's followers.

The most sacred scripture in Sikhism, the Guru Adi Granth, has been housed in the temple complex since 1604. At roughly 5 a.m. every morning it is taken to the Dahar Sahib, a special sanctuary within the temple, where it is placed on a jewel-studded altar. All day long devoted Sikhs sing its various prayers, poems, and blessings to the accompaniment of enchanting music. The beautiful chanting is said to help pilgrims experience a closer connection to God, and is always audible to the many visitors walking by the lake. At roughly 10 p.m. every night the Adi Granth is returned to the Sri Akal Takht Sahib (meaning the Throne of God), where it is kept safely until sunrise.

The Dahar Sahib has four doors, symbolizing the fact that the Sikh faith recognizes and welcomes people of all religions. Indeed, there are almost no restrictions imposed on anyone entering the Dahar Sahib, which is a sacred site where all can find peace with God. Visitors are simply asked not to consume alcohol or drugs, not to eat meat, and to be respectfully dressed. For Sikhs, this involves covering the head and removing the shoes and socks, so that everyone enters the sanctuary barefoot.

The lake surrounding the temple is fed by an underground spring, and its water is believed to be especially holy. The word "Amritsar" literally means "pool of nectar." At all times of the night and day Sikh pilgrims can be seen bathing in the lake to cleanse themselves in anticipation of a direct experience of God, the goal of Sikh spiritual practice. After bathing, pilgrims walk through the great arch known as the Darshani Deorhi, which opens onto the causeway leading to the temple at the center of the island. The Darshani Deorhi is more than 197 ft (60 m) tall and 20 ft (6 m) wide, and opposite it stands the Sri Akal

Takht Sahib, a beautiful building topped with a golden dome, which symbolizes Sikhs' autonomy and political power. In 1988 this precious building—home to the Adi Granth every night—was shelled by the Indian army in a dispute with Sikh militants.

The government then claimed a strip of land next to the lake to be used as a security belt, but strong Sikh resistance meant that this idea was finally abandoned. Instead, the land was used to create a peaceful landscape for a second holy path round the lake, which only adds to the sanctity of the Golden Temple.

A Sikh pilgrim meditates before the temple lake, which is filled by water from a sacred spring.

THE GREAT MOSQUE OF DJENNÉ

LOCATION	Djenné, Mali
SPIRITUAL TRADITION	Muslim
DATE OF CONSTRUCTION	1907 CE
WHEN TO VISIT	Any time of year, although November to January is best because of the milder climate; the impressive annual festival of Crepissage, during which the mosque is ritually replastered, takes place between February and April; non-Muslims can watch the activities outside

The Great Mosque of Djenné is located in Djenné about 217 miles (350 km) south of Timbuktu in central Mali. It is a stunning architectural achievement, being the largest mud-brick building anywhere in the world. The towering monumental structure rises like an apparition above the humble market square in the center of the city.

Djenné has been an important trading center for more than a thousand years. In the 13th century CE the first of many mud-brick mosques was built on the site of the present mosque, the final and present one being completed in 1907 during the period of French control of Mali. A major site for Muslim pilgrimage, the mosque is widely considered to be the acme of sub-Saharan mud-brick building design.

Three huge towers dominate the facade of the mosque, each adorned with spires that are topped by an ostrich egg, thought to symbolize fertility. The main prayer hall is big enough to hold 3,000 worshippers. Its walls are made from sun-baked mud-bricks held together by plaster; the lower walls are more than 1½ ft (0.5 m) thick, the only way to support the enormous weight of the towering structure above. The walls appear to be strengthened by wooden palm beams that protrude to create a beautiful design, but these are actually used by workmen restoring the building during a festival every spring by applying additional mud plaster to the walls. The festival is a joyous event involving men, women, and children, who each have their own traditional jobs to perform, from preparing the mud to climbing the walls.

The massive ceiling is studded with air vents, which are capped during the day by beautiful ceramic plates made by the women of Djenné. The small caps are taken off at night to let in air and cool down the interior of the mosque, which heats up during the day in the intense desert sun. They also help to prevent rain from getting into the Great Mosque, which would lead to its rapid decay.

The magnificent mosque is built entirely from mud bricks which have been baked in the hot desert sun.

HAGIA SOPHIA

LOCATION	Istanbul, Turkey
SPIRITUAL TRADITIONS	Eastern Orthodox Christian, Muslim
ASSOCIATED DIGNITARY	Patriarch of Constantinople
DATE OF CONSTRUCTION	532–37 CE
WHEN TO VISIT	Any time of year

Hagia Sophia—iterally meaning "Holy Wisdom"—is a beautiful Byzantine church in modern-day Istanbul. For nearly a thousand years it was the largest Christian cathedral in the world, dominating the city of Constantinople with its great dome. In a remarkable twist of fate, Hagia Sophia also served as the city's main mosque for 500 years and today it is a much-loved museum, visited by Christians and Muslims alike.

The cathedral was built by the Roman Christian Emperor Justinian between 532 and 537 CE on the site of earlier churches. Upon its completion Justinian is reported to have exclaimed, "Solomon, I have surpassed you!" Many treasured holy relics— apparently including the shroud of Jesus and the Virgin Mary's milk— were brought to the cathedral, which soon became the focal point for the principal religious and official activities of the Eastern Orthodox Church. For almost 700 uninterrupted years Hagia Sophia enjoyed its status as the greatest Byzantine church, only ever requiring repairs to damage caused by fires and earthquakes. More and more treasures were added, including a 164 ft (50 m)-long silver iconostasis—

The interior of the great dome is inscribed with the Light Verse from the Qu'ran.

a wall of icons separating the nave from the altar. Talented artists were commissioned to add beautiful mosaics to the inner walls, which depicted scenes from the New Testament in exquisite detail. Visitors to Constantinople from western Europe were singularly impressed.

In 1204 Catholic Christian crusaders led by Enrico Dandolo, under the command of Baldwin of Flanders, sacked the city of Constantinople. In the aftermath the Latin knights committed a terrible massacre, before desecrating Hagia Sophia in a truly sacrilegious way. They destroyed the great silver iconostasis and burned the vast library of holy books, while drinking consecrated wine. They dismissed the revered Patriarch of Constantinople and replaced him with a common prostitute, an event that severely exacerbated the already deep schism between the Eastern Orthodox and Roman Catholic Churches. In fact, the crusaders behaved so badly towards the Greeks—including raping women and girls—that their actions provoked the condemnation of Pope Innocent III, who had organized the crusade in the first place. Baldwin and his knights stole a vast amount of money from the city, most of which was sent back to wealthy Venetians who had paid for the crusade. Baldwin also looted many treasured holy relics from Hagia

Sophia, including a stone from Jesus' tomb, Jesus' shroud, and the remains of many venerated saints, all of which were taken back to western Europe. To add insult to injury, Baldwin chose Hagia Sophia for his coronation as Emperor of Constantinople.

In 1261 the Byzantines mustered a great army and retook Constantinople, which was by then ruled by Baldwin II. It is said that when they finally re-entered Hagia Sophia, they found the tomb of Enrico Dandolo, upon which they fervently spat, the memories of his terrible deeds still fresh in their minds more than 50 years later. Almost immediately Hagia Sophia reopened as an Eastern Orthodox church, but the city of Constantinople had lost so much wealth and prestige during the intervening years that it never completely recovered its former status and glory.

In 1453 Sultan Mehmed II conquered Constantinople and ordered that Hagia Sophia be turned into a mosque. The holy relics and great altar were removed, and the fine mosaics adorning the walls were covered up. Over time, four minarets were added outside, paving the way for Hagia Sophia to become Istanbul's main mosque—a role it played for almost 500 years. In 1923 the Republic of Turkey came into being and a decision was taken to close the mosque as part of the secularization of

the country. Hagia Sophia was turned into a museum in 1935. Slowly the old Byzantine mosaics are being restored, although to date only those up high have been revealed, in deference to Muslims who do not believe that figurative art should be displayed in a

mosque. In 2004 Pope John Paul II apologized to Eastern Orthodox Christians for the events that took place in Constantinople and at Hagia Sophia 800 years beforehand, and the Catholic and Eastern Orthodox Churches were reconciled.

The great dome of Hagia Sohpia Cathedral is surrounded by four towering minarets.

IL DUOMO, FLORENCE

LOCATION	Florence, Italy
SPIRITUAL TRADITION	Christian
ASSOCIATED SAINT	The Blessed Virgin Mary
DATE OF CONSTRUCTION	1296–1436 CE
WHEN TO VISIT	Any time of year

The fabulous Basilica di Santa Maria del Fiore, known simply as Il Duomo, is located in the Piazza del Duomo in Florence in Italy. Lavishly adorned with fine marble, it boasts the largest brick-built dome ever created. The cathedral contains a significant number of stunning works of art and has long been a sacred site for Catholic pilgrims.

Construction work on the cathedral began in 1296 and was not completed until 1436, when the church was consecrated by Pope Eugenius IV. Il Duomo was then the largest church in the world, topped with an awe-inspiring eight-sided dome designed by Filippo Brunelleschi, whose statue can be seen outside, admiring his crowning achievement. A gleaming lantern composed of a gilt copper ball

and cross was precariously erected on top of the dome, but it was struck by lightning in 1600 and fell down; it was replaced by an even larger one some years later.

Inside the cathedral, exquisite stained-glass windows light up a colossal chamber, which is strangely barren, evoking the stern asceticism associated with medieval Christianity. A huge 15th-century clock sits above the main door, beautifully decorated with frescoes of the four Apostles. Unlike modern 12-hour clocks, this one measures 24 hours; their passing is marked by a single rotation of the solitary hand. Above the clock is a stunning 14th-century stained-glass window, which depicts Christ crowning the Blessed Virgin Mary, to whom this beautiful church is dedicated.

The interior of the dome is painted with dramatic scenes from the Last Judgement, including *Choirs of Angels* and *Capital Sins and Hell*.

The spectacular dome crowned by a copper lantern is the largest brick-built dome ever constructed.

THE KONARK SUN TEMPLE

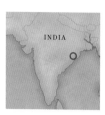

INDIA

LOCATION	Orissa, India
SPIRITUAL TRADITION	Hindu
ASSOCIATED DEITY	Surya
DATE OF CONSTRUCTION	1278 CE
WHEN TO VISIT	Best between October and April; the Konark Dance Festival takes place on December 1–5

The Konark Sun Temple—also known as the Black Pagoda—is one of India's finest and most spectacular temples, located near the town of Konark, close to Puri in Orissa. Widely admired for its lavish sculpted ornamentation, this stunning 13th-century temple was built by King Narasimhadeva I of the Eastern Ganga dynasty. It is dedicated to the Hindu sun god, Surya.

According to tradition, Krishna's son, Samba, behaved so badly—including spying on his father's consort while she was bathing—that Krishna cursed him with leprosy. Samba was told that he could only cure himself if he prayed to Surya by the coast at Puri. Samba set out for Orissa, where he found an image of the sun god seated on a lotus, duly worshipped him, and was cured. The land has been sacred to Surya ever since.

The Sun Temple is modeled on a chariot with 24 intricately carved wheels pulled by seven powerful horses. At the entrance, two lions are

shown crushing a war elephant, in turn crushing a poor human being. The whole surface is adorned with very fine sculptures, depicting birds, animals, musicians, alluring young women, and all manner of interesting geometric shapes.

A second temple—the Nata Mandir—stands in front of the Black Pagoda. This temple is beautifully ornamented with a fine array of evocative and captivating sculptures, including animals and trees, but also naked men and women, sometimes engaged in sexual embraces. Here, dancers would have performed sacred rituals in honor of Surya.

It is thought that the temple was originally designed with a large dome on top, but that the foundations were too weak to support it. However, a local legend insists that the dome was actually built, but with devastating results. Apparently it acted like a giant magnet and caused nearby ships to crash on the coast, so that the dome had to be reluctantly destroyed. It was as a consequence of this supposed intense magnetic force that the temple was nick-named "The Black Pagoda" by European sailors, who were convinced that it was the cause of many shipwrecks that occurred along the coast.

The temple dedicated to Surya is widely prized for its stone ornamentation, often depicting explicitly sexual scenes.

ROCAMADOUR

FRANCE

LOCATION	Occitan, France
SPIRITUAL TRADITION	Christian
ASSOCIATED SAINTS	The Virgin Mary, St. Amadour
DATE OF CONSTRUCTION	*c.* 70 CE
WHEN TO VISIT	Any time of year

Rocamadour is a religious commune splendidly located on a spectacular rocky gorge above a tributary of the River Dordogne, 100 miles (160 km) north of the city of Toulouse. There are many significant religious monuments at this sacred site, but most prominent is the sanctuary of the Blessed Virgin Mary, which has attracted pilgrims—ranging from commoners to kings—for hundreds of years.

According to legend, Zaccheus of Jericho lived at Rocamadour as a hermit. While here, he is believed to have communed directly with Jesus Christ. After Zaccheus' death (c. 70 CE) and subsequent burial, Christian pilgrims began visiting Rocamadour to pay homage.

In 1162 a body was found in a tomb at Rocamadour, and it was generally believed to be that of St. Amadour, the reputed founder of the commune at Rocamadour and Bishop of Auxerre from 388 CE. Over time, St. Amadour and Zaccheus became identified as the same person, although this seems highly unlikely because they lived in different centuries.

Around this time the Church of St. Sauveur was constructed at Rocamadour, and in 1162 a subterranean shrine, the Church of St. Amadour, was dug out of the rock underneath. The church may be visited today and contains many relics of the saint.

In 1479 the present-day version of the Chapelle de Notre-Dame—known as the Sanctuary of the Blessed Virgin Mary—was precariously built halfway up the gorge. To this day, many Christian pilgrims climb up the 216 steps to reach the holy chapel on their knees.

Inside the sanctuary is a wooden statue of the Virgin—the Black Madonna—which legend decrees was brought to Rocamadour by Zaccheus or carved by St. Amadour, although modern dating methods cast serious doubt on both these claims. The black statue is believed to possess special powers, and many pilgrims have reported spontaneous healings and spiritual epiphanies as a consequence of praying while in the sanctuary.

The Sanctuary of the Blessed Virgin Mary is precariously built on a steep rocky cliff. Pilgrims still climb to it on their knees.

SHRI SWAMINARAYAN MANDIR

ENGLAND

LOCATION	Neasden, London, England
SPIRITUAL TRADITION	Hindu
DATE OF CONSTRUCTION	1990–1995 CE
WHEN TO VISIT	Any time of year; people of all spiritual traditions are welcomed, but visitors should be dressed discreetly

The Shri Swaminarayan Mandir is a grand and beautifully domed stone temple in Neasden in north-west London. The first major Hindu temple in Europe, it is a replica of the great Akshardam Temple in Gujarat, India. Neasden Temple attracts more than half a million pilgrims every year.

The Shri Swaminarayan Mandir was dedicated by Pramukh Swami Maharaj in 1995, 25 years after his guru, Yogiji Maharaj, expressed his wish that it be built. Construction began in 1990, with all 26,300 pieces of Italian marble and Bulgarian limestone being carved by a huge team of sculptors in India and then shipped to London. When finished, Neasden Temple was the largest Hindu temple outside India, with the capacity to hold more than 5,000 worshippers in the main hall. It was paid for entirely by donations from the Hindu community, and volunteers carried out most of the building work.

Today, the great temple dominates the local cityscape. Its pristine creamy-white domes and graceful pinnacles rise elegantly above its intricately carved walls, creating a peaceful oasis in its busy London setting. Although it is a Hindu temple, it is also widely used by Sikhs and Muslims, who are attracted by its simple majesty and beauty. The central dome is made entirely from stone, unlike all other large domes in Britain, which make use of steel or lead. Under each of the temple's seven pinnacles is a shrine, and each contains sacred images of Hindu gods on raised altars. These sacred images—known as *murtis*—are looked after by monks, who treat them with a reverence befitting a living god. Every day the *murtis* are bathed, dressed, blessed and offered food, in accordance with sacred rituals described in ancient Vedic texts.

The creamy-white walls, spires, and domes of the great temple are carved from stone and adorned with the finest marble.

ST. VITUS'S CATHEDRAL

LOCATION	Prague, Czech Republic
SPIRITUAL TRADITION	Christian
ASSOCIATED SAINT	St. Vitus
DATE OF CONSTRUCTION	1344 CE
WHEN TO VISIT	Any time of year

Found inside the walls of Prague Castle, St. Vitus's Cathedral is a magnificent Gothic temple. Founded in 1344, it is the most revered Christian church in the Czech Republic.

In 925 CE Wenceslaus I consecrated a small rotunda church to St. Vitus, the patron saint of dancers, diseases, and dogs, on the site of the present-day cathedral. At that time Christians and pagans lived side by side in Prague Castle, but by the middle of the 11th century the Christian congregation was so numerous that Prince Spythinev II built a much bigger basilica in place of the first church to accommodate it. The part of the church containing the tomb of Wenceslaus was preserved.

In 1344 the King of Bohemia, Charles IV, a man of immense wealth and power, helped to found the present-day cathedral in place of the old basilica. He wanted the new cathedral to serve as a place for coronations and to house the most holy relics in the kingdom, as well to be the site of his family crypt. The French architect Matthias of Arras was commissioned to design such a church, and he built an exquisite cathedral with a beautiful triple-naved basilica with flying buttresses, a decagonal apse, and a number of radiating chapels, all in the French Gothic style. Unfortunately Matthias died before his vision was complete, and in 1352 the job was passed to the young Peter Parler, who finished Matthias's designs before adding his own unique contributions, such as the striking double diagonal ribs that span the width of the choir bay, the beautiful dome vault for Wenceslaus's tomb, as well as the breathtaking, undulating window-set walls. While the overall geometry of the building belongs to Matthias, its intricate, compelling detail is a gift from Parler.

The spectacular Gothic facade viewed from within the walls of Prague Castle.

WAT ARUN

LOCATION	Bangkok, Thailand
SPIRITUAL TRADITIONS	Buddhist, Hindu
ASSOCIATED DEITIES	The Buddha, Lord Brahma, Shiva, Indra
DATE OF CONSTRUCTION	18th century CE
WHEN TO VISIT	Any time of year; best approached by boat

Wat Arun—which is also known as the Temple of Dawn—is a spectacular Buddhist temple located on the west bank of the Chao Phraya River in Bangkok. An iconic Thai landmark, the central *prang* or spire of this monumental temple rises to a height of more than 262 ft (80 m) and is surrounded by four smaller prangs, which are no less beautiful.

Wat Arun was built in the mid-18th century CE. In its early days it housed the highly revered Emerald Buddha, which was brought back to Thailand by King Rama I in 1778, before being moved to its present location in the Royal Palace in 1784. King Rama II began work to increase the size of the central prang, a task that was completed by his successor, King Rama III. King Rama IV named the temple Wat Arunrachawararam, which may be roughly translated as the "Temple of Dawn."

Although it is a Buddhist temple, the building is replete with Hindu images and motifs. The huge central prang symbolizes Mount Meru, the mythological abode of Lord Brahma and center of the universe. This highly decorated prang is topped by an ornate seven-pronged spear, known as the Trident of Shiva. In addition, two beautifully carved demons guard the entrance to the Ordination Hall: a white one known as Sahassa Decha, and a green one called Thotsakan, who is the demon Ravana from the great Hindu epic *The Ramayana*. The lavish Ordination Hall is home to a sacred Buddha image said to be have been designed by King Rama II, whose ashes have been buried beneath it.

At the four corners of the central prang are four smaller prangs. These are completely covered with small pieces of porcelain and seashells, creating a stunning visual effect. A series of steep steps lead up from here to two terraces around the central prang. On the second terrace there are four statues of the Hindu god Indra riding a three-headed elephant, the mythological Erawan, who, according to Buddhist mythology, gave his life to the worship of the Buddha.

A view of the stunning Temple from the Chao Phraya River. The central prang symbolizes Mount Meru.

WAT BENCHAMABOPHIT DUSITVANARAM

LOCATION	Bangkok, Thailand
SPIRITUAL TRADITION	Buddhist
ASSOCIATED DIGNITARY	Chulalongkorn, 5th King of Siam
DATE OF CONSTRUCTION	1899 CE
WHEN TO VISIT	Any time of year, but visitors should take care not to interfere with daily rituals in this working Buddhist temple

Wat Bechamabophit Dusitvanaram, also known as the Marble Temple, is one of the most beautiful temples in Thailand. Built in Bangkok from gleaming white marble in 1899–1900, it houses a striking Buddha image—the Phra Buddhahajinaraja—which sits above the preserved ashes of King Chulalongkorn, to whom the temple is dedicated.

Also known as King Rama V, Chulalongkorn was an extremely well liked King of Thailand. Crowned in 1873 at the age of 15, he immediately proclaimed that prostration before the king was to be banned, in an attempt to make the people less subservient. In 1905 he abolished slavery, and he continued to work tirelessly to bring Thailand into the modern age. He died in 1910, and his ashes were buried in the ornate white temple that his half-brother had designed in his honor. In 1920 a great golden Buddha made from bronze, the Phra Buddha-hajinaraja, was placed over his ashes. King Chulalongkorn is still greatly revered in Thailand, and every day Thais meditate before the sacred image in a show of respect to the Buddha and the king.

The design of the Marble Temple is a highly unusual mix of Eastern and European architectural traditions, highlighting King Chulalongkorn's dedication to creating closer ties with the Western world. The front of the building is adorned with fine columns and the walls have beautiful stained-glass windows, but the roof is tiered in traditional Thai pagoda style. Behind the central Bot (the ordination hall) is a cloister, which houses 52 unique Buddha images collected by Prince Damrong Rajanubhab for the king. Their different styles reflect the different Buddhist countries from which they originated.

Behind the cloister is a large bodhi tree, a gift to King Chulalongkorn, which is believed to have grown from a sapling taken from the tree at Bodhgaya in India (see pages 266–267), the sacred fig tree under which the Buddha attained enlightenment. The present King of Thailand studied at the Marble Temple in his youth.

The temple is a striking mix of Eastern and Western traditions: a pagoda-style roof above marble columns and stained glass.

WAT PHRA KAEW

LOCATION	Bangkok, Thailand
SPIRITUAL TRADITION	Buddhist
ASSOCIATED DEITY	The last incarnation of the Buddha
DATE OF CONSTRUCTION	1778 CE
WHEN TO VISIT	Any time of year

Wat Phra Kaew is a revered Buddhist temple located in the grounds of the Royal Palace in Bangkok. Most Thais treat it as the most holy of all the shrines in Thailand, because it houses the Emerald Buddha, a small green statue of immense sacred and societal significance. For this reason the temple is also known as the Temple of the Emerald Buddha. No one but the King of Thailand is allowed to get close to the statue. He dutifully performs rituals on and around this sacred icon on behalf of the people.

Local Buddhists believe that the Emerald Buddha was crafted thousands of years ago, but modern historians dispute this, claiming it is no more than 700 years old. The story goes that in 1434 lightning struck a Thai temple housing a stucco statue of the Buddha. The stucco split open, revealing an intensely green, jade statue of the Buddha. People flocked to the "emerald" statue in droves, whereupon the King decided that this important image should be moved to Chiangmai. He sent out three elephants to collect it, but each elephant took it to the city of Lampang instead. The King saw this as a sign from the Buddha, and decided that the statue should remain in Lampang. However, the King's son successfully moved it to Chiang Mai in 1468. In 1552 the King of Laos "borrowed" the statue, but never returned it. In 1564 he took it to Vientiane, where it stayed until 1778, when King Rama I of Thailand conquered the city and brought the statue home. In 1784 the statue was moved to its present abode in the Royal Palace in Bangkok.

The statue is little more than 1½ ft (0.5 m) tall. It sits on a massive gold altar in the center of the temple, which is adorned with exquisite art. King Rama I had two costumes made for the statue, and King Rama III a third, which the present king changes during a complex ritual three times a year, so the statue is always clothed.

A view of the sacred temple from the grounds of the Royal Palace.

THE CONFUCIAN TEMPLE

LOCATION	Shanghai, China
SPIRITUAL TRADITION	Confucian
ASSOCIATED SAGE	Confucius
DATE OF CONSTRUCTION	1296–1855 CE
WHEN TO VISIT	Any time of year

The Wen Miao Temple—widely known as the Confucian Temple—is located in a tranquil position in the old town of Shanghai. First opened in 1296, the temple has occupied a number of sites since settling on its present location in 1855. Unlike other temples in China, the Wen Miao Temple functions as both a place of worship and a school, highlighting the importance of education in Confucianism.

At the main westerly entrance of the temple complex is a traditional Ling Xing gate made of grey stone and protected by lions. From here a first path leads to the Dacheng Dian, or main hall, which is devoted to public worship. Inside this room is a delightful statue of Confucius, shown teaching. The great philosopher is depicted surrounded by bells and a drum, reputedly his favorite musical instruments. The walls are decorated by a huge number of stone tablets, onto which have been carved the text of the Analects, an ancient compilation of Confucius' sayings and teachings.

It is also possible to enter the Confucian Temple through the Xue, or Study Gate, which leads to a second path through the complex to the old school. Traditionally, only scholars who had passed an examination could enter here. Beyond this gate is another, the Yi, or Etiquette Gate. In the past, students were only allowed entry here if they were suitably attired. This gate opens onto the Nature path, which is surrounded by shrubs and trees and is conducive to contemplation and reflection, which are held in high regard by Confucianism.

Confucius, who lived from 551 to 479 BCE, was primarily concerned with matters relating to life as it was lived in the here-and-now, with little or no attention being paid to the mystical or to God. Wisdom and virtue in daily life were his main concerns, so it is hardly surprising that the Confucian Temple has recently become the site of Shanghai's busiest second-hand book market, where many thousands of people flock every Sunday morning to buy and sell the wisdom that is recorded in books.

Although God plays no role in Confucianism, adherents are committed to ritual and worship. It was customary in the Confucian Temple, as in all confucian temples in China, to perform a "sacrifice" to the spirit of Confucius, which took the form of a ceremonial dance enacted by eight rows of dancers in the main hall.

A stone statue of Confucius teaching welcomes all visitors to his temple in Shanghai.

THE TEMPLES OF MAMALLAPURAM

LOCATION	Tamil Nadu, India
SPIRITUAL TRADITION	Hindu
ASSOCIATED DEITIES	Vishnu, Shiva
DATE OF CONSTRUCTION	7th–8th centuries CE
WHEN TO VISIT	Any time of year

Mamallapuram, otherwise known as Mahabaripuram, is home to an exceptional collection of rock shrines and temples adorned with exquisitely carved sculpture, which have attracted thousands of Hindu pilgrims for centuries. Located near the coast in the Indian state of Tamil Nadu, the temples were constructed in the 7th and 8th centuries CE during the Pallava dynasty.

The most important temple at Mamallapuram is considered to be the Thirukadalmallai Temple, which is formed by three small shrines on the shore. Each shrine is dedicated to a different manifestation of the great Hindu god, Vishnu the Preserver, who is said to have appeared at the site long ago disguised as an old man begging for food.

The Shore Temple is one of the first structural temples ever built in India, as opposed to the more common cave

temples found at Mamallapuram. It was built from granite slabs on a small promontory that stretches out into the Bay of Bengal. Rising to 62 ft (19 m) in height, the main structure is shaped like a pyramid, with a smaller temple attached to the front. It houses three shrines: the main one dedicated to Shiva, a smaller central shrine dedicated to Vishnu, and another shrine also dedicated to Shiva. In the main shrine there is a stone Shiva lingam, which provides a focus for Shiva worship.

The Pancha Rathas are a collection of rock temples carved from granite. Each pyramidal temple is carved from a single rock and is dedicated to Draupadi and one of the five Pandava brothers mentioned in the Mahabharata—Arjuna, Bhima, Nakula, Yudhishtra, and Sahadeva—to whom she was simultaneously married.

The Descent of the Ganges is an enormous bas-relief at Mamallapuram carved into a single rock 95 ft (29 m) wide and 43 ft (13 m) high. In exquisite detail, this breathtaking sculpture depicts the mythical journey of the sacred waters of the River Ganges from heaven to earth.

In 2004 a tsunami caused by an earthquake in the Indian Ocean swept over parts of Mamallapuram. As the waves receded they took with them sandstone deposited over centuries, revealing many ancient animal carvings, including ones of elephants, lions, and a horse.

An artist's impression of the rock temples and animal sculpture at Mamallapuram before it was submerged under the sea.

THE PALACE OF KNOSSOS

GREECE

LOCATION	Crete, Greece
SPIRITUAL TRADITION	Ancient Greek pagan
ASSOCIATED FIGURE	The Cretan Minotaur
DATE OF CONSTRUCTION	2000–1200 BCE
WHEN TO VISIT	Any time of year

The ancient city of Knossos near the city of Heraklion in northern Crete was once the religious center of the Minoan civilization. World-famous today for the largely restored Palace of Knossos —sometimes called the Palace of Minos—the area around Knossos has been inhabited for up to 9,000 years.

The Palace of Knossos was first built around 4,000 years ago, with extensions and refurbishments continuing for up to 900 years. More than 1,000 separate rooms were constructed, many adorned with beautiful frescoes, a great number of which have been painstakingly restored. They typically depict scenes of work and play, and are remarkably free of torment and horror. They conjure up a sense of a society at peace with itself, in striking contrast to the dark legends that are associated with the palace.

According to Greek mythology, King Minos commissioned Daedalus to design a great palace with a subterranean labyrinth that would act as a dungeon for the Minotaur, a monster with the head of a bull and the body of a man. When the design was complete, Minos kept the architect prisoner, fearing that he would reveal its plans. Daedalus made a set of wings for himself and for his son Icarus, and duly escaped. Unfortunately, in spite of his father's warnings, the impetuous Icarus flew too near the sun and the wax holding his wings in place melted, sending the boy crashing to his death in the Aegean Sea. Meanwhile, the palace was built and the Minotaur was trapped in the labyrinth, but he made demands of the King, insisting that he was brought seven boys and seven girls every seven years to eat. King Minos forced the people of Athens to provide him with the children until Theseus disguised himself as one of the youths and entered the labyrinth. Armed with a ball of string given to him by Ariadne, Theseus sought out the Minotaur and killed him. He used the string to find his way back out of the labyrinth and became a hero to the people of Athens, where he has been celebrated ever since.

Modern-day visitors to Knossos can see excavated ruins that are thousands of years old sitting alongside modern reconstructions.

An artist's impression showing what the great palace might have looked like in its full glory more than 3,000 years ago.

EL FUERTE DE SAMAIPATA

LOCATION	Santa Cruz, Bolivia
SPIRITUAL TRADITIONS	Arawak, Inca
DATE OF CONSTRUCTION	3rd–14th century CE
WHEN TO VISIT	Any time of year

El Fuerte de Samaipata is a pre-Inca rock temple carved into the side of a colossal rock in the mountains of central Bolivia. Decorated with an extraordinary array of geometric patterns and stylized animal shapes, it was created by the Arawak people in the 3rd century CE, but was later used by the Incas during the 14th century. Spanish conquistadors built a town next to the site in the 16th century, and its ruins are visible today.

The petroglyphs at Samaipata extend for a huge distance—more than 656 x 164 ft (200 x 50 m), making it the largest carved stone anywhere in the world. On the very summit of the rock, a circle of 12 seats—called the Choir of the Priests—has been carved deep into the sandstone. Inside this 23 ft (7 m)-wide circle are three more seats pointing outward, so that they face the 12 seats looking inward. Historians can only guess at the rituals that would have been performed here. Geometric shapes have been carved into the surrounding walls, but their precise meaning remains obscure. Near the seats what looks like the head of a cat has been fashioned from the stone, and below is a water tank with carved grooves that would probably have streamed water to the valley below, although some believe that they may have been used to stream blood.

The south-facing surface of the rock includes five further temples, and possibly more. Only geometric shapes carved into the walls have survived, and the style is similar those found at other Inca sites, such as Machu Picchu (see pages 84–85). A little further south, a large Inca building that faces these temples across a wide plaza has been found. All the evidence suggests that the Incas found the Arawak temple, then incorporated the site into their own religious ceremonies, adding yet more temples and carvings. Snakes and cougars, which are common at the site, are typical Inca symbols.

Archeologists have recently discovered a deep hole within the Inca ruins, which appears to lead into an underground tunnel, which has yet to be explored.

Deep grooves have been carved beneath the Choir of the Priests; historians believe they were used to get stream water to the valley below.

BAALBEK/HELIOPOLIS

LOCATION	Beqa'a Valley, Lebanon
SPIRITUAL TRADITION	Roman pagan
ASSOCIATED DEITIES	Baal, Jupiter, Mercury, Venus
DATE OF CONSTRUCTION	1st–4th century CE
WHEN TO VISIT	Any time of year

Baalbek is located at the highest point of the fertile Beqa'a Valley, east of Litani River in north-eastern Lebanon. Formerly known as Heliopolis, Baalbek is home to the largest and some of the best-preserved ancient Roman temples anywhere. The site takes its name from the Canaanite god, Baal, who was worshipped here for thousands of years before the Romans arrived.

In 31 BCE the Roman Emperor Octavian came to power. There followed an extended period of stability in the Roman empire, during which the great temples at Baalbek were built. The Temple of Jupiter was erected first, followed by the Great Court. Sadly, only six of the huge temple pillars still stand. In the 2nd century CE the Temple of Bacchus was added, although it is not certain that the temple was in fact dedicated to the young god. This temple is remarkably well preserved and, although much smaller than the Temple of Jupiter, it is

larger even than the Parthenon. Later still came the Temple of Venus, which is tiny by comparison, consisting of just six pillars, which would have supported a dome.

The Temple of Mercury was built on a nearby hill, but only its processional stairway remains today. It is known that building work continued at Baalbek into the 4th century CE, when Rome converted to Christianity under the leadership of Constantine. He had a Christian church speedily built at Baalbek in an effort to curb worship of Venus, which is reputed to have included married and unmarried women offering themselves as prostitutes to strangers.

The Canaanite god Baal has many similarities with the Roman god Jupiter. Baal had a son, Aliyan, and a daughter, Anan, both of whom also bear a close resemblance to the Roman gods Mercury and Venus. This is significant, because the Romans worshipped Jupiter, Mercury, and Venus at Baalbek. What is more, the great statue of Jupiter was adorned with ears of corn and two bulls—motifs directly associated with Baal, indicating that the god worshipped at Baalbek was a fusion of Jupiter and Baal. This suggests that the Romans allowed the local people to continue their worship of Baal, but in a new guise.

The stunning Temple of Bacchus is remarkably well-preserved and larger even than the Parthenon.

CHURCH OF OUR LADY MARY OF ZION

LOCATION	Axum, Ethiopia
SPIRITUAL TRADITION	Ethiopian Orthodox Christian
DATE OF CONSTRUCTION	4th–17th century CE
WHEN TO VISIT	Any time of year, but women are not permitted

The Church of Our Lady Mary of Zion is located in the town of Axum (Aksum) in the Tigray region of northern Ethiopia. It has played a key role in the history of Ethiopia, because for many centuries only a leader who had been crowned here could take the title of Atse, meaning Emperor. It is more famous, however, for supposedly housing the Ark of the Covenant, a small wooden box said to contain the Ten Commandments given to Moses on Mount Sinai.

The first church at the site is believed to have been built during the 4th century CE, during the reign of Ezana, the first Christian Emperor of Ethiopia. This church was destroyed by the warrior queen, Gudit, in the 10th century. A new church was built, but was subsequently destroyed in the 16th century by the Somali Imam, Ahmad ibn Ibrihim al-Ghazi. This church was rebuilt by the Emperor Gelawdewos, who achieved fame for rallying his people against the invading Muslim armies. The present-day church was extended by the Emperor Fasilides in the 17th century. In the 1950s the wife of Emperor Haile Selassie paid for a second church—the Chapel of the Tablet—to be built next to the first church, and this is open to both men and women.

According to the Ethiopian Orthodox Church, the Ark was first brought to Ethiopia by Menelik I, son of King Solomon, and is now kept at the Church of Our Lady Mary of Zion; however, it is believed that the Ark was moved to the Chapel of the Tablet because the immense heat it emitted destroyed its original sanctum. The Ark can only be seen by a specially designated monk, since it is believed to be highly dangerous for non-priests to behold it. The chosen monk spends his whole life confined to the chapel, where he prays incessantly and burns incense. It is claimed that most monks die soon after their appointment with cataracts in their eyes, on account of the great light emitted by the Ark.

Every year on November 30, large numbers of Ethiopian Orthodox Christian pilgrims travel to the Church in order to celebrate the Festival of Zion Maryam.

The Chapel of the Tablet is reputed to house the Ark of the Covenant, a sacred chest containing the ten commandments.

THE FORBIDDEN CITY

LOCATION	Beijing, China
SPIRITUAL TRADITIONS	Taoist, Confucian, shamanic
DATE OF CONSTRUCTION	1406 CE
WHEN TO VISIT	Any time of year

The Forbidden City is a stunning complex of almost a thousand wooden buildings surrounded by huge walls and a moat in central Beijing. Built in the early 15th century CE, it served as the imperial palace for the Chinese royal family for 400 years, until the Qing dynasty was overthrown by the Chinese revolution in 1912.

The Ming Emperor, Zhu Di, relocated the Forbidden City to Beijing from Nanjing in 1406; 16 years later the vast complex of buildings was complete, thus creating a new center for religious and political power in China. More than one million workers had toiled to create this splendid complex of thick walls, monumental gates, imposing towers, ornate squares, sumptuous palaces, and sacred Taoist and Confucian temples, using the finest wood and marble. The city was divided into an Inner Court, which served as the private residence of the royal family, and an Outer Court for civic and religious ceremonies.

At the center of the Inner Court three beautiful halls were constructed: the Palace of Heavenly Purity for the Emperor, the Palace of Earthly Tranquillity for the Empress, and the

Hall of Union between the two, where the royal couple would meet, in accordance with Taoist principles.

In 1644 the Ming dynasty was usurped by the Qing dynasty, assisted by Manchu armies from the north. During the upheaval a number of buildings were burned, and soon afterward Manchu shamanism was introduced into the temples. The last Qing emperor, Puyi, was allowed to remain in the Inner Court of the Palace after the Xinhai revolution in 1912. Thereafter the Forbidden City was no longer the center of power in China, and in 1924 it was turned into the Palace Museum to house the nation's finest treasures. Unlike many sacred sites in China, the Forbidden City was largely undamaged by the Cultural Revolution in the 1970s, in the main because Premier Zhou sent an army battalion to protect it. Today, the Forbidden City attracts millions of visitors from around the world.

An artist's impression of the Forbidden City showing the Palace of Heavenly Purity, the Hall of Union, and the Palace of Earthly Tranquillity at the center.

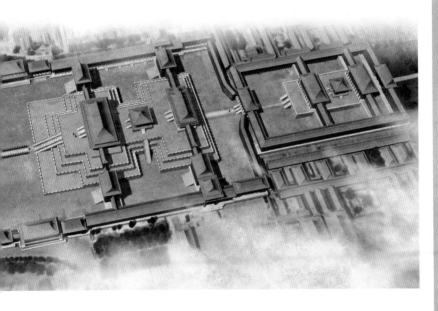

INDEX

ACKNOWLEDGMENTS

Author's Acknowledgments

My heartfelt thanks to all the wonderful people at Octopus who helped pull this book into shape, but especially Sandra Rigby, Clare Churly, Ruth Wiseall, Charlotte Macey and Mandy Greenfield. I am greatly indebted to the many friends and colleagues who freely shared their experiences of sacred sites in remote and inaccessible places. You played a big part in giving this book its depth and breadth. Thank you. Thank you, also, to Susan Mears for encouraging me with my writing and for buying me lunch. And finally, big thanks (and love) to Tim Freke and Mary Anderson for awakening my profound interest in spirituality. Life will never be the same again.

You can contact Anthony J Taylor at: www.anthonyjtaylor.com

Publisher's Acknowledgments

Executive Editor: Sandra Rigby
Editor: Ruth Wiseall
Deputy Creative Director: Karen Sawyer
Designer: Sally Bond
Production Controller: Linda Parry
Picture Researcher: Jennifer Veall

Picture Credits

Alamy/amphotos 247; /Vito Arcomano 252-253; /Yoko Aziz 227; /David Ball 151; /Walter Bibikow/Jon Arnold Images Ltd. 330; /blickwinkel/Hummel 382; /Christophe Boisvieux/Hemis 251; /Charles Bowman/Robert Harding Picture Library 118-119; /Bill Brooks 21, 114; /John Brown 261; /Gary Cook 209; /Derek Croucher 145; /DK 166-167; /Bart Elder 30; /John Elk III 78-79, 104; /Clint Farlinger 6, 23; /Peter Forsberg 74; /Silvana Guilhermino/imagebroker 177; /Bill Heinsohn 211; /Gavin Hellier 355; /Gavin Hellier/Jon Arnold Images Ltd. 13, 14, 40, 225; /Idealink Photography 192-193; /imagebroker 140-141; /Images & Stories 72; /Interfoto 206; /Jon Arnold Images Ltd. 342; /Norma Joseph 317; /JTB Photo Communications, Inc. 301; /Art Kowalsky 371; /Bernd Kröger/INSADCO Photography 275; /Vincent Lowe 122-123; /David Lyons 132-133; /Alain Machet 42; /Oleksiy Maksymenko 367; /Terry Mathews 182-83; /Rod McLean 297; /Megapress 384-385; /nagelestock.com 68, 84; /Charlie Newham 322; /Martin Norris 376; /offiwent.com 26-27; /PhotosIndia.com RM 17 12, 266; /pictureproject 7, 100-101; /Paul Prescott 268-269; /Rolf Richardson 240; /Ghigo Roli/CuboImages srl 186-187; /David Sanger Photography 203; /Darby Sawchuk 372; /Ingo Schulz/imagebroker 18; /Charles Stirling (Travel) 159; /Egmont Strigl/imagebroker 77; /scenicireland.com/Christopher Hill Photographic 112; /Keren Su/China Span 10, 155; /SuperStock 386; /The National Trust Photolibrary 103; /Eric Tormey 109; /Travelpix 90-91; /Ariadne Van Zandbergen 184-185; /Jochem Wijnands/Picture Contact

ACKNOWLEDGMENTS

258; /Andrew Woodley 168-169; /Tengku
Mohd Yusof 237.Corbis/Alan Abraham
164-165; /Jon Arnold/JAI 283; /Yann
Arthus-Bertrand 29; /Atlantide Phototravel
156-157, 178-179; /Edwin Baker/Cordaiy
Photo Library Ltd. 215; /Tiziana and
Gianni Baldizzone 205; /Fernando
Bengoechea/Beateworks 338; /Tibor Bognar
349; /Nelly Boyd/Robert Harding World
Imagery 229; /Richard A. Cooke 116-117;
/Fridmar Damm 273; /James Davis/Eye
Ubiquitous 337; /Destinations 106-107,
148; /Michele Falzone/JAI 152; /Werner
Forman 340; /Michael Freeman 35, 54; /Lee
Frost/Robert Harding World Imagery 138-
139, 146-147; /Mark E. Gibson 318; /Philippe
Giraud 96-97; /Martin Harvey 11, 284-285;
/Dallas and John Heaton/Free Agents
Limited 311; /Chris Hellier 62; /Angelo
Hornak 278; /Rob Howard 160; /Image
Source 375; /Hanan Isachar 182; /Ladislav
Janicek 313; /Andrea Jemolo 189; /Ed
Kashi 335; /Bob Krist 71; /Michael S. Lewis
212; /Bruno Morandi/Hemis 347; /Nabil
Mounzer/epa 4, 234-235; /Michael Nicholson
288, 308; /R H Productions/Robert Harding
World Imagery 306; /Robert Harding World
Imagery 1, 350, 352-353; /Joel W. Rogers 80-
81; /Galen Rowell 39; /Frédéric Soltan 46-47,
362-363; /Frédéric Soltan/Sygma 249;
/STR/epa 233; /Paul Thompson 298;
/Stefano Torrione/Hemis 2, 137; /Vanni
Archive 356; /Francesco Venturi 358-359;
/Steven Vidler/Eurasia Press 134-135;
/Roger Wood 190; /Adam Woolfitt 126;
/Alison Wright 66, 287. Fotolia/Evgenia
194-195, 220-221; /iofoto 36-37; /Liubov
Kinyaeva 314; /Karin Lau 142; /Luis Santos
174-175-175; /David Woolfenden 24.Getty
Images/AFP 50; /DEA/G. Dagli Orti 326;
/Imagno 69; /Courtney Milne 94; /SuperStock
219; /Qassem Zein/AFP 257.OnAsia/Sanjit
Das 222. Photolibrary/Channi Anand 265;
/Jon Arnold 32; /Atlantide SN.C. 58;
/Stefan Auth 216; /Gonzalo Azumendi 292;
/Bhaswaran Bhattacharya 255; /Alan Bailey
360; /Dennis Cox 239; /J. D. Dallet 88;
/DEA/N Cirani 329; /Thien Do 345; /Roger
Hagadone 276; /ImageSource 242; /Inti St
Clair 53; /JTB Photo 9, 48; /Tono Labra 196-
197; /Maurice Lee 369; /Ted Mead 99;
/Brigitte Merz/LOOK-foto 364; /Matz Sjoberg
16-17; /SuperStock 321; /The Irish Image
Collection 280; /Yoshio Tomii 230; /Yoshio
Tomii Photo Studio 111; /Steve Vidler 44-45,
61, 65, 171. wisebrownfox, Australia 92-93

400